Georgeanna Muirson Woolsey Bacon, Eliza Woolsey Howland

Letters of a Family during the War for the Union

Vol. I

Georgeanna Muirson Woolsey Bacon, Eliza Woolsey Howland

Letters of a Family during the War for the Union
Vol. I

ISBN/EAN: 9783337133573

Printed in Europe, USA, Canada, Australia, Japan

Cover: Foto ©ninafisch / pixelio.de

More available books at **www.hansebooks.com**

LETTERS OF A FAMILY

DURING THE

WAR FOR THE UNION

1861-1865

VOL. I

PRINTED FOR PRIVATE DISTRIBUTION
1899

TO THE DEAR MEMORY OF THE
LOVING MOTHER
WHOSE LOFTY FAITH, UNFAILING CHARITY
AND GREAT COURAGE
WERE THE INSPIRATION OF ALL THAT WAS BEST
IN HER CHILDREN
THIS FRAGMENT OF THE WAR-STORY
IS DEDICATED

INTRODUCTORY NOTE

For you, all who are left of our dear nieces and nephews,—
>
> Mary Howland Soley,
> Abby Roberta Howland,
> Georgeanna Howland,
> Eliza Mitchell,
> Hugh Lenox Hodge,
> Alice Bradford Woolsey,
> Una Howland Soley,
> Mary Woolsey Soley,—

we have put together selections from all that are left, of the letters written and received in your Grandmother's family, during the four years of the War of the Rebellion, 1861-65. These few happen to have been saved from a much larger number, which, coming almost daily at times from the brother (Charles), at the Headquarters of the Army of the Potomac, and the sisters in Hospital service, were carefully filed by the eldest sister, Abby, in orderly succession, and, when the home was broken up, were stored in the Morrell warehouse in New York. There, later, with all our Mother's household possessions, they were destroyed by fire, to the deep and lasting regret of all who knew the writers and the times they had passed through.

Dr. Prentiss, our long-time friend and pastor, writes: "The destruction of Charley's letters from the front in the Morrell fire was an irreparable loss, and gave me, I remember, a real shock, for I knew how precious they would have been, sooner or later, not in your family history only, but in the inner personal history of the war."

Out of the few not stored in the warehouse, and by quotations which were made from the army letters, in correspondence with family friends at the time, a sort of connected account has been made, which may help to tell you the story of the family during the Civil War.

As you read, you will see that this was a family of earnest Americans, having no other thought at that time, than to give themselves and their possessions freely—as thousands of other families did—to the service of the men in the field. Some of you were little children then, most of you were not born. You know nothing of the history of the great national sin, slavery, which led to the war, and can never understand the spirit with which a great multitude, ourselves among them, entered into this struggle, unless you can detect it in the first chapter of this story. Of the war itself you know scarcely more, but you will always remember that the willing service of the soldiers of the National Army gave you a country worth caring for. To you your own land is made sacred by the death of half a million steadfast men, and by the thought of the thousands and thousands of broken-hearted women at home, who quietly acquiesced in this great sacrifice out of love and loyalty to their country's flag.

GEORGEANNA WOOLSEY BACON.
ELIZA WOOLSEY HOWLAND.

ABBREVIATIONS

Mother, ...   Your Grandmother, Mrs. Charles William Woolsey, who was Jane Eliza Newton, of Virginia.

Her Children and Children-in-Law (Your Aunts and Uncles):

A. H. W., ...   Abby Howland Woolsey.
J. S. W., ...   Jane Stuart Woolsey.
M. W. H., ...   Mary Woolsey Howland.
G. M. W., ...   Georgeanna Muirson Woolsey.
E. W. H., ...   Eliza Woolsey Howland.
H. R. W. . . . . .   Harriet Roosevelt Woolsey.
C. C. W., ...   Caroline Carson Woolsey.
C. W. W., ...   Charles William Woolsey.
R. S. H., ...   Robert Shaw Howland; Mary's husband.
J. H., ...   Joseph Howland; Eliza's husband.
F. B., ...   Francis Bacon; after the war married to Georgeanna.
H. L. H., ...   Hugh Lenox Hodge; after the war married to Harriet.
E. M., ...   Edward Mitchell; after the war married to Caroline.
Zenie, ...   Arixene Southgate Smith; after the war married to Charles.

Grandchildren:

May, ...   Mary Woolsey Howland.
Bertha, ...   Abby Roberta Howland.
Una, ...   Una Felice Howland.
Baby Georgie, . .   Georgeanna Howland.

CONTENTS

CHAPTER I.

JUST BEFORE THE WAR.

	PAGE
The Fremont Campaign,	1
Mother and Abby at the South,	2
A Slave Auction,	6
John Brown,	15
Some of the Family go to Europe,	18
Election of President Lincoln,	19
The Secession Ordinance,	26
Inauguration of President Lincoln,	34

CHAPTER II.

FIRST YEAR OF THE WAR.

The Firing on Fort Sumter,	37
First Call to Arms,	38
Marching of the 7th New York,	44
Flag Presentation to the 2d Conn.,	52
The Sanitary Commission,	62
J. H. Joins the Army,	71
G. M. W. Studies Nursing,	78
The Sisters Abroad Come Home,	96

xii CONTENTS

	PAGE
J. H's Regiment Passes Through New York,	103
G., E. and C. go to Washington,	109
Camp at Cameron,	116
Mother's Reminiscences,	116
Battle of Bull Run,	121

CHAPTER III.

Three Months' Troops Disbanded,	135
Pioneer Women Nurses,	142
Hospital Work in Washington and at Home,	150
Hospital Chaplains,	161
The Family at Lenox and Astoria,	172
G. and E. dine with General Scott,	183

CHAPTER IV.

Patent Office Hospital,	189
F. B. with the Port Royal Expedition,	197
J. H. has Leave of Absence,	200
H. and C. meet Major Anderson,	208
Thanksgiving Day,	215
Tybee Island, F. B.,	222
The Trent Affair,	227
Christmas,	231

CHAPTER V.

SECOND YEAR OF THE WAR.

A New Year's Call on G. and E.,	237
Washington Jail,	249
Mrs. Abby Hopper Gibbons,	250
Mother goes to Washington,	254

CONTENTS

	PAGE
General Seth Williams,	255
C. C. W. goes to Roanoke Island,	260
"Arbutus from Camp,"	263

CHAPTER VI.

J. H. becomes Colonel of the 16th N. Y.,	268
Manassas Evacuated by the Rebels,	270
The Peninsular Campaign Begun,	272
"A Rainy Day in Camp,"	280
G. and E. Plan to Follow the Army,	285
J. S. W. at Work in New York,	292
H. L. H. goes to the Front,	302
J. H. leaves for the Peninsula,	304

CHAPTER VII.

The Floating Hospital Service,	312
G. and E. Nurses at Large,	312
Mother and Hatty wind up affairs in Washington,	314
Mrs. William Preston Griffin,	316
First Field Patients for E.,	321
Yorktown Abandoned by the Rebels,	326
F. B. with the Wounded Rebels at Fort Pulaski,	333
C. W. W. Joins the Sanitary Commission,	337
The Ocean Queen, Hospital Transport,	338
Battle of West Point, Va., 16th N. Y. engaged,	348
On the Knickerbocker, Hospital Transport,	356

JUST BEFORE THE WAR

CHAPTER I.

When the members of the Woolsey family gave up toys they took up politics. Brought up by a mother who hated slavery, although her ancestors for generations had been Virginia slave-holders, they walked with her in the straight path of abolitionism and would none of the Democratic party.

The Fremont Campaign. As long ago as 1856, when the Fremont campaigners, with misguided zeal and loud enthusiasm, proposed to sing the "Pathfinder" into the White House, night after night this family, with the many young men who flocked to their standard, sang, doors and windows being all open, hour after hour, the patriotic doggerel of the campaign song book; and many a song went hot from No. 8 Brevoort Place, the New York home, to the campaign printing office, and was shouted at political meetings for the furtherance of a result which a merciful Providence averted.

We all cut our political teeth on the New York Tribune, and were in the right frame of mind to keep step with the steady march to the inevitable through the Kansas perplexities, the John Brown raid and the election of Mr. Lincoln, to the firing of the first gun by the rebels upon the national flag at Fort Sumter.

Mother and Abby in the South.

In the spring of 1859, Abby not having been very well during the winter, Mother planned a little trip to the South for her benefit, making up a party with Robert, Mary, and little Mary.

They spent several days in Charleston, and vexed their righteous souls with the sights and sounds of an auction of slaves.

Abby writes to her cousin, Harriet Gilman:

CHARLESTON, S. C., Feb. 6, 1859.

Slave auctions are of daily occurrence, and one of these we attended, seeing what perhaps no lady-resident of Charleston has seen. But for that sad insight we might have thought things had a pretty fair aspect, generally. Certainly nothing forced itself unpleasantly on our attention, only every black face in the street reminded us of the system. I enclose you the list of some we saw sold. It is the list of only "one lot" put in by one trader. I could not get a full catalogue of sale; it seemed very long, and the men who held them were marking off the names and the prices which they brought. One man, a great stout thorough African, ran up to $780, but that was "cheap." The sale was in Chalmers street — a red flag indicating the spot — hardly a stone's throw from the hotel. The slave yard was probably the largest in Charleston — a great empty square, with high walls on three sides and a platform where the auctioneer stood and around which the bidders were grouped. On the fourth side was a five or six-story brick building, dirty, ragged-looking, like our rear tenements, where the poor crowd were lodged. The gentlemen of our party, Mr. Robert Howland, and Mr. Charles Wolcott of Fishkill (who is here with his wife on a hasty tour), went in among the bidders. We ladies stood at the gate and looked in. Whole families of all ages were standing back against the walls, being questioned by purchasers and waiting their turn. A poor old woman, her head bowed, was sold with her son. They told us families are never separated except on account of bad behavior when they wish to get rid of some bad fellow — that this is so much the custom that the opposite course would not be tolerated. But mortgages, sheriffs' sales, sudden death of the owner, etc., must often, as we can imagine, infringe on this custom. Among the saddened lookers on, all colored women except ourselves, was a middle-aged black woman, with a child in her arms. Mother had much talk with her. "Ah! Misses," she said, "they leave me some of the little ones. They sell my boys away, but I expect that, and all I wish is that they may get a good Master and Misses. There! Misses, that's one of my boys on the stand now! I don't mind that, but its hard to have the old man (her husband) *drifted away*. But what can I do? My heart's broke, and that's all." He had been sold some time ago, and was gone she didn't know where. We turned home sickened and indignant. The bidders were gentlemanly-looking people, just such as we met every day at the hotel table. The trader had come down with this very gang in the cars with the Wolcotts the day before, and was so drunk then he could hardly stand. Isn't Dr. Cheever justified?

. . . March, 1859.

Though this is March, the Japonicas are just passing out of blossom and the roses are in their first fresh glory — yellow and white Banksia, the Lamarque, and all those choice fresh varieties. I'll just run down in the garden here and pick you a rosebud. There it is — my voucher for the floral stories.

While we were at the Pulaski in Savannah, the great sale of Pierce Butler's slaves took place, and there all the gentlemen interested were congregated. You would never suppose the young meek pale little man, Pierce Butler, to be either a slave-owner or Mrs. Kemble's husband. He is the indignant vestryman, I am told, who walked ont of Rev. Dudley Tyng's Church when that sermon was preached. I am glad to hear that Mrs. Kemble has never drawn a dollar of her alimony, $3,000 a year, but allows it to accumulate for the children. She has the honest pride of maintaining herself, under the circumstances. Of course, you have read the Tribune's account; the girls sent it to us, and we have kept it well concealed, I assure you, for there are fire-eaters in the house, who would not hesitate to insult us. But now it is copied into the New York Herald — the only northern daily sold here — and has gone all through the city. There is a shrewd Philadelphian here, with his wife, Mr. Ashmead. He knew the agent at that sale. He attended the sale; took notes of course, as every northerner had to do, and now and then made a modest bid — to appear interested as a buyer. He says: "All I can say of Doe-stick's account is it does not go one bit beyond the reality — hardly comes up to it, indeed." He heard all the remarks quoted about Daphney's baby; says the story of Dorcas' and Jeffrey's love is true; and it was to himself and one other that the negro driver's remarks about the efficacy of pistols were made. He thought Mr. Ashmead was one of the same sort! The latter was a Buchanan man; he goes home an Abolitionist, and says: "Now I can believe that everything in Uncle Tom's Cabin might really happen."

As properly part of the history of the war, the following New York Tribune's account of this sale is valuable. It was found among Abby's papers, dated March 9th, 1859:

A GREAT SLAVE AUCTION.
400 MEN, WOMEN, AND CHILDREN SOLD.

"The largest sale of human chattels that has been made in Star-Spangled America for several years took place on Wednesday and Thursday of last week at the Race Course, near the City of Savannah, Georgia. The lot consisted of four hundred and thirty-six men, women, children and infants, being that half of the negro stock remaining on the old Major Butler plantations which fell to one of the two heirs to that estate — Mr. Pierce M. Butler, still living and resident in the city of Philadelphia, in the free state of Pennsylvania. They were, in fact, sold to pay Mr. Pierce M. Butler's debts.

"The sale had been advertised largely for many weeks, and as the negroes were known to be a choice lot and very desirable property, the attendance of buyers was large. Little parties were made up from the various hotels every day to visit the Race Course, distant some three miles from the city, to look over the chattels, discuss their points, and make memoranda for guidance on the day of sale. The buyers were generally of a rough breed, slangy, profane and bearish, being, for the most part, from the back river and swamp plantations where the elegancies of polite life are not, perhaps, developed to their fullest extent.

"The negroes were brought to Savannah in small lots, as many at a time as could be conveniently taken care of, the last of them reaching the city the Friday before the sale. They were consigned to the care of Mr. J. Bryan, auctioneer and negro broker, who was to feed and keep them in condition until disposed of. Immediately on their arrival they were taken to the Race Course and there quartered in the sheds erected for the accommodation of the horses and carriages of gentlemen attending the races. Into these sheds they were huddled pell-mell, without any more attention to their comfort than was necessary to prevent their becoming ill and unsalable.

"The chattels were huddled together on the floor, there being no sign of bench or table. They eat and slept on the bare boards, their food being rice and beans, with occasionally a bit of bacon and corn bread. Their huge bundles were scattered over the floor, and thereon the slaves sat or reclined, when not restlessly moving about or gathered into sorrowful groups discussing the chances of their future fate. On the faces of all was an expression of heavy grief.

"The negroes were examined with as little consideration as if they had been brutes; the buyers pulling their mouths open to see their teeth, pinching their limbs to find how muscular they were, walking them up and down to detect any signs of lameness, making them stoop and bend in different ways that they might be certain there was no concealed rupture or wound.

"The following curiously sad scene is the type of a score of others that were there enacted:

"'Elisha,' chattel No. 5 in the catalogue, had taken a fancy to a benevolent-looking middle-aged gentleman who was inspecting the stock, and thus used his powers of persuasion to induce the benevolent man to purchase him, with his wife, boy, and girl. 'Look at me, Mas'r; am prime rice planter; sho' you won't find a better man den me; no better on de whole plantation; not a bit old yet; do mo' work den ever; do carpenter work, too, little; better buy me, Mas'r; I'se be good sarvant, Mas'r. Molly, too, my wife, Sa, fus rate rice hand; mos as good as me. Stan' out yer, Molly, and let the gen'lem'n see.'

"Molly advances, with her hands crossed on her bosom, and makes a quick, short curtsy and stands mute, looking appealingly in the benevolent man's face. But Elisha talks all the faster. 'Show Mas'r yer arm, Molly — good arm dat, Mas'r — she do a heap of work mo' with dat arm yet. Let good Mas'r see yer teeth, Molly — see dat, Mas'r, teeth all reg'lar, all good — she'm young gal yet. Come out yer Israel; walk aroun' an' let the gen'lm'n see how spry you be'—

"Then, pointing to the three-year-old girl who stood with her chubby hand to her mouth, holding on to her Mother's dress and uncertain what to make of the strange scene,— 'Little Vardy's on'y a chile yet;

make prime gal by and by. Better buy us, Mas'r; we'm fus' rate bargain'—and so on. But the benevolent gentleman found where he could drive a closer bargain, and so bought somebody else.

"In the intervals of more active labor the discussion of the re-opening of the slave-trade was commenced, and the opinion seemed to generally prevail that the reëstablishment of the said trade is a consummation devoutly to be wished, and one red-faced Major, or General, or Corporal, clenched his remarks with the emphatic assertion that 'We'll have all the niggers in Africa over here in three years—we won't leave enough for seed.'

"One huge brute of a man, who had not taken an active part in the discussion save to assent with approving nod to any unusually barbarous proposition, at last broke his silence by saying in an oracular way 'You may say what you like about managing niggers; I'm a driver myself, and I've had some experience, and I ought to know. You can manage ordinary niggers by lickin' 'em and given' 'em a taste of the hot iron once in a while when they're extra ugly; but if a nigger really sets himself up against me I can't never have any patience with him. I just get my pistol and shoot him right down; and that's the best way.'

"The family of Primus, plantation carpenter, consisting of Daphney his wife, with her young babe, and Dido a girl of three years old, were reached in due course of time. Daphney had a large shawl, which she kept carefully wrapped around her infant and herself. This unusual proceeding attracted much attention, and provoked many remarks, such as these:

"'What do you keep your nigger covered up fer? Pull off her blanket!'

"'What's the fault of the gal? Ain't she sound? Pull off her rags and let us see her!'

"'Who's going to bid on that nigger, if you keep her covered up? Let's see her face!'

"At last the auctioneer obtained a hearing long enough to explain that there was no attempt to practice any deception in the case — the parties were not to be wronged in any way; he had no desire to palm off on them an inferior article, but the truth of the matter was that Daphney had been confined only fifteen days ago, and he thought that on that account she was entitled to the slight indulgence of a blanket, to keep from herself and child the chill air and the driving rain.

"Since her confinement, Daphney had travelled from the plantations to Savannah, where she had been kept in a shed for six days. On the sixth or seventh day after her sickness she had left her bed, taken a railroad journey across the country to the shambles, was there exposed for six days to the questionings and insults of the negro speculators, and then on the fifteenth day after her confinement was put up on the block with her husband and her other child, and, with her new-born baby in her arms, was sold to the highest bidder.

"It was very considerate in Daphney to be sick before the sale, for her wailing babe was worth to Mr. Butler all of a hundred dollars. The family sold for $625 apiece, or $2,500 for the four.

"There were some thirty babies in the lot; they are esteemed worth to the master a hundred dollars the day they are born and to increase in value at the rate of a hundred dollars a year till they are sixteen or seventeen years old, at which age they bring the best prices.

"Jeffrey, chattel No. 319, being human in his affections, had dared to cherish a love for Dorcas, chattel No. 278; and Dorcas, not having the fear of her master before her eyes, had given her heart to Jeffrey.

"Jeffrey was sold. He finds out his new master; and, hat in hand, the big tears standing in his eyes and his voice trembling with emotion, he stands before that master and tells his simple story:

"'I loves Dorcas, young Mas'r; I loves her well an' true; she says she loves me, and I know she does; de good Lord knows I love her better than I loves any one in de wide world — never can love another woman half so well. Please buy Dorcas, Mas'r. We'll be good sarvants to you long as we live. We're be married right soon, young Mas'r, and de chillun will be healthy and strong, Mas'r, and dey'll be good sarvants, too. Please buy Dorcas, young Mas'r. We loves each other a heap — do, really, true, Mas'r.'

"At last comes the trying moment, and Dorcas steps up on the stand.

"But now a most unexpected feature in the drama is for the first time unmasked; Dorcas is not to be sold alone, but with a family of four others. Full of dismay Jeffrey looks to his master who shakes his head, for, although he might be induced to buy Dorcas alone, he has no use for the rest of the family. Jeffrey reads his doom in his master's look, and turns away, the tears streaming down his honest face.

"And tomorrow Jeffrey and Dorcas are to say their tearful farewell, and go their separate ways in life to meet no more as mortal beings.

"That night, not a steamer left that southern port, not a train of cars sped away from that cruel city, that did not bear each its own sad burden of those unhappy ones."

Abby's account from Charleston goes on:

On Sunday Mother and I went to the African Baptist Church, and had a most interesting service, remaining to their communion. The new members, nine of them, were seated in the front pews; the young women, in white dresses, shawls, and white ribbons on their straw bonnets. We had a seat of honor just behind them. The pastor, a slender, meek man in spectacles — a black man you know — "Dr. Cox," gave them the right hand of fellowship, with many touching words of counsel and passages of scripture. He and we, too, were equally moved, as to one (free) woman he said, "If the Son shall make you free, ye shall be free indeed," and to another, "Stand fast, therefore, in the liberty wherewith God shall make you free." He is free himself, I hear, but the Methodist minister is a slave. He is well taken care of — given his whole time, and is considered in an enviable position. The church was crowded — bandannas of every shade, and style of tie — and no small sprinkling of the gayest bonnets. The minister was a quiet, excellent speaker; "two broders" who assisted were roaring ones, and the "broder officers" who officiated were such real darkies, and the singing was so like stories I have read, that altogether I had more a sense of sight-seeing than of worshipping, I am afraid. The service was very solemn, however, and we were deeply interested. There must have been three or four hundred communicants, for it was not close communion. The bread and wine were carried to every one, and up in the galleries too, and the eight baskets were emptied and the eight goblets were all emptied and filled three times. We shook hands with "Dr. Cox," who seemed gratified that we had remained, and as for us, we would not have missed it for a great deal.

<small>John Brown.</small> Abby's heart was full of the thought of the slave market when, six months later, John Brown put his belief into action and attempted to bring about the forcible liberation of the slaves, acting as he thought and said "by the authority of God Almighty." Death by hanging was his reward. He left the jail at Charlestown and met his fate "with a radiant countenance and the step of a conqueror."

At the hour appointed for the execution, December 2d, 1859, thousands of Northern hearts were with him, and in Dr. Cheever's church, New York, prayers were offered.

A. H. W. to E. W. H.

8 BREVOORT PLACE, Dec. 5, 1859.

My dear Eliza: I went round to Dr. Cheever's lecture room for half an hour. I found it crowded with men and women — as many of one as the other — hard-featured men, rugged faces, thoughtful faces, some few Chadband faces; plain, quiet women; none that looked like gay, idle, trifling people. I entered just as some one suggested five minutes of silent prayer, which I have no doubt every soul of us made the most of, and then Dr. Cheever, who had the chair, gave out that hymn, "Oh, glorious hour! Oh, blest abode! I shall be near and like my God," etc. Mr. Brace made a fervent prayer for John Brown. Then a Methodist brother made a few remarks — said "it did him good to cry Amen. It proved you to be on the right side and that you were not afraid to make it known, and it didn't need a polished education to help you do that much for truth." Then they sang, "Am I a Soldier of the Cross?" everybody singing with a will, and, indeed, throughout the meeting there was much feeling — some sobs and many hearty Amens.

The public feverish excitement constantly increased and carried our family along in its stream.

Abby writes:

8 BREVOORT PLACE, Dec. 17, 1859.

Dear Eliza: Georgy has gone to Professor Smith's class on church history and Jane has been out for a little air and exercise, to see if her head would feel better. She is in a highly nervous state, and says she feels as if she had brain fever, the over-excitement being the result of last night's meeting at the Cooper Institute, with speeches from Dr. Cheever and Wendell Phillips. She and Georgy went with Charley, and they say that the moment Dr. Cheever opened his mouth, Pandemonium broke loose. There seemed to be a thousand mad devils charging up and down the aisles with awful noises, and one of the rowdies near them plucked Charley and tried to draw him into a quarrel. This frightened Jane, but though Charley grew very white with rage he stood firm, and then Mr. Rowse joined them, and, as they couldn't get out, by degrees they worked their way to the platform, over the backs of the seats, and were high and dry and safe, and heard Phillips through. He was not so ornate in style as they expected, but a charming speaker.

All this had such an exciting effect on Jane that in her sleep last night she walked about; went into the little room next to ours and locked herself in; barricaded the door with baskets and chairs, throwing one of the latter over and breaking it. She had previously closed the doors between our room and Mother's, so that Mother only heard the sounds indistinctly. Jane lay down on the little bed, without covering, and toward morning the cold waked her, to her great bewilderment.

<small>Some of the Family go to Europe.</small> In the summer of 1860 Robert and Mary, with little Mary and Bertha, went to Europe, taking with them Hatty and Carry, and on November 20th, 1860, Mary's fourth little girl, baby Una, was born in Rome at the Casa Zuccara, via Quattro Fontane. She was christened Una Felice, in water brought from the Aqua Felice fountain. Mother's note refers to it all, and several of the following letters give peaceful little touches of home life before the storm broke:

SATURDAY MORNING, Dec., 1860.

My dear Eliza: Your very modest little, "may I Mother?" leads me to an immediate reply. Yes, my dear child, come and welcome, just as often as you possibly can and never feel it necessary to ask if you may *come home*, for this you know is only another home. I am happy to enclose you a foreign letter bringing still further pleasant news. How much we have all to be thankful for that the travellers have so much enjoyment and so little interruption to it. Dear Mary finds, I dare say, comfort enough in the little new baby to compensate in a great measure for all the suffering consequent upon its arrival.

What do you think of Felice added to Una? Our opinions will be useless now, however, as before the last letters reach, the baptism will have *been done*. Did you see the paragraph stating that the continual assassinations in the streets of Rome render it unsafe to strangers and to residents after dark! This is very comforting to anxious families who have friends there! Hatty and Carry are certainly having a gay time at Naples. Just think of Vesuvius, a hurried dinner, rush to the Crocelli to meet a party of naval officers, a fourteen-oared boat excursion, dancing, and other festivities on board the Admiral's ship-of-war, supper, etc., etc., all on one day! And after that the return civility of an egg nogg party! I am very glad they are under the care of a clergyman and his wife!

<small>Election of President Lincoln.</small>

J. S. W. to a Friend in Paris.

NEW YORK, Dec. 5, 1860.

We came down to Centre Harbor on the 6th of November (the great day) and there the Republican majorities came rolling in for Abraham Lincoln. Our host in that place was of a practical turn, and, having no artillery and having some rocks to blast in the garden, laid his trains and waited for the news; and when the stage coach came in from Meredith village he "stood by to fire," and all the rocks went off at once and made a pretty good noise. Georgy and I stopped in New Haven for a visit and had some delicious breezy, rushing, sparkling little sails in the bay and in the sound. We took to the salt water with a keen relish after nearly five months of mountains. Miss Rose Terry was in New Haven. She has just published a little volume of poems, and is writing New England stories for the magazines. Think of our national bird being in danger of splitting at last, like that odious fowl, the Austrian Eagle — a step toward realizing the vision of a "Bell-everett" orator in the late campaign, whose speech I read, and who saw the illustrious biped with "one foot upon the Atlantic shore, one on the golden strand, and one upon the islands of the main!" Not that I care for secession; let them go! We are told we "mustn't buy too many new dresses this winter," but *still* I say no matter — no compromises. Millions for defence, not one cent for tribute. I can live on a straw a day. "So can *I*," Georgy puts in here, "if one end of it is in a sherry cobbler." But what a sight we must be to other peoples. Just as morning breaks over Italy with sunshine and singing, this evil cloud comes up in our heaven. Must there be a sort of systole and diastole in civilization, and must one nation go down in the balance as another goes up, till the great day that makes all things true? You read all this stuff in the papers: how the North "hurls back with scorn the giant strides of that Upas Tree, the slave power!" and how the South will no longer be "dragged at the chariot wheels of that mushroom, the Northwest!" The money men look blue and the dry-goodsy men look black. Charles Rockwell has just gone to Georgia, rather against the advice of some of his friends, for the R's are stout Republicans and given to being on their own side. Now and then an incident "comes home" that doesn't get into the papers. Here is one that came under my own knowledge. A young lady, being rather delicate, decided three or four weeks ago to go to her friends in Georgia for the winter. For some reason they could not send for her, or even meet her at Savannah, so she set out alone. During the little voyage there was some talk in the cabin about John Brown. "But we must allow he was a *brave* man," she said:— nothing more. The steamer arrived in the night, and she with some others waited on board till morning. Soon after daybreak, while she was making ready to go ashore, three gentlemen presented themselves to her; "understood she had expressed abolition sentiments, regretted the necessity," etc.—the usual stuff—"if she would consult her safety she would leave immediately by the Northern train; her luggage *had already been transferred;* they would see her safely to the station." She denied the charges, told who her relatives were (staunch Democrats), etc., in vain. They, with great politeness, put her into a carriage, escorted her to the station, presented her with a through ticket and sent her home, where she arrived safely, a blazing Abolitionist.

Thanksgiving day is lately past, and the burden of the sermons was peace, peace and concession. Mr. Beecher preached a tremendous Rights-of-Man and Laws-of-God sermon, and I was told that once when a fine apostrophe to freedom came in, and there were movements to hush signs of enthusiasm, he paused a moment, and said in his peculiar manner: "Oh, it isn't Sunday!" and all the great audience broke into long applause. And why not? In the Church's early days they used to applaud and shout "Pious Chrysostom!" "Worthy the Priesthood!" And in the meantime:

Garibaldi! The word is a monument and a triumphal song. I should like to have one of the turnips from that island farm of Caprera. Now, when the "deeds are so few and the men so many" it is surely a great thing to find a noble deed to do, and to do it! What a scene that was, the meeting and the crowning at Speranzano; for *that* was the real crowning, when Garibaldi said to Victor, "King of Italy!" We fairly cried — don't laugh — over that scene. And now he is like Coleridge's Knight:—

>"In kingly court,
>Who having won all guerdons in the sport
>Glides out of view, and whither none can find."

While I am writing they are screaming "President Buchanan's message" in the streets. I capture an extra and try to make "head and tail" of it for you, without success. Our family friends are snugly settled in Rome, and "as quiet as in North Conway." Baby Bertha begins to speak, and her first articulate word is "Viva!"

G. M. IV. to the Sisters in Europe.

PHILADELPHIA, Dec., 1860.

Dear Girls: Mother and Abby have just come down from Fishkill, Mother declaring that she feels like a different person in consequence of her visit. We are none of us making a time over Christmas presents this year. Abby has had a little bureau just to fit shirts made for Mr. Prentiss, who was in high delight while they lived abroad because he had *a drawer* to keep his things in. No calls will be received at No. 8 this New Year and indeed I don't think there will be many made, people are so depressed about the times.

The papers today report from Washington that "alarming news has been received from Charleston. Apprehensions of immediate collision with the Federal government are entertained. Influential Northern men are doing their utmost to avert the calamity. The intention of the people of North Carolina is to seize the forts and arsenals and to prevent the government from collecting the revenues. Despatches have been received stating that the forts would be taken in less than twenty-four hours. The Cabinet is in council. It has not transpired what course the government will pursue. A naval fleet will probably be despatched to Charleston. The amendment of the Constitution to settle the controversy between North and South forever, by a division of the country from ocean to ocean on the parallel of the Missouri line, is the great subject of discussion." Notwithstanding all this trouble, and the secession ordinance which was published on Saturday, "the stocks of the North have gone up steadily for some days both before and after the fulmination of the ordinance. Never was the strength of the business condition of the northern and central states more decisively proved than now." I hope you are interested in all this; politics are the only things talked of among all classes of men and women here in this country, now, and foreign affairs relating to the "state of Europe" are comparatively of no importance. In fact, all interest given to Italy centres in the "Casa Zuccara" and especially on our 'Donna and child. We only wish the Southerners could see how prosperous and happy we look, on the outside at least! "O, yes, Doctor," one of them said the other day to Dr. Hodge, "it's a beautiful city this of yours, but in a little while the grass will be growing in the streets." Lenox's reports from down town are that it is suggested that the governors of the states should have the troops of the different states in readiness for any emergency, since the South is busy making its preparations, and thus far we have been doing nothing. I took the news word for word from the paper this morning, from the Washington correspondent, and you must take it for what it is worth. People think it worse than anything thus far, though Mr. Seward predicts that in sixty days the troubles will have past away. Only think how jolly! There's an ordinance in Charleston forbidding the sale of Boston crackers and including farina.

Several pleasant surprises came to lessen the depression of this Christmas. Mr. Martin, a young gentleman returning from Rome, brought to Mother a promised ring —"a Mosaic of a carrier pigeon, which lifted up and displayed a shining curl of the new little baby's hair," and Abby writes: "Uncle Edward* gave me some of Father's early water-colors, interesting to us — the work of a boy of fourteen, — and when Mother and I drove in after spending the day with him what do you think we found besides? — a box with a scarlet camel's hair shawl for Mother with Cousin William Aspinwall's best wishes." (This shawl is now Alice's.)

The Secession Ordinance. On December 20th, 1860, South Carolina "in convention assembled" had declared the union subsisting between that state and other states to be "hereby repealed." Other southern states were rapidly following the insane example.

All sorts of efforts, private and public, were made to compromise and patch up,

---

*Our dear Uncle and guardian, Edward John Woolsey, of Astoria, L. I.

and family friends and relatives on both sides made last attempts to join hands. Abby writes Eliza, "What do you think? I wrote Minthorn Woolsey a long letter the other day asking for information as to the position he holds on secession."

[When we were all children and spending, as usual, our summer with Grandfather Woolsey at Casina there arrived one day a new and charming cousin, Benjamin Minthorn Woolsey, from Alabama. He belonged to the Melancthan Taylor branch of the family, and none of us had ever seen him before. A warm friendship began and was continued until the mutterings of secession were heard. Abby, unwilling to give him up, argued and entreated in vain. The letter from which the following extracts are taken was probably her last to him and will give an idea of her clear and forcible thinking and writing. Many families decided at this point to meet again only as enemies.]

My dear Cousin: I hasten to answer your letter, for, as events march, mail facilities may soon be interrupted between North and South. When the great separation is a recognized fact postal treaties, along with others, may be arranged. Meantime, it is one of the curious features of your anomalous position that you are making use of a "foreign government" to carry your mails for you, on the score of economy. Congress may cut off the Southern service and occasion some inconvenience and delay, but I am told it will save the government about $26,000 weekly, that being the weekly excess of postal expenditure over revenue in the six seceding states.

I thank you very sincerely for your letter. It was very kind in you to write so promptly and fully and in so sedate a tone. But what a sober, disheartening letter it was! We have been slow to believe that the conservative men of the cotton states have been swept into this revolution. I could not believe it now but for your assurance as regards yourself and your state. "Not a hundred Union men" as we understand it, in Alabama! We had supposed there were *many* hundreds who would stand by the Union, unconditionally if need be, and uphold the Constitution, not according to any party construction, but as our fathers framed it, as the Supreme Court expounds it, and as it will be Mr. Lincoln's wisest policy to administer it. Not a hundred Union men in your state! Truly not, if Mr. Yancey speaks for you and Alabama when he avows himself as "utterly, unalterably opposed to any and all plans of reconstructing a Union with the Black Republican states of the North. No new guarantees, no amendments of the Constitution, no repeal of obnoxious laws can offer any the least inducement to reconstruct our relations." Then compromisers in Congress, in convention, everywhere, may as well cease their useless efforts. Not a hundred Union men in Alabama! Who then burned Mr. Yancey himself in effigy? Have those delegates who refused to sign the secession ordinance yet done so? and what constituencies do they represent? Why was it refused to refer the action of convention to the people?

Whatever the Border states may have suffered, and, as in the case of the John Brown raid, have swiftly and terribly avenged, you of the Gulf states can hardly think that your wrongs have been so intolerable as to make revolution necessary. True, you describe us as standing with a loaded pistol at your breast, but the heaviest charge we have ever put in is non-extension of slavery in the territories. If slavery cannot stand that; if, surrounded by a cordon of free states, like a girdled tree it dies, then it cannot have that inherent force of truth and justice — that divine vitality which has been claimed for it. This is as favorable a time as we could have to meet the issue and settle it peacefully, I trust, forever. And here comes up the subject of compromises, the Crittenden measures particularly. How does it happen that the Southern demands have increased so enormously since last year? *Then* the Senate declared by a vote of 43 to 5 that it was not necessary to pass a law to protect slavery in the territories. *Now*, you "secede" because you cannot get what Fitzpatrick, Clay, Benjamin, Iverson, and others declared you did not need. *Then* you asked the Democratic convention at Charleston to put a slavery code into the party platform, and you split your party about it. *Now* you come to the opponents who fairly outvoted you and your platform and ask them to put the same protective clause, — where? — *into the Constitution!* We can never eat our principles in that way, though all fifteen of the states secede. The right of eminent domain, by which South Carolina claims Fort Sumter, inapplicable as it is, is a respectable demand compared with what has been practiced further south — the right of seizure. If you attack Sumter you may precipitate a collision. Meantime, never was a people calmer than ours here, in the face of great events. We have scarcely lifted a finger, while the South has been arming in such hot haste and hurrying out of the Union, in the hope of accomplishing it all under Floyd's guilty protectorate. We all hope much from the new administration. We think well of a man who for so long has managed to hold his tongue. We shall try to help him and hold up his hands, not as our partisan candidate but as the President of the Nation. If we become two confederacies we shall not shrink from this race with *your* Republic, which in the heart of christian America and in the middle of the Nineteenth Century lays down slavery as its corner stone, and finds its allies in Spain, Dahomey, and Mohammedan Turkey.

A. H. W. to E.

8 BREVOORT PLACE, Feb. 1, 1861.

My dear Eliza: As Charley was away at Astoria Georgy sent round for young Herdman, and she and I went with him to hear Wendell Phillips' lecture. I never saw him before, and found it a perfect treat. A more finished and eloquent sketch I never heard, enlivened by telling anecdotes, and that quiet, shrewd wit which distinguishes the speaker. He made the lecture an indirect argument of course for the negro race; twice in the course of it mentioned John Brown's name, which was received with a storm of applause, and once, in speaking of the courage of the blacks, he said: "Ask the fifty-two thousand of LeClerc's soldiers who died in battle. Go stoop with your ear on their graves! Go question the dust of Rochambeau and of the eight thousand who escaped with him under the English Jack! and if the answer is not loud enough, come home!" and (dropping his voice) "*come by the way of quaking Virginia!*" There was a great crowd, but we went early and had excellent seats, and were perfectly charmed.

On Friday Rose Terry (who is at the Danas) and Dr. Bacon are to dine here. Rose wrote the "Samson Agonistes" it seems, — the fragment about John Brown in the Tribune which we all liked.

J. S. W. to Cousin Margaret Hodge.

Feb. 7, 1861.

Night before last a Virginia gentleman said to us: "Don't be too sanguine. Union does not mean in Virginia what it means in New York. There it means only delay — it means Crittenden's compromise; it means secession, not today but tomorrow." The same gentleman said: "Floyd was no gentleman. No Virginia gentleman would ask him to dinner" (the climax of earthly honors I suppose) and that "he was intoxicated at the Richmond dinner and not responsible for his speech." This Virginian said he would "stake his existence," or something of the sort, on the honor of the South in paying, to the last cent, everything it owes the North. As an offset to this, Mr. Lockwood last night repeated to us the contents of three letters he had read yesterday, sent to acquaintances of his in answer to requests for payment. One said: "I shall pay, of course, every farthing I owe you, in cash, but not till I pay it in the currency *of the Southern Confederacy.*" Another sent a note to the effect: "I promise to pay, etc., five minutes after demand, to any Northern Abolitionist the same coin in which we paid John Brown, endorsed by thousands of true Southern hearts." The third said: "I cannot return the goods, as you demand, for they are already sold, and the money invested in muskets to shoot you — Yankees!" Georgy was at a party last night at Amy Talbot's, where nothing but politics was talked. Uncle Edward has just popped in, for a minute, and says: "All *I* am afraid of now is that Virginia and the other Border states *will stay in*; and we shall have the curse of their slavery on our shoulders without the blessings of a complete union."

Dr. Roosevelt dined with us on Saturday, and I said: "What do you go for,

Doctor?" "I go for gun-powder!" he answered. Mrs. Eliza Reed hears from her brother-in-law, a clergyman in Beaufort, S. C., that she "ought to be very thankful that her property is safely invested at the South" (partly in his own hands) and that he is "sorry he is *not able to forward her the interest now due*," the fact being that she has not had a cent of her income this winter.

One more anecdote and then my gossip is over. Mrs. Dulany overheard two negresses talking on a corner in Baltimore. "Wait till the fourth of March," said one of them, "and then won't I slap my missus' face!"

Inauguration of Mr. Lincoln.

ABRAHAM LINCOLN was inaugurated President of the United States on the fourth of March, 1861. In closing his inaugural address he said to the Southern seceders: "In your hands my dissatisfied fellow-countrymen, and not in mine, is the momentous issue of Civil War. You can have no conflict without being yourselves the aggressors. You have no oath registered in Heaven to destroy the government, while I shall have the most solemn one to preserve, protect, and defend it."

FIRST YEAR OF THE WAR
1861

CHAPTER II.

The Firing on Fort Sumter. The rebel batteries in the neighborhood of Charleston had been built and armed in the last three months of the imbecile administration of Mr. Buchanan and his traitorous Cabinet, and on April 12th, 1861, they opened fire upon Major Anderson, Fort Sumter, and the national flag, and easily forced a capitulation from troops left by the government without food or ammunition.

A. H. W. to E. W. H. April 14, 1861.

What awful times we have fallen upon! The sound last night of the newsboys crying till after midnight with hoarse voice, "Bombardment of Fort Sumter," was appalling. Cousin William Aspinwall was seen at a late hour going into the Brevoort House — no doubt to give what little comfort he could to Mrs. Anderson. This storm, which has been raging a day or two at the South, and has just reached us, has scattered the fleet sent to reinforce and provision Fort Sumter, and the vessels can neither rendezvous nor co-operate with Major Anderson who is there without food, without help, and without instructions. Is Providence against us too?

First Call to Arms. April 15th, 1861, President Lincoln issued the first call to arms, summoning the militia of the several states to the aggregate number of 75,000 men to serve for three months, and ordering the oath of fidelity to the United States to be administered to every officer and man.

At once the Governors of all the Northern states called out their militia, and preparations for war began in earnest, with a great burst of patriotic self-devotion on the part of men, women, and children. Regiments almost immediately began to arrive in New York en route for Washington. Mother and all her family enlisted promptly for the war, and the home, 8 Brevoort Place, New York, became a sort of headquarters for all the family friends. The little strong mahogany table which our uncle Commodore Newton had had made for Charley, on his flagship, the "Pensacola," and which Charley and the younger sisters had used at their play in the old Rutgers Place nursery, was brought down and established in the parlor. A bandage-roller was screwed to it, and for months bandage-rolling was the family fancy-work, and other festivities really ceased.

A. H. W. to E.
April 19, 1861.

My Dear Eliza: Your's and Joe's note and the box of birthday flowers for Charley came yesterday morning, and the latter we have all had the benefit of. Charley did not want to give any away, so we used them for the dinner-table and parlor, and looked and smelled "lovely" last night when we entertained eight young men callers. Charley did not have any of his friends to dinner or supper. On Wednesday he said he should keep his birthday on Thursday, and on Thursday he said he had kept it the day before. I think he preferred not having any special celebration this year. Meantime, the candy pyramid stands untouched, consolidating gradually into a huge sugary drop. The city is like a foreign one now; the flag floats from every public building and nearly every shop displays some patriotic emblem. Jane amused herself in shopping yesterday, by saying to everyone: "You have no flag out yet! Are you getting one ready?" etc. Shopkeepers said in every instance: "No — well — we mean to have one; we are having one prepared," etc. She met Mr. Charles Johnson, of Norwich, who had been down to see the Massachusetts contingent off — a splendid set of men — hardy farmers, sailors from Marblehead, some in military hats, some in fatigue caps, some few in slouched felts — all with the army overcoat. C. J. had a talk with some of them in their New England vernacular, which he described as very funny, "thought there might be some fightin', but by golly! there's one thing we want to do — a lot of us — just pitch into an equal number of South Carolinas." C. J. says a few gentlemen in Norwich came in to the "Norwich Bank" to his father and authorized him to offer Governor Buckingham $137,000 as a private subscription. This is beside the $100,000 offered by the other bank the "Thames."

Yesterday Mother and I went round to see Mary Carey, who was out, but seeing policemen about the door of the Brevoort House, colors flying, and a general look of expectancy on the faces of people in opposite windows, we hung round and finally asked what was going on? "Why nothing ma'am, only Major Anderson has just arriv'." Sure enough, he had driven up rapidly, reported himself at General Scott's headquarters, and then driven round to the hotel. In five minutes the crowd on foot had got wind of it and came surging up Eighth street with the Jefferson Guard, or something of that sort — a mounted regiment — who wished to give the Major a marching salute. Band playing, colors flying, men's voices cheering lustily, and everywhere hats tossed up and handkerchiefs waving — it was an enthusiastic and delightful tribute! We clung to an iron railing inside an adjoining courtyard and, safe from the crush of the crowd, waved our welcome with the rest and saw Major Anderson come out, bow with military precision several times and then retire. He looked small, slender, old, wrinkled, and grey, and was subdued and solemn in manner. Charley Johnson was on hand, of course — he is up to everything — and later in the day pressed his way in with some ladies, shook hands impressively and prayed, "God bless you, Sir!" "I trust He will!" said Major Anderson, and expressed himself honored by the interest felt in him. Our Charley went round in the evening, found Mr. Aspinwall in close conversation with the Major in the parlor, but not liking to intrude, looked his fill at him through the crack of the door.

Yesterday was "one of the days" in 10th street — a steady stream of people all day. While Mother and I went out for a few calls and had our little adventure, as above described, Jane took a short constitutional. C. Johnson, whom she met, gave her a flag, and as she walked up Broadway a large omnibus, with six horses, passed, gaily decked with flags and filled with gentlemen — some delegation — going to wait on Major Anderson as they supposed. Jane said she could not help giving her flag a little twirl — not daring to look to the right or left — and instantly the whole load of men broke out into vociferous cheers. They tell us that quantities of Union cockades were worn in the streets yesterday, and I should not be surprised if they should become universally popular. Just at dusk Will Winthrop came in to say good bye. To our immense surprise, he said he and Theodore joined the Seventh Regiment a week ago — he as a private in the ranks and Theodore in the artillery in charge of a howitzer — and they were all to leave this afternoon for Washington. It seemed to bring war nearer home to us. Mother was quite concerned, but I cannot but feel that the Seventh Regiment is only wanted there for the moral influence. It will act as guard of honor to the Capitol and come home in a fortnight. However, the demand for troops in Washington is very urgent. They are telegraphing here for all the regular officers. Even Colonel Ripley, the Dennys' cousin, who arrived on government business yesterday on his way to Springfield, was overtaken by a telegram as he took his seat in the New Haven train and ordered back by night train to Washington. Other men received similar despatches, and the idea is that Washington may be attacked at once now that Virginia has gone out, and the fear is that if done this week it may be taken. Troops are hurrying on. The Rhode Island contingent passed down at nine this morning, the Seventh goes at three — that will be a grand scene! We shall be somewhere on Broadway to see them pass. Georgy has been busy all the morning cutting up beef sandwiches and tying them up in white papers as rations. Each man tonight must take his supply with him for twenty-four hours, and Theodore Winthrop, who was in last night, suggested that we should put up "something for him and Billy in a newspaper." The Seventh is likely to have more than it needs in that way; it is being greatly pampered; but it all helps to swell the ardor of those who stay behind I suppose. The more troops who can be sent off to Washington the less chance for fighting. The immensity of our preparations may over-awe the South. Last night we had rather jolly times, joking and telling war anecdotes, and worked ourselves up into a very merry cheerful spirit. It is well that we can sometimes seize on the comic points of the affair or we should be overwhelmed by the dreadful probabilities.

J. S. W. to Cousin Margaret Hodge.

April, 1861.

Marching of the 7th New York.

My dear Cousin Margaret: I fancy that you may like to know how we have gone through the dreadful tumoil and excitement of the last few days, and so I send you an incoherent line tonight, though my wits are scarcely under command of my fingers.

The three great local incidents this week have been the arrival of Major Anderson, the leaving of the Seventh Regiment, and the great mass-meeting today in Union Square, or rather whose centre was Union Square, for the huge sea of men overflowed the quadrangle of streets where the speakers' stands were, and surged down Broadway, up Broadway, through Fourteenth street and along Fourth avenue far beyond the Everett House. We were in a balcony at the corner of Union Square and Broadway and saw the concourse, though we could not distinguish the words of any speaker. We could only tell when the "points" were made by the thousands of hats lifted and swung in the air and by the roar of the cheering. Every house fronting the square, and up and down the side streets, was decorated with flags and festoons, and the Sumter flag, on its splintered staff, hung over the stand where the gentlemen of the Sumter command were. The Puritan Church had a great banner afloat on its tower. Trinity set the example to the churches yesterday, when a magnificent flag was raised on its tall spire with a salvo of artillery. The sight was a grand one today, and in some of its features peculiar. As the tide rolled up under our balcony we could see scarcely a man who was not earnest-looking, grave, and resolved, and all seemed of the best classes, from well-dressed gentlemen down to hard-working, hard-fisted draymen and hod-carriers, but no lower. There was not a single intoxicated man as far as we could see, or a single one trying to make any disturbance or dissent. You will see by the reports of the meeting who were the officers, speakers, etc., and judge how all colors of opinion were represented and were unanimous. New York, at any rate, is all on one side now — all ready to forget lesser differences, like the household into which grief has entered. Almost every individual, man, woman and child, carried the sacred colors in some shape or other, and the ladies at the windows had knots of ribbon, tri-colored bouquets, and flags without number. There was not a policemen to be seen from our outlook, though no doubt there were some about the square, but the crowd kept itself in order and perfect good nature, and whenever the flag appeared at the head of any procession or deputation it fell back instantly and respectfully to let it pass through. The resolutions, Committee for Patriotic Fund, etc., you will see in the papers.

I have given the first place to the meeting because it was the most recent, but yesterday was a more exciting and saddening day than this. Beside Meredith Howland, Captain Schuyler Hamilton, Howland Robbins and other friends and acquaintances in the "Seventh," our two cousins Theodore and William Winthrop went. All these are privates except Merry, who is on the staff — Paymaster. The Winthrops came in their accoutrements at one o'clock to get their twenty-four hours' rations (sandwiches which Georgy had been making all the morning), and we filled their cases and liquor flasks, with great satisfaction that we were able to do even such a little thing for them. We gave them a hearty "feed," helped them stow their things with some economy of space, buckled their knapsack straps for them, and sent them off with as cheerful faces as we could command. They were in excellent spirits, on the surface at any rate, and promised to come back again in glory in a little while. We in our turn promised to go down to them if they needed us. Poor fellows! It was heart-sickening to think of any such necessity. Then we went down to a balcony near Prince street, in Broadway, and saw them off. The whole street was densely crowded, as today, and the shops and houses decorated — only there were three miles of flags and people. After long waiting we began to see in the distance the glimmer of the bayonets. Then the immense throng divided and pressed back upon the sidewalks, and the regiment came, — first the Captain of Police with one aid, then the Artillery corps, then company after company, in solid march, with fixed faces, many of them so familiar, so pleasant, and now almost sacred. The greeting of the people was a thing to see! The cheers were almost like a cannonade. People were leaning forward, shouting, waving handkerchiefs, crying, praying aloud, and one block took up the voice from the other and continued the long, long cry of sympathy and blessing through the entire route. Some friends of the soldiers who marched all the way with them to the Jersey cars, said the voice never ceased, never diminished, till they reached the end of that first triumphal stage of their journey. It was a triumph though a farewell.

At Ball and Black's Major Anderson was in the balcony with Cousin John's and Cousin William Aspinwall's families, and each company halted and cheered him as it passed. Except for this, they looked neither right nor left, but marched as if at that moment they were marching into the thick of battle. They were not long in passing, and the crowd closed in upon them like a parted sea. We watched the bayonets as far and long as we could see them, and the last we saw was a late warm beam of sunshine touching the colors as they disappeared.

Great anxiety is felt tonight about their arrival in Washington and what they may meet there. Many gentlemen here think the forces in the District quite inadequate and blame anybody and everybody for not hurrying on more troops. A gentleman was here late this afternoon looking for Cousin William Aspinwall. They were hunting him up everywhere where there was any chance of his being found, to make instant arrangements for steam vessels to take reinforcements tomorrow. Several regiments are ready, only waiting orders and means of transit. Uncle Edward came to the meeting today — very grave indeed — and I don't doubt very efficient and open-handed, as usual, in anything that needed his help. He has ordered a great flag for the "barrack." Joe has set one flying from his house-top. He (J. H.) has joined a cavalry company in Fishkill who are drilling for a Home Guard or a "reserve." Charley has joined a similar company (foot) in town. He is uneasy and wants to "do something." Uncle Edward says: "Stay at home, my boy, till you're wanted, and if the worst comes to the worst I'll shoulder a musket myself!"

Major Anderson was the hero of Cousin Anna's party last night. Only Charley represented us; we didn't feel "up to it." C. said it was a very handsome party, as usual with their entertainments, and that a portrait of Major Anderson was hung in the picture gallery, wreathed with laurel, and all the "Baltic's" flags decorated the hall and supper room. Thirty of the expected guests had marched at four o'clock with the Seventh. Major Anderson is very grave, almost sad, in expression and manner, as a man may well be who has been through such scenes and looks with a wise eye into such a future; but if anything could cheer a man's soul it would be such enthusiasm and almost love as are lavished on him here. He says "they had not had a biscuit to divide among them for nearly two days, and were almost suffocated." They say he talks very little about it all; only gives facts in a few modest words. He is "overwhelmed" with the sight of the enthusiasm and unanimity of the North; "the South has no idea of it at all." He says that he "felt very much aggrieved at being attacked at such disadvantage;" that "for four weeks he only received *one* message from government, and was almost broken down with suspense, anxiety, and ignorance of what was required of him." He went to all the stands today at the mass-meeting, and was received with a fury of enthusiasm everywhere. Yesterday he was obliged to leave the balcony at Ball and Black's, the excitement and applause were so overpowering; and he goes about with tears in his eyes all the time.

Mrs. Gardiner Howland is very anxious and sad about Merry in the Seventh. She says she is "no Spartan mother." Mary G. G. has sent to Kate Howland withdrawing her invitations for her bridesmaids' dinner on Tuesday. She is not in spirits to give it.*
Two regiments start tonight instead of tomorrow to go by rail to Philadelphia and thence by steamboats, outside. There are the gravest fears that they may be too late.

. . . I have been writing while the others have gone to the Philharmonic concert. They have come back and had a splendid scene at the close — singing of the Star-

---

* Kate Howland was married April 2, 1861, to Richard Morris Hunt.

Spangled Banner, solo, and chorus by the Lierderkranz and the whole huge audience, standing, to the hundred stringed and wind instruments of the orchestra, while a great silken banner was slowly unrolled from the ceiling to the floor. Then followed rounds of vociferous applause, and three times three for everything good, especially for Major Anderson, and the Seventh.

The Massachusetts contingent passed through on Thursday, and then we got the news of the cowardly assault in Baltimore.* The poor fellows tasted war very soon. Tonight the city is full of drum-beating, noise and shouting, and they are crying horrible extras, full of malicious falsehoods (*we hope*). G. G., we hear, is going from home to his Mother's and back again, all the evening, contradicting them. There should be authentic news by this time of the progress of the Seventh, but people will not believe these horrible rumors, and refuse to believe anything.

There is the most extraordinary mixture of feeling with everyone — so much resistless enthusiasm and yet so much sadness for the very cause that brings it out. It

---

*The Sixth Massachusetts, crossing Baltimore to the Washington depot, were set upon by a furious mob of roughs and pelted with stones and brickbats. Two soldiers were killed and eight wounded, and the troops forming in solid square with fixed bayonets at last forced their way through the crowds.

seems certainly like a miracle, this fresh and universal inspiration of patriotism surmounting the sorrow, like a fire kindled by God's own hand from his own altar — and this alone ought to inspire us with hope of the future.

Flag Presentation to the Second Conn.

The following letter from our special cousin, Sarah Chauncey Woolsey, to G. M. W. describes the making of the Connecticut flags and their presentation, and the farewell to the Second Connecticut Volunteers on the New Haven Green. Dr. Bacon (now "Uncle Frank") marched with them as Assistant Surgeon:

Our beautiful flags are nearly done and are to be presented to the Second Regiment before they leave. The regimental banner is worked with the arms of the state, which are far more beautiful than those of any other state, with a heavy wreath of palm worked in gold-colored silk around the shield and mounted on a staff headed with a battle-axe and spear plated with gold. Won't it be beautiful? The other flag is the Union flag and just as handsome in its way. F. B. was here last night with stripes on his trousers, but wisely withholding the full splendors of his "milingtary" attire until we become gradually accustomed to it. He looked very handsome and is as coolly delighted at the chance of a little fighting as anyone I have seen. We are both highly entertained just now by the pertinacity with which our friends here persist in engaging us to each other. I was telling him last night of a lady who called the other day and would not listen to any denials on my part, asseverating that Miss ——— assured her that she knew it to be a fact; whereon Frank, putting himself in an attitude, informed me that "being on the eve of battle and about risking his life in his country's defence, he *could not* feel that it was his duty to engage the affections of any young and lovely female and withdraw her from the bosom of her own family," whereon I begged him not to apologize, and explained that "being on the point of joining the Nightingale Regiment and putting myself in the way of catching a fever, *I* could not feel justified in allowing my naturally susceptible feelings to run away with me," etc. I don't know why I tell you all this stuff—only it makes you laugh a little. . . .

Later.— Dora and I went up at four o'clock to see our flags given to the Second Regiment, on their way to the "Cahawba," which waited to carry them off, no one knows where, under sealed orders,—but probably to Washington or Fortress Monroe.

The colors were presented on the Green at the foot of the liberty pole, where the Home Guard formed a hollow square enclosing all the ladies who had worked on or were interested in the flags, and when the regiment marched up they took their places inside the square, which widened and kept off the crowd outside. Two pretty girls held the flags, assisted by two gentlemen. Mr. Foster made a short and spirited address to the regiment, and their Colonel replied in a few brave words, and then Dr. Leonard Bacon read the twentieth Psalm, "in the name of our God we will set up our banners," etc., and made a beautiful prayer, and amid the shouts and cheers of the crowd, the frantic waving of handkerchiefs and flags and the quiet weeping of some who were sending off their dearest ones to all the chances of war, the glittering waving splendors were lifted aloft and the regiment swept on — carrying in its ranks Frank, who found time in the midst of the confusion to ride his horse round to the place where we stood, and hold my hand tenderly for two or three minutes while he whispered some good-bye words, especially his "farewells to Miss Georgy," greatly to the satisfaction of some old ladies near, who, fondly fancying that I am engaged to him, probably wondered at my comparative composure. Yes! the good-byes are hard enough even if it is for the country, and I have had a heartache all day at the thought that I shall see the dear fellow no more for so long a time, and of how much we shall all miss him. He looked tired, with these last days of hurry. We stood two hours nearly, on the Green. We heard all about the doings in Norwich from Captain Chester and Lieutenant Coit of the "Buckingham Rifles." They are both pleasant young fellows, and we made their acquaintance while sewing green stripes on the trousers of the company and brass buttons on their coats — the very garments which were made on Sunday by the Norwich ladies. It was funny work, as the men all had to be sent to bed before we could be put in possession of their apparel, and the officers being in the same quandary all were comfortably tucked up in their quarters and their trousers under way when sixteen Norwich gentlemen called to see them, and had to be received by them "lying in state!"

About this time the national flag was printed in colors on note paper, and on slips for use in books and wherever it could be displayed on anything, and this next letter of Jane's bears it, as a matter of course, on the first page.

J. S. W. to the Sisters Abroad.

Seventh Regiment safe and jolly. No fighting yet,— April 29th, 1861.

Eliza has been making a flag for their church. It was her part to cut out and sew on the stars. She sent for a large number of very small testaments, for knapsacks, for the Fishkill Regiment, and we have found some sheets of flags on paper, like stamps, to paste in them, each with an appropriate verse — "Fight the good fight;" "Endure hardness as a good soldier of Jesus Christ," etc.

On Thursday evening Charley had a few friends to supper — a substitute for the birthday party — and we decorated the table with flags, bunting, red, white and blue mottoes, etc. They seemed to have a gay time and sang many songs to a squealing accompaniment from Pico. It is by no means unlikely that a Home Guard will be needed with all the militia ordered away and seditious people biding their time in town. Mansfield Davies is with his regiment at Fort Schuyler, drilling. They go south next week. George Betts goes today as Lieutenant-Colonel Second Zouaves. The great barracks in the park are nearly finished — meant as a mere shelter for troops in transit and there is a camp in the Battery — officers' marquee and a whole fleet of tents.

We hear from Norwich that last Sunday was spent by Dr. Bond's congregation in making red flannel shirts for the regiment who were to leave next day. Mr. Davies asks us for bandages, etc., for their surgeon, which we shall supply with great readiness. Mother has made a great deal of beautiful lint. There is an organization of medical men to train nurses for the camp; lectures are to be given and bands of ten ladies are to walk some wards in the hospitals, as a preparation. Georgy has been to some of the lectures with Mrs. Trotter, and would like to go as a nurse, but would no doubt be rejected, as none but "able-bodied and experienced" women are to be taken. While I write a company goes down Broadway with the eternal Reveille. We had a grand patriotic sermon last Sunday from Dr. Prentiss, and now we have only patriotic prayers and psalms, with the petition for the President borrowed bodily from the Prayer Book.

This morning I got, to my surprise and pleasure, an official document containing a letter from Will Winthrop of the Seventh, written, no doubt, in acknowledgment of the little kindnesses we were able to show him on leaving. I quote, as it's far too bulky to send: "Washington, April 26. Dear Cousin: Here we are in "marble halls" the adored of everybody, the heroes of the hour. Members of Congress frank our letters; hotel men fetch the sparkling wines; citizens cheer us with tears and rapture. Wherever we appear vivas greet us — now the triple cheer, now the *"bully for you!"* This p. m. we paraded in the Capitol grounds, and forming in a grand square took the oath of allegiance, all together, repeating it sentence by sentence after the migistrate. Green grass was soft under foot, trees in spring attire exhaled fragrance, the marble halls gleamed on every side. Every man was clean and beautiful of moustache, pipe-clayed as to belts of snowy whiteness, well-dinnered internally. Brass plates and bayonets glistened in the sun. The band played the national hymns and the Valence polka. Abe and wife walked happy and beaming along the line. All was brilliant and imposing. Night before the last we were staggering along the line of railroad from Annapolis, wearied to exhaustion, stiff with cold and swamp damps, almost starved, with nothing but a little salt pork or jerked beef in our haversacks and no water in our canteens, feet sore with tramping—wretched beyond expression; yet all the time forced to build bridges destroyed by the enemy, and relay railroad track, torn up (rails and sleepers); also to push along before us heavy platform-cars carrying our howitzers;

also to scout in the van and watch on all sides for the enemy who might be ambushed anywhere. This we had done during the day, now under a hot sun, now rained on by heavy showers; but at night in the dark and fog and cold it was cruelly severe, and to all of us the most terribly wearisome experience of our lives. Whenever we halted to hunt missing rails and lay track, our men who were not thus employed would sink down and instantly fall asleep, and often could not be roused without violent shaking. Many a time during the night did I thank (1) the cherub that sits up aloft for having put me in the way of roughing it in Minnesota; (2) the blessed women whose brandy helped to give heart to many a miserable beside myself. On the day before this forced march we were in clover in Annapolis doing parade drill on the Academy ground, sniffing the sea breeze and the fruit blossoms, swelping down oysters on the demi-shell. On the day before this, we were packed in the transport, either stifled in the steerage in odors of uncleanness and water drips, or broiling on the deck, each man with a square foot or two to move in, and all subsisting on the hardest of tack. The day before, we woke at dawn in Philadelphia and foraged for provisions around the railroad station, bearing off loaves on our bayonets, entertained by Quakers with eggs and cakes, lingering all day at the station, utterly in doubt about the future — ending with a hot fatiguing walk across the city to take the transport. The day before, the triumphal march down Broadway! Such are the vicissitudes of a week, the most eventful and strange in the lives of all of us — a week of cheers, tears, doubt, peril, starvation, exhaustion, great dinners, woe, exultation, passion. And the sweetest thing of all has been the brotherhood and fraternization. We share in common, give, relieve and love each other. . . . We were disappointed that we could not have a chance at Baltimore; also that we had no brush with the enemy in Maryland. We only saw them scampering over the distant hills. They could tear up the track, but were too craven to meet us. There were but few troops here in Washington; everybody was in doubt and dread, and when we marched up toward the White House with colors flying, full band playing and perfect lines, the people rushed out in tears and shouting welcome. Our importance is, of course, over-estimated, but *moi* I feel that I never before was so useful a member of the Republic.

We are quartered in the stunning Representatives Hall and march down three times a day to our browsings at the hotel. This is luxury, but pretty soon we go into camp on Georgetown heights. Regiments arrive all the while and the city is awake and brilliant — guards and watchings everywhere. Washington is not in immediate danger, but all are ready to resist an attack at any moment." All very graphic and interesting. Now we shall be eager to know how *you* take all this stupendous news, and whether it affects in any way your plans. Perhaps you will think best to spend the summer abroad — Isle of Wight, or something. For many reasons we should be quite satisfied to have you. Perhaps on the other hand you will be for rushing home; — natural but after all, useless. One thing, look out for Jeff. Davis' privateers, and don't come in any ship that hasn't arms of some sort on board. This sounds ridiculous, so did the siege of the Capitol, ten days ago; so did the prophecy that New York would be nothing but a barrack full of marching regiments.

Uncle E. has a turn of gout. Abby is going out to spend the day there. Some day soon Mr. Aspinwall is going to drive Major Anderson out, for Aunt E.'s gratification. I shall keep my letter open for tomorrow's news. Nothing immediate is expected, but a collision *must* come soon. We shall send every day's papers and you must look out for them. Tuesday.—The news this morning is the final departure of Virginia and the call for more troops by the President. We can send as many as are wanted and more.

<small>The Sanitary Commission.</small> On April 25th, 1861, the first steps were taken by fifty or sixty New York women towards organizing systematic work for the sick and wounded.

From this "Woman's Central Association of Relief," together with Boards of Physicians and Surgeons proposing to furnish hospital supplies in aid of the army, came the first suggestion to the Department of War at Washington that a "mixed commission of civilians, medical men and military officers" be appointed, charged with the duty of organizing and directing the benevolence of the people towards the army.

As the result of this petition the great United States Sanitary Commission, was, on the 13th of June, 1861, duly appointed by Simon Cameron Secretary of War, with the signature and approval of President Lincoln.

While retaining its independence, the Woman's Central Association became at its own instance an auxiliary branch of the commission, and other branches sprang up all over the northern states.

The headquarters of the commission were in Washington, where also was stationed Mr. Frederick Law Olmsted, its life and soul. With its work we, as a family, were associated from the beginning.

Eliza and Joe were just taking possession of their beautiful new home, "Tioronda," at Fishkill, and all the little details of E.'s home letters have a pathos of their own in view of the speedy closing of the house and the sudden change from peaceful loveliness to the grimness of civil war. Meantime, E. was busy, as all of us began to be, in work for the disabled soldiers.

E. W. H. to A. H. W.

"TIORONDA," WEDNESDAY EVENING.

Dear Abby: I was just going to write you a note this p. m. when the Kents came in for a long call and stayed on for an early tea. We sat in the *library* where the books are now all arranged and the cushion we ordered at Soloman and Hart's in its place in the bay-window. To be sure there is no carpet down, and we have no tables or chairs, but it already has a very habitable look, and we feel quite at home in presence of our old book-friends. They make a very good show, though there are still a number of empty upper shelves which will fill up by degrees. James Kent had been in town for a couple of days and had a good deal to say about military matters. While Joe was in town I did a good deal of cutting out and have three dozen army pillow-cases and six double-gowns under way. Tomorrow I shall attack the drawers and night-shirts, for which I borrowed a good simple pattern of Mrs. Kent. I smile when I think of the sang-froid with which you and I discussed the cut of drawers and shirts with that pleasant young doctor the other day. I see that Georgy is excluded from the corps of nurses by being under thirty.

A. H. W. to E.

FRIDAY.

Dear Eliza: We got off our first trunk of Hospital supplies for Colonel Mansfield Davies' Regiment yesterday and feel today as if we were quite at leisure. You have no idea of the number of last things there were to do, or the different directions we had to go in, to do them. Mr. Davies came in at breakfast yesterday, in his regimentals, quite opportunely, to tell us what to do with the trunk. It went down to his headquarters at 564 Broadway and thence by steamer to Fort Schuyler for the sick soldiers there. Charley and Ned drove out there yesterday afternoon from Astoria to see the drill, and saw the box safely landed within the walls. It was the old black ark which you and G. had in Beyrout, Syria, marked with a capital H, which now answers for *Hospital*. There were in it as follows — for you may be curious to know: —

  42 shirts,
  12 drawers,
   6 calico gowns,
  24 pairs woolen socks,
  24 pairs slippers,
  24 pocket handkerchiefs,
  18 pillow sacks,
  36 pillow-cases,
  18 damask napkins,
  36 towels,
  24 sponges,
   4 boxes of lint,

beside old linen, oiled silk, tape, thread, pins, scissors, wax, books (Hedley Vicars and the like), ribbon, cloth, etc., and fifty bandages.

This morning Mother has been putting up a tin box of stores for Mr. Davies — sardines, potted meats, arrow root, chocolate, guava and the like, with a *box* of cologne, a jar of prunes and a morocco case with knife, fork and spoon, fine steel and double plated, "just out" for army use.

Lots more. The box, a square cracker box, holds as much in its way as the trunk. I am glad you are in the library at last. You will grow accustomed to it and find it pleasanter even than the dining-room.

J. S. W. to a Friend in Paris.

    8 BREVOORT PLACE, FRIDAY, May 10, 1861.

I am sure you will like to hear what we are all about in these times of terrible excitement, though it seems almost impertinent to write just now. Everything is either too big or too little to put in a letter. Then one can't help remembering sometimes that you are that august being, a "Tribune's Own," and as unapproachable on your professional pinnacle as the ornament of the Calendar whom Georgy *will* persist in calling Saint Simeon Stalactites. But the dampest damper to enthusiastic correspondents on this side is the reflection that what they write as radiant truth today may be "unaccountably turned into a lie" by the time it crosses the "big water." So it will be best perhaps not to try to give you any of my own "views" except, indeed, such views of war as one may get out of a parlor window. Not, in passing, that I haven't any! We all have views now, men, women and little boys,

"Children with drums
 Strapped round them by the fond paternal ass,
Peripatetics with a blade of grass
 Betwixt their thumbs,"—

from the modestly patriotic citizen who wears a postage stamp on his hat to the woman who walks in Broadway in that fearful object of contemplation, a "Union bonnet," composed of alternate layers of red, white and blue, with streaming ribbons "of the first." We all have our views of the war question and our plans of the coming campaign. An acquaintance the other day took her little child on some charitable errand through a dingy alley into a dirty, noisy, squalid tenement house. "Mamma," said he, "isn't this South Carolina?"

Inside the parlor windows the atmosphere has been very fluffy, since Sumter, with lint-making and the tearing of endless lengths of flannel and cotton bandages and cutting out of innumerable garments. How long it is since Sumter! I suppose it is because so much intense emotion has been crowded into the last two or three weeks, that the "time before Sumter" seems to belong to some dim antiquity. It seems as if we never were alive till now; never had a country till now. How could we ever have laughed at Fourth-of-Julys? Outside the parlor windows the city is gay and brilliant with excited crowds, the incessant movement and music of marching regiments and all the thousands of flags, big and little, which suddenly came fluttering out of every window and door and leaped from every church tower, house-top, staff and ship-mast. It seemed as if everyone had in mind to try and make some amends to it for those late grievous and bitter insults. You have heard how the enthusiasm has been deepening and widening from that time.

A friend asked an Ohio man the other day how the West was taking it. "The West?" he said, "the West is all one great Eagle-scream!" A New England man told us that at Concord the bells were rung and the President's call read aloud on the village common. On the day but one after that reading, the Concord Regiment was marching into Fanueil Hall. Somebody in Washington asked a Massachusetts soldier: "How many more men of your state are coming?" "All of us," was the answer. One of the wounded Lowell men crawled into a machine shop in Baltimore. An "anti-Gorilla*" citizen, seeing how young he was, asked, "What brought you here fighting, so far away from your home, my poor boy?" "It was the stars and stripes," the dying voice said. Hundreds of such stories are told. Everybody knows one. You read many of them in the papers. In our own little circle of friends one mother has sent away an idolized son; another, two; another, four. One boy, just getting over diphtheria, jumps out of bed

---

*That was the newspaper's way of spelling "Guerilla."

and buckles his knapsack on. One throws up his passage to Europe and takes up his "enfield." One sweet young wife is packing a regulation valise for her husband today, and doesn't let him see her cry. Another young wife is looking fearfully for news from Harper's Ferry, where her husband is ordered. He told me a month ago, *before Sumter*, that no Northman could be found to fight against the South. One or two of our soldier friends are surgeons or officers, but most of them are in the ranks, and think no work too hard or too mean, so it is for The Flag. Captain Schuyler Hamilton was an aid of General Scott's in Mexico, and saw service there, but he shouldered his musket and marched as a private with the Seventh. They wanted an officer when he got down there, and took him out of the ranks, but it was all the same to him; and so on, indefinitely.

The color is all taken out of the "Italian Question." Garibaldi indeed! "Deliverer of Italy!" Every mother's son of us is a "Deliverer." We women regretfully "sit at home at ease" and only appease ourselves by doing the little we can with sewing machines and patent bandage-rollers. Georgy, Miss Sarah Woolsey and half a dozen other friends earnestly wish to join the Nurse Corps, but are under the required age. The rules are stringent, no doubt wisely so, and society just now presents the unprecedented spectacle of many women trying to make it believed that they are over thirty!

The Vermont boys passed through this morning, with the "strength of the hills" in their marching and the green sprigs in their button-holes. The other day I saw some companies they told me were from Maine. They looked like it — sun-browned swingers of great axes, horn-handed "breakers of the glebe," used to wintering in the woods and getting frost-bitten and having their feet chopped off and conveying huge fleets of logs down spring-tide rivers in the snow and in the floods. — The sound of the drum is never out of our ears.

Never fancy that we are fearful or gloomy. We think we feel thoroughly that war is dreadful, especially war with the excitement off and the chill on, but there are so many worse things than gun-shot wounds! And among the worst is a hateful and hollow peace with such a crew as the "Montgomery mutineers." There was a dark time just after the Baltimore murders, when communication with Washington was cut off and the people in power seemed to be doing nothing to re-establish it. It cleared up, however, in a few days, and now we don't feel that the "social fabric" — I believe that is what it is called —

FIRST YEAR OF THE WAR

is "falling to pieces" at all, but that it is getting gloriously mended. So, "Republicanism will wash"—*is* washed already in the water and the fire of this fresh baptism, "clothed in white samite, mystic, wonderful," and has a new name, which is *Patriotism*.

J. H. joins the Army. From the first moment of the firing on Fort Sumter J. H. had felt that "solemn and compelling impulse" that forced men, almost in spite of themselves, into the service of the government. Making his decision quietly, seriously, he gave up the new home and all that it meant, and early in May, 1861, joined the Sixteenth New York Volunteers—a fine regiment from the northern counties of the state, then forming at Albany under the command of Colonel Thomas A. Davies,—into which he was mustered as Lieutenant and Adjutant.

E. W. H. to Mother.

May 11, 1861.

Dear Mother: Joe had a note from his Colonel last night requesting him to report himself at headquarters, 678 Broadway, on Wednesday of this week. This may be merely to take the oath, receive his commission, etc., but he will arrange matters to stay if required. He is now under orders and not his own master. It is generally known now that he is going, and hearty blessings and congratulations pour in upon him. He wrote to Uncle Edward and his sisters last night, and was busy till a very late hour settling business matters and explaining things to me. He goes off with rather a sad heart, but he feels that he is *doing right*, and I can give him nothing but encouragement. Our friends here have been most kind in their sympathy and in offers of service to me; and, as for me, if I can have all or any of you here I shall be very courageous. Don't forget our big house in making your summer plans. I would rejoice in having you with me.

Uncle Edward to J. H.

May 13, 1861.

My dear Joe: My eyes are so weak that I must use your Cousin Emily's pen to express the surprise caused by the announcement in your letter that your sense of duty had obliged you to accept the adjutancy of a regiment.

Had the question been propounded to me, I should have replied that I did not think you possessed the physical endurance needed for such a post, nor the requisite knowledge of military law and tactics; also that you could be ten times more usefully employed in aiding the cause than by a *personal* devotion to the duties of an officer of the army. If there had been a deficiency of able men anxious to serve, then the duty might have been imperative to stand forward and offer personal services. There are, however, five men offering to each man required. All this I state, because you wish my candid opinion, though I am fully aware that now, having taken the step under your own sense of duty, it is perhaps well that you had not an opportunity of consulting me previous to your decision.

May God's presence accompany you; and if during your absence I can be of any use to Eliza let her come to me as freely as to a father.

Your Cousin Emily joins with me in all love and desires to do anything in her power for you or Eliza.

Yours with sincere affection,
E. J. Woolsey.

From Mother.

May 15, 1861.

My dear Eliza: Thank you and Joe for your letters received this morning. I was hoping to see you here today, and on reading these letters telling of Joe's sudden departure, and thinking of you as all alone at your house, I at once concluded to go up, Charley and I, by the three o'clock train. I was all packed up to start when your telegram was brought in. I felt relieved to get it, because I was going off in a little uncertainty as to whether we might not possibly pass you on the road, on your way to us. I hope you will come, and Joe too, if he can. He must now I suppose *obey orders*—a somewhat new position for him! Should the regiment be ordered to Washington, perhaps you might feel like going on there for a while, at least, But remember, my dear child, your home is with us still, for as long as you choose.— Indeed, I think you had better come to us altogether—at any rate we must manage to keep an eye over you, and all of us must look on the bright side and hope for the best. How comforting to fall back at such times to that invisible arm which is ever ready for our support and which, I trust, is leading in all this movement. Charley waits for the letter, and I will only add my tender love to you both. Many thanks to Joe for his letters.

Your loving Mother.

Among many kind notes from friends at this time was the following from Mrs. Professor Smith:

My dear Mrs. Howland: I thank you very much for the beautiful flowers, which are a great delight to us all, and I thank you especially for thinking of our pleasure when your heart must have been so full. I could hardly be reconciled at first to Mr. Howland's going, but now I am glad that such a man should go. Surely the cause is worthy of the best and noblest, and he will have the same Protector there as at home, and the constant loving prayers of many hearts will be like a shield of defence.

A. H. W. to E.

FRIDAY, May 17, 1861.

My dear Eliza: Your nice long letter of yesterday from Albany came this morning at breakfast. I say your "nice" letter in the sense of its being long and circumstantial. That anything concerning Joe's going off is nice, I shall never be brought to say. It seems as if you both had been snatched up and swept away from us by some sudden and awful fate. No time for thought about it and no use for regrets! I hardly think he himself realized all he was pledging himself to — the bothering duties, I mean, of an Adjutant's office, a great deal of work and no glory; a sort of upper servant to an exacting Colonel; though some people tell us that the Adjutant's post is a highly military one, requiring fine military education — a knowledge, at least, of theories and laws, etc.

I am glad that Colonel Davies impresses you pleasantly.

Do find out from Joe's Dr. Crandall what style of garments he thinks best for hospital wear, as we are constantly cutting them out, and may as well make them with reference to his wants. Should the nightshirts be of unbleached or canton flannel, and drawers ditto? Should the shirts be long or short? and are extra flannel shirts necessary for hospital wear? I am going to the Cooper Union today to try and get some simple pattern for calico gowns. They advertise to supply paper patterns of garments to ladies, and their published circular, a copy of which I have seen, is far more particular and satisfactory in its directions than the one we have had.

I went to Astoria day before yesterday and came back yesterday noon. Aunt E. and I spent all the time in Casina library. The women dusted the books and I checked them off on the catalogue to see if they were all right and to leave them in good order for G. G. Howland, who moves up next week. I saw the transport go up to Riders' Island with George Betts' Zouaves — the Hawkins' Zouaves as they are called. We can see the barracks built for them from Casina. I thought if Robert were at home he would be flying about in his sailboat, visiting these points, and could make many a call on Joe if he were to be at Fort Schuyler. I found on coming home from Astoria that Georgy had fairly begun at the hospital — the City Hospital on Broadway — but as she has requested me not to "discuss her" with anybody I had better leave her to tell her own story. She and Mrs. Trotter go down daily at twelve o'clock, and yesterday, Mother tells me, they went before breakfast beside, at 6 a. m. Two such visits a day, when a singing lesson and a German lesson come in between, are rather too much, *I* think, but this insane war is making men and women insane,— Mr. ——— of Alexandria, for instance. Mother had a letter from him this morning written in the true Southern style — so highfalutin — with abuse and melancholy, martial ardor and piety, beautifully commingled. Mother wrote the other day to find out something about them, and this letter was to say that her's had been received and forwarded to his wife and daughters at Lexington, Va., where he had removed them "to be out of the reach of the licensed outrages of our Northern outcasts, who make up the Northern army!"

Today we are going to try and decide on our wedding presents for Jenny Woolsey. Just think of Susan Johnson, too! and now Sarah Winthrop tells us of *her* engagement to Mr. Weston, a friend of her brother Will's. It reminds me of the days of Noe when there was marrying and giving in marriage and the flood came and drowned them all. Love to Joe. What is his title now? We cannot call him plain Mister!

G.M.W. Studies Nursing. As part of their excellent work, the Woman's Central Relief Association organized a nursing staff for the army, selecting one hundred women and sending them to the various hospitals in New York city for such drill as could be secured in a few weeks, through the kindness of the attending staff. The Sanitary Commission undertook to secure recognition for these women from the War Department with the pay of privates; and they were sent on to the army hospitals on requisition from Miss Dix and others, as needed.

I (G.) still have my blue ticket, or pass, signed by (Mrs.) Christine Kean Griffin, Secretary of the Ladies' Committee, and Dr. Elisha Harris, of the Hospital Committee, on which I, "No. 24," was admitted to the old New York Hospital for a month's seasoning in painful sights and sounds.

[The old New York Hospital property comprised a square on Broadway bounded by Worth street on the north and Duane on the south. Great office buildings now take its place on the Broadway front, and the rest of the site has become the centre of the dry-goods trade. One hundred years ago your great-great-uncle, Mr. William Walton Woolsey, was one of the governors of this charity, and the family is still represented on the Board by your cousin, Theodorus Bailey Woolsey.]

Later in the war it happened that the Sanitary Commission wanted contributions to the "SPIRIT OF THE FAIR," published during the great Fair held for the Commission, and I gave them my experiences in getting ready to be a nurse three years before. They may interest you and I quote from them. You will be amazed to know that your aunt was considered by some of the committee as too young and too pretty! to be sent to the front. That was thirty-seven years ago though!—

"It was hard work getting myself acceptable and accepted. What with people at home, saying 'Goodness me! a nurse!'

'All nonsense!' 'Such a fly-away!' and what with the requisites insisted upon by the grave committees, I came near losing my opportunity.

"First, one must be just so old, and no older; have eyes and a nose and mouth expressing just such traits, and no others; must be willing to scrub floors, if necessary, etc., etc. Finally, however, by dint of taking the flowers out of my bonnet and the flounce off my dress; by toning down, or toning up, according to the emergency, I succeeded in getting myself looked upon with mitigated disapprobation, and was at last sat upon by the committee and passed over to the Examining Board. The Board was good to me. It had to decide upon my physical qualifications; and so, having asked me who my grandfather was, and whether I had had the measles, it blandly put my name down, leaving a blank, inadvertently, where the age should have been, and I was launched, with about twenty other neophytes, into a career of philanthropy more or less confused.

"Then began serious business. Armed with a blue ticket, I presented myself with the others at the door of a hospital and was admitted for instruction. 'Follow me,' said our guide, and we followed in procession. 'This will be your ward; you will remain here under so and so, and learn what you can; and this, yours; and this, *yours.*' That was *mine!* I shall never forget the hopeless state of my mind at this exact point. To be left standing in the middle of a long ward, full of beds, full of sick men — it was appalling! I seized another nurse, and refused to be abandoned. So they took pity, and we two remained, to use our eyes and time to the advantage of the Army of the Potomac which was-to-be. We took off our bonnets and went to work. Such a month as we had of it, walking round from room to room, learning what we could — really learning something in the end, till finally, what with writing down everything we saw, and making elaborate sketches of all kinds of bandages and the ways of applying them, and what with bandaging everybody we met, for practice, we at last made our 'reverses' without a wrinkle; and at the end of the month were competent to any very small emergency, or very simple fracture."

In looking over my little note book of those first days at the New York Hospital I find it full of extracts from the lectures of Dr. Markoe and Dr. Buck at the bedside of the patients, and with sketches of four-tailed, six-tailed and many-tailed bandages. I remember it gave me a little shock that first day in the ward to hear the young "house" say peremptorily: "Nurse, basin!" I presented the basin promptly, and as promptly tumbled over in a faint at seeing a probe used for the first time. I came out from this ignominy to find that my associate-nurse was dashing my face with water from a tumbler in which she dipped her fingers before offering it to me to drink from.

"Before the summons from the army, though, came sickness among our soldiers passing through the great cities. Measles and typhoid fever began almost immediately. New wards in hospitals had to be opened, and the beds were filled faster than we could make them. Such nice fellows, too, from the country villages as were brought in.

"My first patient of the war was a Duryea's Zouave, not a country boy though, but one of those poor desolate creatures, so many of whom the army has sheltered, giving them the first *home* they have ever known. My Zouave was dying when he enlisted; he had no friends, no place to live in, no place to die in, so he told me, and came into the army for the sake of finding one. 'I felt the sickness coming on, and I knew if I was a soldier they would put me into a hospital, and *then* I could die there.'

"Poor soul! he was young and refined, in look and manner, and so comforted by little attentions, so appreciative of them;— and never to have had anything of the kind given him through all his lonely life!

"Now, in these few last days of it there was a satisfaction in doing everything for him, in being as good to him as possible, in bringing him all that a gentleman's son might have had. So, with his poor tired head on my arm, I fed him with jellies and ices, and in little ways tried to comfort him. We owed him all the blessing we could bring into these last few moments of a dreary life.

"My Zouave died, and they buried him in his fine new clothes — the best he had ever had — and put him to sleep in his own bed; now, at last, *his own*, that no one would dispute with him; no one grudge him possession of forever."

What our common soldiers understood the war to mean is shown in this extract from a letter of one of them, taken ill on the march through New York from Connecticut and nursed by me in the New York Hospital. The rough draft in my hospital note book is sandwiched between directions for a "figure of 8" bandage and a receipt for boiling farina. The letter was to his old mother in Ireland:

"We are having a war here in America. The Southern states want to have a flag of their own and as many slaves as they can buy or steal. The North wants to keep the old flag and the country as Washington left it, and not to have slavery go any further; so they have gone to war about it, and I have enlisted and hope to fight for right and the country."

This gives the cause of the war in a very few words.

What the spirit was which these Northern men and women had to meet when they "enlisted for the war" is shown for instance in the proceedings of the "open session of the Confederate Congress," May, 1861, where the "assistance of The Most High" was impiously asked with the following blatherskite: "To protect us from those who threaten our homes with fire and sword; our domestic circles with ruthless lust; our fathers' graves with the invader's feet, and our altars with infidel desecration."

As soon as J. H. was mustered in, G. began to urge that she and E. should go as army nurses. Mother writes: "Georgy is more earnest than ever about being a nurse for the soldiers. *I shall never consent* to this arrangement unless some of her own family go with her."

G. herself writes to E.

May 15, 1861.

I supposed you would go to Albany; I am sure I should, and I hope you will take into serious consideration the small plan I suggested to you about being a nurse —at any rate about fitting yourself as far as you can for looking after the sick, if you go, as I suppose you will want to, to Washington in the fall with Joe. I invite you to join me. Mrs. Trotter and I were yesterday examined by the Medical Committee, Drs. Delafield, Wood and Harris, and with ten other women admitted to the course of instruction at the New York Hospital. We are to learn how to make beds for the wounded, cook food properly for the sick, wash and dress wounds, and other things as they come along in the proper care of the wards — fresh air, etc. Not that we have any idea of really going south now, no one will till the fall, and two or three companies of ten each who are fitting themselves at Bellevue Hospital will at any rate go first. Then if there is really a necessity for more nurses we shall send substitutes agreeing to pay their expenses,—unless the opposition in the family has come to an end, in which case, having tested our strength and endurance a little in this training, we shall be very glad to carry out our plan and go. We three might very usefully employ ourselves in Washington if we went no further south, and I shall not be satisfied at all to stay at home while Joe is down there. So, my dear, be keeping the little plan in view in making your arrangements, and don't say a word to anybody about our being at the Hospital; I don't want to have to fight my way all through the course, and be badgered by the connection generally, besides giving a strict account of myself at home. We all mean to be very brave about Joe, and I am sure you will be;—it's a way you have; especially as you and I, and perhaps Mrs. Trotter, will be near him in Washington at one of the hotels or hospitals.

A. H. W. to the Sisters Abroad.

[Robert and his family and Hatty and Carry were still in Europe, but hurrying their return on account of the breaking out of the war.]

NEW YORK, May 21, 1861.

Dear Girls: We hope soon to have more particulars about your interview with Mrs. Browning, what *she* said, and "said he" and "said they."

I hardly know what to tell you about home. I have been trying to think what questions about public affairs you are longing to have answered, the whys and wherefores of things, but am afraid I might hit on the very wrong ones. We cannot see into details ourselves; we live only on newspaper rumors, and the only peace of mind we get is by mentally consenting to leave everything in the hands of Scott, satisfied of his patriotism, wisdom and skill. The best statesmanship of the country is at work for its good; many knowing heads are contriving and planning; many brave hearts and steady hands are executing the will of government; the monied men, who have so much to save or lose, feel that their only hope of extrication is in the vindication of our laws and constitution; the military men know the true weakness of the South and predict its ultimate ruin; and above all and over all, as Mr. Prentiss preached to us on Sunday, "this continent belongs to Christ. He has a greater stake in it than any of us, who are here only for our little day, can have. If it should be destroyed, where on earth has God such another country so suited to His great providential designs? Be sure He will see to it that America is delivered out of all her troubles in His own time."

We hear the bugle-call now constantly floating down the streets. It is used as a rallying sound in the field — as in Europe — by the French and the German volunteers, and by some of our own regiments, I think. Going down Broadway you pass a great many "headquarters" or recruiting offices, and the crossed bayonets at the door or the sentry marching up and down have a very foreign look. You should see Charley in his Home Guard martial array. It is a sight to strike awe into feeble sisters — a grey tight-fitting coat, with red cuffs and collar edged with white cord, and a red and grey cap trimmed with white braid.

From Eliza and Joe at Albany we hear as follows: Joe was summoned there to report for duty, as the regiment is quartered in barracks, along with others, four thousand troops in all. The regiment and officers were sworn into United States service last Wednesday, drawn up in a long line, and the sound of their cheers rolling down the field like thunder. Two men refused to swear from some cause or other, and a third, who had hesitated but finally stepped into the ranks, was cheered by his comrades till the tears ran down his cheeks.

They say they are "able to lick their heft in wild cats" and are pronounced the finest regiment so far accepted — all six feet or more high and experienced riflemen. Joe is well, so far, and busy, and does not for a moment regret the step he has taken. The duties of adjutant are honorable and responsible ones, and purely military.

A. H. W. to the Sisters still Abroad.

June, 1861.

We are gradually growing accustomed to things that a few weeks ago would have appalled us, or which we should have received as horrid jokes — such, for instance, as Georgy's training at the hospital. She comes home fagged-looking but determined to "stick it out." Did you know, Carry, that Miss Bessie and Miss Mattie Parsons are walking the hospitals in Boston? Some of the ladies there fainted every day for a week, when Dr. Bigelow made them very mad by telling them "they had tried it long enough; they were unfit for it and must go home." It will not surprise us if by and by Georgy starts for the wars. *Nothing* astonishes us nowadays; we are *blasées* in revolutions and topsy-turvyings; or, as Joe elegantly expresses it: "How many exciting things we have had this winter! First, parlor skates, and now, civil war!"

I am reminded to say that the best thing

that Theodore Winthrop has ever done, after volunteering for this war, is to write an account of the eventful journey of the Seventh Regiment in "THE ATLANTIC" for June. You will get it in England — Sampson and Low no doubt receive it. It is very bright — just sentimental enough — and has its value given it in the fact that his feelings went along with it in the writing and our feelings go with it in the reading. He describes the fraternization of the New York Seventh with the Massachusetts Eighth, and says they began to think that there was *nothing* the Eighth couldn't do. All trades and professions were represented. The man that helped to build the locomotive, you know, stepped out of the ranks to repair it, at Annapolis; others sailed the good ship Constitution; others laid rails; others mended leaky canteens, as tinsmiths; and Theodore says he believes if the order had been given, "poets to the front!" or "sculptors! charge bayonets!" a baker's dozen would have stepped from each company in answer to the summons.

Don't let me forget to give you Charley's message which is to countermand the purchase of his carriage blanket and to beg you to buy his gloves a trifle larger than the size he mentioned, as his hands have spread, as well as his appetite, since he began to drill.

Mr. Dayton, the new French minister, will have arrived in Paris before you leave, and perhaps Mr. Charles Francis Adams may be in London in time for you to see him. I hope Robert will see and consult one or both of them as to the state of things at home and the safety of taking passage in an American steamer. You can do nothing, of course, but take the best advice and then do what seems best to yourselves. The summer is going to be a broken one at any rate. We have given up our rooms in Conway. We cannot leave Eliza *entirely alone*, as she will be at Fishkill. Joe has gone "for the war" if he lives and it lasts, and Eliza reverts to our love and protection. The summer will be harassed by skirmishes in Virginia — possibly a great battle may be fought if General Scott thinks we are ready. He is bothered more than anything by the haste of ignorant, injudicious men who think they are great military geniuses, and want to push the matter on. June is a great month for battles in the world's history — *we* may add another to the catalogue — but it looks more as if the hard work, especially that in the far South and in the gulf, would be postponed till fall. A rebellion that has been thirty years in maturing isn't going to be put down in a day.

We went on Sunday night to a grand

meeting of the Bible Society where reports were read of the distribution of Testaments and Bibles to the volunteer troops. Twenty-three thousand have been given away, and many interesting anecdotes were told and most stirring addresses made by Professor Hitchcock and Dr. Tyng. They began in a very sober Sunday-night spirit, but before we got through there was the most rampant patriotism — stinging sarcasms about Jeff Davis; kissing of flags which draped the platform; storms of applause, and a great time generally. . . . You would not judge by the streets that we were at war. The shops are thronged by gay women making cheap purchases. Indeed, it seems difficult to pay *more* than two and sixpence a yard for a new dress — double width at that.

E. fancying at first that she ought to stay behind to care for "the stuff" when J. went to the war, sent cheerful bulletins to him of home matters:

E. W. H. to J. H. at Albany.

FISHKILL, May 21, 1861.

Everything goes on nicely. I have made the rounds this morning and the report is all satisfactory. Thomson has bought a very nice bay mare to take Dick's place for $130, and a third pig, as there was too much food for the others. The men are all at work, the potatoes in and the corn will be finished tonight. Then the sodding and grading will be resumed. Mechie has bought dahlia poles and is now finishing the flower beds outside the greenhouse, which looks finely. A superb box of flowers came up this morning. . . . Everyone expresses the greatest interest in you and your movements. Moritz says the country wasn't as "lonesome" all winter as it was the first few days of your absence. . . . I don't doubt James will go with you, but I wouldn't let him decide hastily. Thomson would go with you himself in a minute but for his family. . . . I have had a very busy morning and haven't had a chance to miss you.

SUNDAY (between churches), May 26.

I am going over to the Dutch Church at the Corners more, I confess, to hear the news from Washington than for the sermon's sake. The rumor by telegraph this morning was that Washington was on fire. I am restless and anxious. There *must* be important movements on one side or the other before long, now that we have advanced beyond the Potomac.

In yesterday's papers the great camp preparing on Staten Island is described — 10,000 acres on the southeast slope of the island, with room for the tents and evolutions of an army of 60,000 men. Is it likely that you will be ordered there?

Mr. Masters told me this morning to tell you you were not forgotten in the village, for the boys have organized a company and are drilling under the name of the "Howland Guard." Mother thinks it should be called *Mrs.* Howland's Guard. . . . .

May 27. This morning I deposited Mother with the papers at the old chestnut tree seat and helped Thomson and Mechie get a good line for the turf on the carriage road. It is not right yet, but shall be made so. Thomson says: "We'll na gie it up, ma'am, till you say it's right." The sodding round the door and kitchen end* is a great improvement and gives quite a finished look. We all took a turn in the wagon after dinner, stopping for me to get some cut-out work from the Women's Army Association, which is fairly under way now, with Mrs. David Davis as President, Mrs. James Kent Secretary and Miss Rankin Treasurer. Five or six dozen shirts were given out today. . . . I have a note this morning from L. H. H. asking me to make them a visit at Newport and saying Mr. H. would come on for me and bring me

---

* Where the rhododendrons are now twelve to fifteen feet high.

back. It is very kind, but I shall stand by my post here this summer. . . . . .

Mr. Masters told us an anecdote of old R—— who was in a tavern barroom the other day with a party of rough fellows discussing the war, when one of them declared that "any man who would refuse to go *now that Mr. Howland had gone* ought to be drummed out of the community."

A. H. W. to E.

June 1, 1861.

Dear Eliza: We had a funny communication from Theodore Winthrop this morning written at Fortress Monroe, where he is acting as Military Secretary to Major General Butler, in the very middle of the middle of things — "Headquarters Department of Virginia." He tells about the negroes who are flocking to them, and begs that on the sly we will manage a patriotic job for them — get some sort of kepi, turban or headgear, which shall make them more respectable to look at and more formidable to the enemy. Of course, General Butler is to know nothing of it *officially*, but since the poor ragged fellows must be clothed they will be glad to have a sort of coarse uniform for them — shirt, trousers and cap — if the ladies will do it privately, and forward to Fortress Monroe.

Last night and night before G. and I each made three havelocks, and Georgy is going to take them down to the Battery Encampment and distribute the six to the six men who fled the hospital. *They*, at least, must be supplied, as they had had inflamed eyes already from wearing the hot caps. If the Fishkill ladies want work say there is a demand for 3,000 havelocks, 3,000 grey flannel shirts and 3,000 grey or red drawers, and more will be needed. *Those* are needed today.

Yesterday Charley went about a good deal trying to find a room as a depot for receiving and distributing books and magazines for the troops. He had seen one or two notices on the subject in the papers, but last night's Post showed us that some gentlemen of the Evangelical Alliance are already in the field.

The Sisters abroad come Home.

E. W. H. to J. H. at Albany.

8 BREVOORT PLACE, June 13, 1861.

We are waiting for our travellers who are due now at any moment by the "Adriatic." Abby and I came down this morning from Fishkill leaving a lovely summer morning behind us, but bringing some of it in the shape of flowers, strawberries and vegetables. Mother has everything in nice order for the girls, cribs for the babies, little novelties and conveniences for the girls, plenty of lovely flowers, etc., etc. It will be a tight squeeze to accommodate them all, but it will be done, with Mother's usual faculty, and there would have been a place for you, too, if you could have come. . . . How wretched the Southern news is; such bungling and such frightful and unnecessary loss of life. That battle of Bethel must injure us very much and give strength to the rebels. I suppose you have seen the death of poor Theodore Winthrop — one of its victims. It has shocked us all and brought the matter very close.

Major Winthrop was shot in the fight at Great Bethel, June 10th, 1861. From the Yale College Obituary Record this extract is taken:

"While gallantly leading a charge on the battery he fell mortally wounded and died in a few minutes. His body was buried near the spot where he fell. It was subsequently disinterred, and after obsequies in New York City was brought to New Haven, where, on the 28th of June, 1861, with unusual demonstrations of respect from military, civic and academic bodies, and from the people-at-large, it was laid to rest in the burial-place of his father."

All the students and faculty marched in procession to the grave.

As the coffin was brought through New York it was taken to the Seventh Regiment Armory. There Mother and G. saw it resting on a gun carriage, when they went for a last farewell. They had, so short a time before, helped to pack and buckle on his knapsack!

E. W. H. to J. H. (still in Albany.)

NEW YORK, June 14, 1861.

At 10 p. m. the expected telegram arrived saying the "Adriatic" would be at her wharf by 11, and Charley and Mr. S. left at once in carriages to bring the girls up. The travellers all look remarkably well and by no means as seedy and sea-sick as they ought to by rights. Molly has a sore throat, but is bright and very smart in spite of it, and the other children are lovely as possible. Bertha is the *stranger* after all, for Una is like most other sweet babies — round and plump and laughing — but Bertha is a little darling, unlike May and unlike Elsie, unlike all other children — not belonging to anyone, in likeness or manner. She is a mere baby herself; just running about and beginning to talk, saying, "*I will*" and "*I won't*" in the sweetest and most winning way.

Robert has been out to the country with Charley, and the rest of us have had a grand "opening" of foreign traps. . . . . Aren't you glad Harper's Ferry has been evacuated without bloodshed?

The middle of June, 1861, J. H.'s regiment, the Sixteenth New York, suddenly received orders to be ready to march, and after some little further delay it left Albany for Washington and the front. The family were now fairly in the war.

Rev. G. L. Prentiss to J. H.

NEW YORK, June 19, 1861.

Abby has just told my wife that you are ordered South. Is it so? If I were not strong in faith about you, I don't know what I should say. But the path of duty is the path of safety and of honor, and if you were my own brother (you seem to me more like a younger brother than anything else) I could not lift a finger against your going — assuming always that your health and strength hold out. God bless you and have you ever, dearest friend, in His holy keeping.

Most affectionately yours,

GEORGE L. PRENTISS.

G. M. W. to E.

WEDNESDAY.

My dear Eliza: You must feel that I am ready and glad to go anywhere and at any time with you and dear Joe. You will probably go with him to Washington, at any rate. You and I could be companions for each other at the hotel as long as the regiment camps near the city, and, judging from the way the other regiments have been disposed of, that is likely to be the arrangement for them for some time. We should be able to see them every day and perhaps go even farther south. Since Joe has taken the sick under his care we *perhaps* shall be able to be a part of the regiment, as other women have been, and may keep together in this way, doing what we can.

You know we three have travelled over rough roads together before, and have now only to take up our little bundles and commence our march again. We shall like it and we will do it if possible. Two of our bands of nurses have been sent on from the Hospital already, and with a letter of introduction from our association (which is accepted by government) *I* shall probably be able to go where I please, as far south as hospitals have been established; and so we may be able perhaps to keep up with the Sixteenth. If you can, don't you think you had better come down and be introduced to Dr. Elizabeth Blackwell and others, and go for a few days to one of the hospitals opened to us, so that you may be able to give references from our association, if necessary? It may save you some delay and be useful to you in other ways. I am ready, or shall be at the shortest notice, to do as you say. I cannot tell you how we all feel about this. We shall try and not feel at all, only our hearts are with you and Joe always.

E., who had by this time definitely abandoned the idea of trying to stay behind, alone, writes to G. from Tioronda, June 20:

We will go together, as you say, and will keep as near Joe as possible, though where it may be is entirely uncertain. They will march like others, with sealed orders. I go to Albany on Friday to see them in camp again before they leave. Will you go too? Joe has ordered a mess-chest and camp-table, and wants a *cookery-book*. I think I have seen one for army use advertised. Will you get me a simple one of any kind, civil or military, and send or bring it up? Simple directions for soups, gruels, stews, etc., are all he wants. His advice to me is to close up my affairs here and go to Mother for a while, till he can reach Washington and spy out the land. He wants us to be all ready to move but not to move hastily, and he says we must take Moritz with us as body-servant wherever we go. If any of you are near Tiffany's the next few days you might hurry the flags up.

E. W. H. to J. H.

TIORONDA, June 23, 1861.

. . . . I write chiefly to remind you of the stand of colors which Tiffany is making and promises for Wednesday. You may want to have them presented to the regiment the day they pass through New York, and, if so, will have to arrange the affair with the Colonel. *I* do not wish to appear in the matter, but you can present them in my name, or, if you like, perhaps Charley will be willing to, but don't have any fuss or parade about it, and *don't* let the men tramp through the city *à la* McChesney till they are exhausted. The colors will remain at Tiffany's till the Colonel sends for them or notifies me.

Mary and Robert and the children are still here and all well. Mary broke the news of my going to the servants, who were very sorry for me and for themselves. In the course of next week I shall wind up my affairs — pay my debts, etc., and go to Mother's. I shall go down on Wednesday when the regiment passes through New York, at all events, for the day and night, unless I hear to the contrary from you.

J. H.'s Reg't Passes through New York. The Sixteenth left Albany for the seat of war via New York, June 25th, and, reaching the city early in the morning of the 26th, marched to Washington Square. Here at 3.30 before embarking for the South the regiment was presented with a stand of colors, state and national, made by Tiffany and Co.,— Eliza's gift.

Mr. Robert S. Hone made the presentation in E.'s name, and Colonel Davies responded for the regiment,— also saying "already my command is deeply indebted to Mrs. Howland and her family for many articles which they needed while in Albany."

Colonel Davies then delivered the state flag to the color-sergeant, who bore it to the line. Waving the national flag before the regiment, he asked each company if they would defend it. A prolonged "yes" rang from one end of the line to the other, followed by deafening cheers and waving of caps. That promise was faithfully kept.*

---

*At Gaines' Mill the color-bearers were three times shot down, and all except one of the color-guard were either killed or wounded.

The regimental banner was in every march and every battle in which the regiment participated. At Crampton Gap Corporal Charles H. Conant was instantly killed by a minie ball through the head while

That same afternoon of the 26th the regiment left by transports for Elizabethport and from there by rail to Washington, via Baltimore. Before entering the last place ammunition was issued, in remembrance of the brutal attack of the mob there on the Massachusetts Sixth and other national troops. The Sixteenth New York was the first regiment to march through that city without some form of attack.

J. H. to E. W. H.

WASHINGTON, June 30, 1861.

Our journey on was a hard one. We reached Harrisburg late Friday p. m., and Baltimore at sunrise Saturday. Our passage through Baltimore was unmolested, but was one of the most impressive scenes imaginable. We marched through about 8 o'clock without music and with colors furled, in perfect silence, marching in quick time, only pausing once to rest. The streets were full of people, but we did not get one word of welcome or a single smile except from two little girls in an upper

---

holding one of the flags, and Corporal Robert Watson, of the color-guard, was shot through the leg in this action.

These flags are now deposited with other battle-flags in the Capitol at Albany.

window and half a dozen old darkies standing in doorways. At the head of the column of eight hundred stern-faced men walked the Colonel with his sword sheathed and a hickory stick in his hand. Once a rough fellow in the crowd (a city official) asked tauntingly, "Where's your music?" and Colonel Davies, gritting his teeth, replied, *"In our cartridge boxes!"* We were all fully armed and supplied with ammunition, and had received full instructions how to act in case of an attack. Tramp, tramp, tramp, went the Sixteenth through Baltimore in the early morning, and the crowd looked cold and bitter at us, and we looked stern and ready at them. All the road from Harrisburg to Washington is guarded by strong bodies of federal troops, *and they are needed.*

We got here safely at noon yesterday, and, after a couple of hours' delay under the shade of the trees of the Capitol grounds, we marched out to "Camp Woolsey," for so this camp is named in your honor! There are 100,000 soldiers in Washington.

I hope to see you very soon. I don't know what you will do with yourself here, but, if you want to come, your coming will make me very happy. God bless you!

G. M. W. to E.

NEW YORK, SUNDAY.

My dear Eliza: In anticipation of a possible march on Tuesday I have got myself ready and hold myself under orders for any moment. As for some sort of a hospital costume, if we chance to need one, I have *two* grey cottonish cross-grained skirts, and a Zouave jacket giving free motion to the arms — so the skirts can be, one of them, always in the wash; and a white Zouave will take the place of the waist when that is in the tub. Four white aprons with waists and large pockets; two stick-out and washable petticoats to take the place of a hoop, and a nice long flannel dressing-gown, which one may put on in a hurry and fly out in, if the city is bombarded or "anything else." Then for quiet and civil costume, I have only one dress made of black grenadine, like Mary's, and a black Neapolitan straw with green ribbon will make it all very nice. I shall make up a trunk of towels and old scraps of linen and cotton, soap, cologne, oil-silk, sponges, etc., and have it stored away in the hotel in Washington for use, if necessary. Any towels or old sheets you may have to dispose of we shall probably find useful if we are able to do anything for the sick. I have also under consideration a small camp cooking affair, about two feet square, with lamp and all complete, which I shall probably get — cheap and very useful in an emergency — could cook up little things for ourselves at any rate. If we find that we shall be allowed to march with the regiment, or rather *ride*, we could easily have grey flannel skirts and shirts made in Washington. So I don't see that we may not be very comfortable and useful, and consequently happy, even in following the war.

A. H. W. to J. H.

NEW YORK, July 3, 1861.

My dear Joe: It was a satisfaction to us, at least, to receive your telegram of yesterday morning about half-past four in the afternoon. I was sorry that Eliza could not have seen it before she and Georgy left, at 3 p. m. But she was in good spirits, having received your letter with the account of your strange, safe march "through Baltimore," "that luke-loyal, flagless city," as somebody from the Garibaldi Guard, writing to the Post, calls it. By the way, I think your camp and the Babel-camp of the Garibaldians must be near each other, from the accounts. I am glad yours is on that high open ground — a hitherto undefended part of Washington, too, I think. "Camp Woolsey," has a strange sound to us, there never having been any military association with the name in our family. *Naval* officers you know we have had, and there is a little village of five houses down at Pensacola named after the Commodore — "Woolsey."* I send by this mail some maps for Georgy and Eliza. Carry, Jane and I are living very quietly and miss you all sadly. Mother and Hatty intend to spend the Fourth at Astoria.

Every morning I wake up to bright sunshine and familiar sounds and sights, and think for a second that perhaps all this pageant and preparation of war has been a horrid dream! A busy reality to you I dare say, hardly giving you time to read this or even to remember

Yours affectionately,
A. H. W.

---

*Abby forgets the service during the Colonial wars of Colonel Melancthan Taylor Woolsey (brother of our great-grandfather, Benjamin Woolsey), who, according to the inscription on his tombstone, at Dosoris, L. I., "departed this life 28th of September, 1758, in the service of his country against the French in Canada."

There was also our great ancestor, Captain George Woolsey, our grandfather's great-grandfather, who was commissioned Captain in the Burgher Guard of New York, in 1696; and a brother of our great-grandmother, Anne Muirson Woolsey, Heathcote Muirson, a revolutionary soldier, was mortally wounded in an attack by the British on Lloyd's Neck, L. I., July, 1781.

<small>G. E. and C. go to Washington.</small> We — Charley, E. and G. — left New York, July 2d, to join the army and J. H. in Washington, stopping on our way over night with Cousin Margaret Hodge in Philadelphia.

G. M. W. to Cousin Margaret Hodge.

WASHINGTON, July 8, 1861.

My dear Cousin Margaret: I should have begun by dating my letter Ebbitt House, we having been established here since Saturday, spending the first three days of our visit, or probation, at the "National," in the fifth story, a prey to several inconveniences, but refreshingly near processions. Joe sent his man down to meet us, and came himself after evening drill. He looks brown and well; is dashing round on horseback all day from camp to the War Department, and back again to camp, where he must spend seven hours a day drilling. Then all the cracks are filled up with our society out there. We go out every day in time for evening drill, and stay till it is time to shut up for the night, having a nice time in the door of Joe's tent "in the cool of the day," and this sort of thing we fondly thought was going to last an indefinite length of time, till yesterday, when Joe surprised us by the news that they were ordered into Virginia, and would leave on Tuesday or Wednesday. The Colonel has been made an acting Brigadier-General, and he and Joe were eight hours in the saddle yesterday, flying round selecting three regiments to form the Brigade with the Sixteenth. Joe has been in today on the same business, being entrusted to decide upon them and take whichever he thought best; and has chosen the Eighteenth, Twenty-first and Thirty-first — all from New York. So on Wednesday I suppose they will move over the bridge, and then we shall deliver our letters of introduction and plunge into occupation of some kind.

Washington is the stillest place for a city I have ever been in; nobody knows anything, or has anything to say. Everything is guess work. A few doleful little boys call the evening papers round the doors of the hotel, but in a tone that fixes a gloom upon you. I hate the "Eve-ening Star" already, and our only news comes via New York. The Tribune, Times and Herald have a great deal of information about what goes on here, and it generally proves true. . . . One longs now and then for a real living and lying "Extra" boy, with his mouth full of fearful statements, all disproved by his paper which you imprudently buy. We went, of course, to the opening of Congress and also to hear President Lincoln's message, read on the fifth.

Charley has been about visiting the camps at Alexandria, Georgetown and Arlington, but for all this a pass is necessary, which can only be procured through General Mansfield on introduction by some one known to him. If Lenox knows anyone at home who knows the General it would save him half a day to get his letter before coming on. Charley got his through Colonel Davies who is a relative of the General's. I hope Lenox will come on, but it is too bad that he will not see Joe. . . .

Here comes a regiment down *this* street. About 15,000 men have gone over into Virginia since we came on. Joe goes up in rank with his Colonel as his aid — is now Captain and Assistant Adjutant General — and the Brigade will be in McDowell's Division. . . . The regiment has marched past — the Massachusetts Eleventh just from Harrisburg, all in beautiful order, gray uniforms and large clean havelocks. New England doesn't do anything by halves. . . . And here goes another company, guarding thirteen well-filled baggage wagons and followed by its regiment. We have only to flourish our handkerchiefs and the dear fellows will kiss their hands, twirl their hats and manifest affection for the entire woman population of the North. They are the Fourth Maine, and are going over into Virginia. I must put up my letter and watch them marching along. Our love to the Doctor and the boys.

C. W. W. to G. M. W.

NEW YORK, July 9, 4.30 p. m.

It is not quite one day since I left the "Ebbitt House," dear G., and here I am writing to you from the table in my room with Pico by my faithful side—no! the other way. I arrived at the house an hour ago for all the base lies that the railroad guide tells, and am waiting in a serene perspiration the arrival of my trunk by express from the station. Journey on long and fearfully dusty. Passed, just out of Washington, a long train full of ambulances and took a walk in Baltimore. Everyone sat on his doorstep and every group without exception was talking *about* the war.

The Ebbitt House in Washington was a rambling, untidy place on F street, which became a sort of Army Headquarters, filled with officers and men connected with the service. We (G. and E.) were given a large parlor on the second floor, where cot beds were set up for us, and we began a sort of half army-life, with bundles of hospital supplies stacked in all the corners and extemporized arrangements for comfort. We were close by Willards and in the midst of all that was going on, and just opposite the headquarters of the Sanitary Commission.

Charley, having seen us established, hurried home. Rather later Uncle Edward Woolsey, Robert Howland and some gentlemen friends came on for a brief view of what was going on, and took us to Mr. Lincoln's reception at the White House, where we are glad to think his great hand grasped ours for a moment. Mr. Seward, who was receiving too, was rather gruff and gave us welcome with the remark that "the fewer women there were there the better."

As soon as possible we called on Miss Dorothea Dix, who had, by a general order, been recognized in the following words:

"Be it known to all whom it may concern that the free services of Miss D. L. Dix are accepted by the War Department, and that she will give at all times all necessary aid in organizing military hospitals and by supplying nurses; and she is authorized to receive and disburse supplies from individuals or associations, etc., etc.

Given under the seal of the War Department, April 23, 1861. (Signed.)
SIMON CAMERON, *Secretary.*

G. M. W. writes:

Miss Dix received us kindly and gave us a good deal of information about the hospitals, and this morning we went out to the Georgetown Hospital to see for ourselves. We were delighted with all the arrangements. Everything was clean and comfortable. We shall go again and take papers and magazines.

H. R. W. to G. and E.

NEW YORK, MONDAY, July 15, 1861.

My dear Girls: I might as well give you the benefit of a scrawl just to thank you for the big yellow envelope in Georgy's handwriting lying on the library table by me. It has just come and I think you are two of the luckiest fellows living to be where you are, down in the very thick of it all, with war secrets going on in the next tent and telegraph-wires twitching with important dispatches just outside of your door. "Who *wouldn't* be a nuss" under such circumstances? or would you prefer staying at home to arrange flowers, entertain P. in the evenings, devise a trimming for the dress Gonden is making for you, and go off into the country to fold your hands and do nothing?

I tell you, Georgy, you are a happy creature and ought to be thankful. Jane and Abby have been in Astoria all the week. It was a triumph of ours to make Abby loosen her hold of those abominable old women of the widow's society. She won't get back to them for some time either. . . . Mother and I went up to Northampton, Mass., one evening last week to look up summer quarters. We went via New Haven by the 11 o'clock boat. Charley saw us on board and we got to bed about twelve. Quite a good night for a boat. Mother says she slept well, and was prime for a walk over to the depot before breakfast the next morning. She is certainly made of more enduring material than the rest of us, and, after getting through our business, wanted to come back in the express train at 5.30 that evening. Mr. Frank Bond and Mr. Thomas Denny spent the other evening here. F. B. is going on to Washington very soon, and is to be with General Tyler, something or other to him, and charged me when I wrote to let you know he was coming, and renewed his invitation to you to accompany them into Virginia as chief surgeon!

Mary has cut Bertha's hair square across her forehead, which makes her look more sinful and unregenerate than ever. Polly has had her's cut, and is more comfortable. Did Robert mention the box of old wine for General Scott, from Uncle E.? Think how glorious a part to take—propping up the government with rare old wine from one's own cellar."

Camp at Cameron.
Our regiment, the Sixteenth New York, was about two weeks stationed at "Camp Woolsey," near the Capitol, and then crossed the Potomac and pitched its tents on Cameron Run, a little west of Alexandria, in the fields which were once the property of our great-great-Aunt Ricketts, whose plantation was famous for its flour, ground by the mill on the Run. This Aunt Ricketts, a sweet-faced woman, whose likeness was among those taken by Saint Memin about 1805, brought up your dear grandmother (left an orphan in 1814), whose letter of July 19th speaks of those days:—

Mother to G. and E.
8 BREVOORT PLACE, FRIDAY, July 19, 1861.

My dear Girls: A loving morning kiss to you both, and three hearty cheers for the success of the grand forward movement thus far. I have just been devouring the "Times"—that part of it, at least, and that only, which tells of the war movements—everything else is passed over with a very slighting glance. We feel the intensest interest now in every tramp of the soldiery as they advance southward, and wait with great impatience from night till morning, and from morning till night again, for our papers. Georgy, how deeply interesting was your letter to us, written in the doorway of the tent at Alexandria!—not the first tent letter we have had from you, but how different the circumstances of this last from any other! and how strange to me that poor old Alexandria, where all of my eleven brothers and sisters were born, and where my father and mother and relatives lie buried, should be the scene of such warfare—the camping ground of my children under such circumstances! You must have been very near the graves of your grandparents, and that of my dear venerated great-aunt, Mary Ricketts, who was a loving mother to me after the death of my own, and in whose house Abby was born. Cameron, too, was one of the places and homes of my childhood. It was the country-seat of this same good aunt, and on the grounds, some distance from the dwelling-house, stands a dilapidated building, in its day a fine "mansion" for that part of the country, which was the original home of the family, and where my mother was married to a then "affluent merchant" of Alexandria.

"Cameron Run" was the scene of all our childish sports, where we used to fish and sail and bathe and have all sorts of good times; it was then a wide deep stream, and formed the boundary line along the bottom of the garden at Cameron, and was lined on either side by magnolia trees; and when the old family coach, with its grey horses, was called up to the door on Sunday mornings to take us into town for church, we each had our magnolia in hand, showing where our morning walk had been, and *our side* of the old church was known by its perfume. All this is as fresh in my memory as though *fifty years* had been but as many days! I perfectly remember every spot about the old place;—but everything had changed almost entirely when I was last there, though I look back to it still as it was in my childhood. More than ever do I now regret my not having kept a diary of my early life, which might have been interesting to my children.

I feel very much as you do, my dear Eliza, that "somehow or other I cannot write letters now," and, indeed, I cannot sit down very long at anything. My mind is in a state of unsettledness, if I may coin a word —a sort of anxious suspense, all the while, and I feel better when on the jump, going about. I have been making up a lot of currant jelly, some of which I will send on to the hospitals. I am going out by and by to get a work basket for little May—her birthday present. She is to keep her birthday and little Bertha's together, to-morrow, by having a tea-party on the lawn. I shall fill the basket with goodies for them. . . . What an imposing sight it must have been when the troops all set forward together, and then the arrival at Fairfax! and then at Centreville! the rebels flying before them and leaving all their goods behind! I hope this may be the case all along, that they will throughout have a bloodless victory! . . . We look any instant for your letters. I say constantly to myself, "What will be the next news?" I dread to hear from Manassas, but hope the enemy will continue to retreat, until the whole land is clear of rebels. I cannot help thinking it will be an easy victory, and without bloodshed. May God bless and keep you, my dear children, and graciously prepare us for whatever may be his will. Give my love and blessing to Joe when you write.

Most tenderly and lovingly yours,
MOTHER.

Our letters from Camp Cameron were among those lost in the Morrell fire, but late in the war, when the Sanitary Commission wanted items for its paper, G. sent the following sketch of the camp:

"It was a pretty spot, our camp in a valley in Virginia—the hillside, covered with white tents, sloping to a green meadow and a clear bright little river. The meadow was part of my great-great-aunt's farm years ago, and in the magnolia-bordered stream my grandfather's children had fished and paddled. Now, we, two generations afterwards, had come back and pitched our tents in the old wheat fields, and made ready for war, and there were no magnolia blossoms any more.

"On the hills all about us the army was gathering, white tents springing up like mushrooms in the night. With their coming, came sickness, and sickness brought men of the next brigade into a poor little shanty close behind our headquarters. There we found them, one day, wretched and neglected, and 'most improperly' at once adopted them as our own. We asked no one's permission, but went to work; had the house cleaned from top to bottom, shelves put up and sacks filled with straw; then we prescribed the diet and fed them just as we pleased. All this was a shocking breach of propriety, and I have no doubt the surgeon of the regiment was somewhere behind a fence, white with rage. Never mind, our men were delighted, and one dear little blue-eyed boy, who had blown his lungs through his fife, was never tired of saying and looking his thanks. Finally we persuaded the General to break up the little den, and order all the sick sent to general hospitals, and our breaches of etiquette came to an end."

Our regiment had only been camped a few days on Cameron Run when the advance against the enemy at Manassas was ordered, and we two (G. and E.) watched the brigade break camp and march down the peaceful country road, carrying Joe away from us. We stood alone, and looked after them as long as they were in sight, and then made our way back to Washington.

Battle of Bull Run.

After skirmishing at Fairfax Court House and Centreville, in which the regiment was engaged more or less, the battle of Bull Run was fought, July 21st, the regiment taking position on the extreme left at Blackburn's Ford.

Here Colonel Davies, owing to the unfortunate condition of Colonel Miles, was left virtually in command of the reserve division.

J. H. writes from Camp near Centreville.
July 19, 1861.

We had hardly got here yesterday when we heard heavy cannonading in the S. W. It proved to be the firing at Bull's Run, where our troops were repulsed. A complete blunder—the old story of a masked battery and an insufficient infantry force sent against it. We expected a renewal of the fight last night. We slept on our arms, and were prepared for action at any hour. Nothing occurred, however. Our scouts bring in word that the enemy are receiving large reinforcements, and we on our side are also getting them. Everything points to a great battle.

July 20th. We march at 6 p. m., and there will be a great battle within twenty-four hours unless the rebels retreat. Our brigade takes the advance on the left wing. We can see the enemy from a high hill near here concentrating their troops. Our pickets were firing all night, and we slept on our arms. I am well, though I feel the want of sleep and the constant anxiety. We are all in good heart, officers and men.

On the battle-field near Bull Run,
Sunday, 21, 12.45 p. m.

Our brigade is making a demonstration in the face of the enemy and a fight is going on on the right of the line five or six miles off. The enemy's batteries do not return our fire. We see immense masses of troops moving, and the supposition is that the enemy is trying to outflank us on the left. We started (from Centreville) at half-past two this morning.

The following little note, hardly legible now, written in pencil on a scrap of soiled and crumpled paper, made its way to us at Washington and told the rest of the story:

EVENING. Half-past seven.

A complete rout. The Sixteenth safe. We are making a final stand.   J. H.

Mother to G. and E.

MONDAY, July 22, 1861.

My dear Girls: We have had an exciting night and morning. Just as we were going to bed last night we heard the distant sound of an "Extra;" it was very late; everybody in bed. We had been out to the meeting of the Evangelical Alliance at Dr. McAuley's Church. We were all undressed, but waited with anxiety till the sound approached nearer and nearer; but made up our minds not to rush down and buy one, as it might be a hoax—till at last a tremendous howl of three boys through 10th street gave us the news of a "great battle at Bull's Run." "Rebels defeated! Batteries all taken!" We thanked God for this much, and went to our beds to try and sleep patiently till morning. We have now had the newspaper accounts as far as they go, but long for further and later. Your two letters of Saturday, Georgy, we have also this morning; many thanks for both; rejoiced to hear good news from Joe so direct, and that you are both well and *busy*. It is better so. I feel this morning as if I could fly right off to Washington, and can scarcely resist the impulse to start at once. Would you like to see me? . . .

The girls are packing a box for your distribution at the hospitals,—Jane rolling a fresh lot of bandages. Poor Kate, our housemaid, looks quite distressed to-day, thinking her brother may have been foremost in the ranks, as the paper stated "the First Massachusetts led in the advance, and had suffered much." . . . Dr. Tyng made an inspiriting address last night to a densely crowded audience. He said he was greatly surprised to see such an assemblage when he had supposed the city deserted, and thought such an audience was a sufficient appeal without a word from him, as showing the deep interest manifested in this "righteous" cause—"I say *righteous*, for I firmly believe if there ever was a righteous, holy war, direct from the hand of God, this is one." . . . There were some very interesting letters read from the different chaplains, and some from the men themselves of different regiments. Dr. Hoge has resigned, and left his charge to Dr. Spring, on account of his attachment to the South! and his desire to be there at this time. *I* say joy go with him, but some of the people are unwilling to receive his resignation. . . . I have no news for you; we see no one, and are supposed to be out of town. It is perfectly cool and comfortable here, and we are at present better satisfied to be here. By and by we may run off for a while. God bless you both, my dear children! I wish I were close at your side.

        Your loving Mother.

A. H. W. to G and E.

July 22, 1861.

My dear Girls: Since Mother's letter was sent this morning we have had some heavy hours. At noon we got the first extra with the despatch announcing the defeat and retreat of our troops—defeat, because retreat, or *vice versa*, whichever it was. It is a total rout of our grand army of the Union. All guns gone, etc.; but the saddest is the vast number of wounded and half dead. I have no doubt your hands are full, at some one of the hospitals. Hour after hour to-day went on and we heard nothing from you; had nothing but the horrible extras and our consciousness of your anxiety and suspense. We packed the trunk for you very busily and tried not to think too hard. At five p. m. your despatch came, dear E., and such a load was removed from our hearts. Joe not only was safe, but you had seen him. Thank Heaven! We could hardly make out from the confused papers what his position had been in the fight. . . .

Mary and Robert drove in at six to hear what we had heard, and met Ned at the Ferry, carrying out your despatch. Robert brought his valise in case Mother wanted him to escort her to Washington, but the immediate anxiety she felt for you having been relieved, she feels it is safest to wait till she gets a letter from you. So many troops will probably encumber the roads on the way to Washington to-morrow, and there is so much chance of a riot in Baltimore, as Robert suggests—that it is more prudent to wait. She wants to go for her *own* satisfaction as well as yours you know, so you must not think it desirable for you to oppose it. If she could only have been with you these two horrible days she would have been so glad. She is anxious to do something for the army and thinks she ought to go on and be matron in the Alexandria Hospital. We laugh, and remind her of her fortitude when Dr. Buck tried to vaccinate her! . . . And now for the boxes. Mrs. Willard Parker is ready to make the largest grants. Has packed one box to-day, and is anxious to have it go to you that she may know what disposition is made of the things. Let us know when you receive them—one French black trunk, one wooden packing box. Mrs. Parker has a huge box packed, but I shall advise *that* one going to the Sanitary Commission. Your box has six dozen sheets in it from her, and the trunk is filled with our shirts, slippers, etc.

In haste and with all love,

A. H. W.

P. S. Also one box of currant jelly. All will be directed to the Ebbitt House, except Mrs. Parker's box.

Thread and needles are invaluable in camp. We hear that after every march bits of uniforms fly all over the camp, and that one man patched his black shoulder with a sky-blue scrap begged from a brother volunteer. You know the men haven't always a sixpence to spare for the sutler every time a button is needed, and our two hundred thread cases will go very little way in a regiment. . . . Everybody is knitting yarn socks for the men—all the young girls and all the old women. Everybody means to make one pair each before winter. Cousin Margaret Hodge has set all her old ladies at work at the Asylum. We have set up four to-night for ourselves, and Kate and Mary the cook are to have their turn too. . . . But the deed of Mrs. Lowell of Boston, sister-in-law of the poet, puts all others to insignificance. She being a lady of means and leisure, took the Government contract for woolen shirts in Massachusetts and is having them cut and made under her own eyes by poor women at good prices, and the sum that would have gone into some wretched contractor's pocket has already blessed hundreds of needy women.

Mother to E. and G.

TUESDAY MORNING, July 23, '61.

God be praised for that telegram! What a day was yesterday to us; and what a day must it have been to you, my dear Eliza! The terrible news, the conflicting reports, the almost unendurable suspense we were in, the distance from you at such a time! Altogether it was a time to be remembered!

We are thankful indeed, unspeakably so, to hear this morning by your nice letter, Georgy, of Joe's quiet sleep upon the sofa at your side! How mercifully are we dealt with! when we think of the families in our land who are this day in sorrow as the result of this terrible battle. . . . There is a tremendous sensation throughout the city in consequence of this news—crowds are rushing continually to the news offices, and all we have seen are wearing looks of sadness and disappointment, following as this does so immediately upon the accounts of the easy manner in which Fairfax, Centreville and Bull's Run were captured, and the flying of the enemy before our soldiers.

G. M. W. writes:

WASHINGTON, July 22, 1861.

My dear Cousin Margaret: This is the third attempt I have made to finish a letter to you. Joe is safe and quietly sleeping on the sofa by us. You know all about this total defeat—our army is entirely broken up, all the army stores, three of the batteries, ammunition, baggage, everything, in the hands of the enemy—Centreville retaken by them, Fairfax C. H. retaken, and our troops scattered in and about Washington. Everything was in *our* hands and success seemed certain at Bull Run, when from some cause or other a panic was created, our men fell back, the rebels seized the moment for a bold rush and we were entirely routed. Joe says there never was a more complete defeat. All last night the soldiers were arriving in all sorts of conveyances, and on horses cut from ambulances and baggage wagons. An officer from Bull Run told us he saw four soldiers on one horse; and so they came flying back to Washington in all directions. Colonel Miles' division, in which Joe's regiment was, was held as a reserve at Blackburn's Ford on the left and only came into active duty when the rout began—they had a sharp engagement with 5000 in a "gully"—lost only two men from the Brigade and none from the 16th and retired in order, first to Centerville, where orders met them to fall back on Fairfax C. H. Here they slept half an hour last night, when they were again ordered to retreat to Washington, which order they have followed as far as Alexandria, and expect now to be stationed there some little time. The dead and wounded were left in the hands of the enemy, and one of the officers told me it would be unnecessary to ask for the sick, for the rebels were killing them: he knew it had been done in some cases, and undoubtedly would be in all. Colonel Davies and two of the officers came up from their camp at Alexandria with Joe, and all four of them were wretched-looking men, dirty, hungry and utterly tired out. Joe had not had his high boots off since he left Alexandria on the 16th. The day that McDowell's division marched south, Eliza and I were out at the camp to see them pass, and our own regiment march. Eleven thousand fine-looking fellows filed past us as we stood at the cross-roads,—and disappeared down the quiet country lane. What a horrid coming back it has been! "We shall not see this place very soon again," they said as they packed up their things at Alexandria, and marched off, singing as they went. And in spite of all this, and in full knowledge of the great outnumbering of our men on the other side, General Scott sat quietly in St. John's Church that battle-Sunday through a tremendously heavy sermon, shook hands with me at the church door, and told us all that "we should have good news in the morning and that we were sure to beat the enemy." Colonel Davies has seen him this morning too, and he is quite cheerful and composed. The Zouaves, one Massachusetts regiment, and the 69th and 71st New York have been the greatest sufferers—very few of the Zouaves are left. The fighting was all from behind masked batteries on the enemy's side. Lieutenant Bradford told me that he had to ride down the lines and give the order to retreat. Our men were all lying on their faces, and the air filled with shot and shell and not a rebel's head to be seen. When Colonel Davies was asked what lost the day, he said "green leaves and fine officering on the enemy's side." In open field, they all say they should have beaten the rebels entirely. . . . Now he and Joe are off on business in a hard rain, and go to Alexandria at two, where the regiment is established in the old camp—at Cameron Run. Yesterday and last night were hard to bear, but what with General Scott's assurances, General Ripley's, Mr. Dixon's and Judge Davies' comforting little visits, we got along, jumping up every few moments through the night whenever a horse dashed by the house or an ambulance rumbled along. Now we shall be as much as possible at the camp in Alexandria,—for how long I can't say. . . . We have had an encounter with Miss Dix—that is rather the way to express it. Splendid as her career has been, she would succeed better with more graciousness of manner. However, we brought her to terms, and shall get along better.

Eliza adds, also to Cousin Margaret:

The sick and wounded are doing well. Georgy and I have been to all the hospitals and find them very well supplied, for boxes of garments and stores of all kinds have poured in ever since the battle. It has been the one cheering thing of the times. . . . We hear from the surgeons we have met here that very many of the wounded who were left behind had their wounds carefully dressed before the rout began, and they are constantly being brought into the city in ambulances, having reached the camps on the other side by slow stages.

In this same battle of Bull Run the 2d Conn. was in the thick of the fight, and its surgeon, Dr. Bacon (your Uncle Frank), found himself separated from the troops and in the midst of a group of southern wounded, for whom he cared under the impression that *we* were victorious and he within our own lines. He ordered them to surrender their arms, threw most of these into a pond near by, and saved a pistol and two dangerous knives as trophies. They are those that afterwards hung on the banisters of his house in New Haven. One of the knives was more than a foot long and home-made from a horse shoer's file, with rough home-made scabbard; the other, an ugly dirk, was made in England and engraved *there* " Arkansas toothpick." The revolver belonged to the wounded commanding officer, Lieutenant-Colonel Gardner, leading a Georgia regiment. He insisted upon giving his watch to Dr. B. as a return for the good care received.—(It was afterwards returned to him.)—When the arms were in the horse pond and the rebels cared for, the Doctor made the startling discovery that he was alone—our army in retreat, and he virtually a prisoner to the rebels. He left hastily, before the truth dawned upon Colonel Gardner's mind!

R. S. H. to G.
Astoria, July 23.

We are trying to look things in the face,—like the great apostle, cast down but not disheartened.

Of course the first thought of us civilians is to take care of the wounded. I send enclosed a cheque from Cousin Edward and one from myself. If you find you cannot use these amounts satisfactorily at Washington let us know and we will send materials as they may be wanted. Telegraph to Howland and Aspinwall (to G. G. for me) if anything is wanted immediately. . . . If you want *anything* specifically in the way of hospital stores, wines, currant jellies, &c., telegraph first and write more fully afterwards.

H. R. W. to E.
New York, July 23.

Abby is in the front parlor reading the papers. It is quite useless to say anything about going into the country just now. If we are away from the daily papers, or if they are delayed an hour the girls get into a perfect fever; besides, Abby, you know, has decided never to go to the country again! Because she took a sea bath at Mary's and felt weak after it, she thinks the country doesn't agree with her! . . . Aunt Emily is going up to Lenox the last of next week, I believe. I hope so, for Uncle E. needs change; he looks miserably, has a constant cough, and seems quite run down; though when Aunt E. says, "You don't feel very bright to-day, do you, dear?" he is quite indignant and makes a feeble attempt to sing "the Cock and the Hen," or to whistle "Dixie."

CHAPTER III.

The regiments called out for three months were now about disbanding, though a large number of the men at once re-enlisted for the war. *Three months' troops disbanded.*

A. H. W. to E.

July 27, 10 a. m.

My dear Eliza: I have just been up to the corner to see a sorry sight, the return of the 69th Regiment—oh, so shabby, so worn and weary—all sorts of hats and shirts and some with hardly any clothes at all, staggering along under their knapsacks which they should never have been allowed to carry up Broadway. The surging mass of men and women locking arms and walking with the soldiers, was wonderful. It was a wild, tumultuous, promiscuous rush—not a march. Yesterday afternoon the 8th came through. I could see from the balcony how brown they looked and sturdy, and trimmer than the 69th. The girls and Mother saw them from Brady's window. The cheers and applause they got down town, I suppose. There was not much of it up here—there was too much crying. Even policemen were in tears. What a dreadful collapse the "Grand Army" of the Potomac suffered. I don't think the North needed such a lesson! Perhaps they did—perhaps the people have felt as if they could march down to Richmond whenever they chose. . . . Scott sent an inefficient general (known as a perfect windbag among brother officers) without commissariat, without organization, without proper regimental officers, against what he knew to be a fortified camp of a hundred thousand men. The one great blunder was that the battle was fought at all. All other minor blunders—and how many there were! are included in this. . . .

Jefferson Davis is free now to do what he pleases—flushed with success. Everyone says this battle has been as good to him as an increase of a hundred thousand fighting men. . . . He will perhaps attack Washington itself. The papers speak of the danger of this—and we all feel that the city is in greater peril than it was in those April days. Under such circumstances we do not quite relish your idea of going to Alexandria. You would be cut off at once, in that town, from communication or escape. One thought that checked Mother's desire to go immediately to Washington last Monday was the idea that on reaching there she might find that women and children had been ordered to leave—for fear of an attack from Beauregard. That order may come yet. My dear sisters, I do not want to write anything depressing, but you must make up your minds after this disaster for a *long war*, an impoverished country, many reverses. So far, you have had but one thought —that of immediate success. General Scott's plan of closing in on the rebels in Virginia and crushing them as in his fingers, is blown to the winds. We are to have a protracted and somewhat equal struggle, but the North is in earnest; its fault has been *over*-eagerness. Men there always have been enough of,—let them have proper officers; and as to money, Congress ought to be ashamed to haggle about direct taxation but pass the bill at once and provide ways and means. . . . I am very glad the boxes had all arrived safely. Next day you would get Aunt Emily's two barrels, and Uncle Edward's $250 in money. Buy whatever you see is needed or the surgeons and nurses want. Don't wait for red tape. If it is mattresses, cots, pillows, spirit lamps, food, sheeting, flannel, etc. to wrap wounded men in, or what not. You can have plenty of money, and it could not be better spent than in fitting up a hospital even if that *is* government work. Carry wanted me to send you some money for her, but I told her I would wait and see whether you could buy the things you needed in Washington, or whether it had better be spent here. Please let me know. We shall have enough more things to fill a barrel early next week. Shall we put in the bandage roller, or are the hospital surgeons provided? I am sorry that Mrs. Leavitt did not send you a list of the contents of *her* boxes. . . .

Don't save up things if you see them needed. It is easy to buy more slippers and mosquito net here, and it does not cost us any time or a stitch of effort to send more clothing. The Society has plenty on hand. Mrs. Parker jumped up with pleasure when we sent round the other day to see if she could let us have a few things for the trunk, and granted enough, as you saw, to fill two boxes and over. She was delighted at the idea of their being distributed where she could hear about it, and I must manage to put some scraps of your accounts together and tell her what you say. There is a fresh lot of handkerchiefs under way. Maria Gilman hemmed them on her machine.

Mother to E.

BREVOORT PLACE, Late in July.

My dear Eliza: If the regiments are all to be stationary for some time you and G. might run on for a *visit*. I have given up my plan of going to you for the present unless you should need me. We are now talking again of Lenox for the summer.— Abby and Jane are both wilting daily in the hot city, and I feel troubled at their being here, though we are unwilling to move off further away from you girls. We don't know at what time the Southern army may make an attack. I have no idea that *they* will wait patiently till fall, though our side might, and the daily expectation of another battle keeps us here. It is intensely hot, noisy, dusty and distracting. The streets seem filled with a perfect rabble all the while. . . . Mary and the children are looking perfectly well. Baby Una grows fat and lovely by the hour— she is a splendid child. Bertha is a witch, but fascinating in her badness. Little May is very much interested in hemming a handkerchief for some poor soldier, which I basted for her, and am to send on to you when finished! She feels as if she had the whole army on her hands! in this important piece of work. . . . It is pleasant to know of your seeing so many friends. I think you are right to stay in Washington instead of Alexandria—the latter place must be intolerable,—but don't wear yourselves out.

Social formalities were entirely abandoned in Washington in war time. The Ebbitt House public parlors were on a level with F street and the windows were always open. Any friends in passing would catch a glimpse of us and happen in for comradeship, giving bits of news, and offering kindly services. One group of four Philadelphia officers were especially friendly and helpful. The lack of conventionality now and then, though, had its drawbacks, as G's note shows—addressed to "Mrs. Howland—Parlor" and sent down from the bedroom one evening to E., who, not fortunate in escaping, was captured by the enemy :—

"Find out incidentally before Dr. E. goes, where Mr. Channing is to preach. Mind, I don't want to accept an invitation to go with *him*. I saw him, when I was shutting the blinds up here, pass the windows of the parlor, and stop and look in, and go on, and stop, and turn back and come in—! and then I banged the blinds with glee, and am just popping into bed. Shall expect you up about midnight."

A. H. W. to E.

10TH STREET, July 31.

My dear Eliza : We were quite touched by a note and a message from your farmer Thomson, and I write at once that no time may be lost in carrying out the generous wishes of the people on the place. As soon as they received the particulars of the battle of Bull Run, Thomson took up a subscription among them, for the wounded soldiers, and raised *twenty dollars*. He took it to Mrs. Wolcott, asking her to put it into the Society's fund for buying hospital clothing. But she suggested that a more satisfactory way would be to send it to you, to be spent on the spot, in any way you thought best. . . . Thomson preferred this himself, and hopes to hear from you that the twenty dollars are well laid out.

E. to J. H. in camp.

WASHINGTON, August —.

Hurrah for you, to be offered the Colonelcy of the regiment! I am glad, however, that you have no wish to take it. I shrink from any such responsibility for you.

Dr. Bacon came in last evening and we had a nice pleasant chat. His regiment, the 2nd Connecticut, goes home to-day to be mustered out. We saw them march down yesterday to give up their arms and were struck with their fine manly appearance and precision in marching. Dr. Bacon is anxious to come back to the army and hopes that one regiment at least may be formed of the three just returning, in which he may serve. He has left one of his patients at the new Columbian College Hospital and commended him to our care. We shall see him this afternoon and take him jelly, slippers, etc. The slippers are from a large boxful which Lenox

Hodge has sent us, our commission. They are scarce at the hospitals and in great demand. Cousin M. Hodge writes of her happiness at hearing of your safety and welfare. Columbian College Hospital is just opened and only half organized, but already crowded. It *will* be nice, but now they have few comforts or conveniences, scarcely any sheets, no water, etc. One of G's nurse friends is there working like a slave, as are the other five women nurses. We spent the morning there helping them, reading to the men, writing letters for them, etc.

G. writing in 1864 of the annoyances of those first days, said:

" No one knows, who did not watch the thing from the beginning, how much opposition, how much ill-will, how much unfeeling want of thought, these women nurses endured. Hardly a surgeon whom I can think of, received or treated them with even common courtesy. Government had decided that women should be employed, and the army surgeons—unable, therefore, to close the hospitals against them—determined to make their lives so unbearable that they should be forced in self-defence to leave. It seemed a matter of cool calculation, just how much ill-mannered opposition would be requisite to break up the system.

Some of the bravest women I have ever known were among this first company of army nurses. They saw at once the position of affairs, the attitude assumed by the surgeons and the wall against which they were expected to break and scatter; and they set themselves to undermine the whole thing.

None of them were 'strong-minded.' Some of them were women of the truest refinement and culture; and day after day they quietly and patiently worked, doing, by order of the surgeon, things which not one of those gentlemen would have dared to ask of a woman whose male relative stood able and ready to defend her and report him. I have seen small white hands scrubbing floors, washing windows, and performing all menial offices. I have known women, delicately cared for at home, half fed in hospitals, hard worked day and night, and given, when sleep must be had, a wretched closet just large enough for a camp bed to stand in. I have known surgeons who purposely and ingeniously arranged these inconveniences with the avowed intention of driving away all women from their hospitals.

These annoyances could not have been endured by the nurses but for the knowledge that they were pioneers, who were, if possible, to gain standing ground for others,—who must create the position they wished to occupy. This, and the infinite satisfaction of seeing from day to day sick and dying men comforted in their weary and dark hours, comforted as they never would have been but for these brave women, was enough to carry them through all and even more than they endured.

At last, the wall against which they were to break, began to totter; the surgeons were most unwilling to see it fall, but the knowledge that the faithful, gentle care of the women-nurses had saved the lives of many of their patients, and that a small rate of mortality, or remarkable recoveries in their hospitals, reflected credit immediately upon *themselves*, decided them to give way, here and there, and to make only a show of resistance. They could not do without the women-nurses; they knew it, and the women knew that they knew it, and so there came to be a tacit understanding about it.

When the war began, among the many subjects on which our minds presented an entire blank was that sublime, unfathomed mystery—'Professional Etiquette.' Out of the army, in practice which calls itself 'civil,' the etiquette of the profession is a cold spectre, whose presence is felt everywhere, if not seen; but in the Medical Department of the Army, it was an absolute Bogie, which stood continually in one's path, which showed its narrow, ugly face in camps and in hospitals, in offices and in wards;

which put its cold paw on private benevolence, whenever benevolence was fool enough to permit it; which kept shirts from ragged men, and broth from hungry ones; an evil Regular Army Bogie, which in full knowledge of empty kitchens and exhausted 'funds,' quietly asserted that it had need of nothing, and politely bowed Philanthropy out into the cold.

All this I was profoundly ignorant of for the first few months of the war, and so innocently began my rounds with my little jelly pots and socks knit at home for the boys—when, suddenly, I met the Bogie;—and what a queer thing he was! It was a hot summer morning, not a breath of air coming in at the open windows—the hospital full of sick men, and the nurses all busy, so I sat by a soldier and fanned him through the long tedious hours. Poor man, he was dying, and so grateful to me, so afraid I should tire myself. I could have fanned him all day for the pleasure it was to help him, but the Bogie came in, and gave me a look of icy inquiry. My hand ought to have been paralysed at once, but somehow or other, it kept moving on with the fan in it, while I stupidly returned the Bogie's stare.

Finding that I still lived, he quietly made his plan, left the room without saying a word, and in ten minutes afterward developed his tactics. He was a small Bogie—knowing what he wanted to do, but not quite brave enough to do it alone; so he got Miss Dix, who was on hand, to help him, and together, they brought all the weight of professional indignation to bear upon me. I 'must leave immediately.' 'Who was I, that I should bring myself and my presumptuous fan, without direct commission from the surgeon-general,' into the hospital? 'Not only must I leave at once, but I must *never return.*'

This was rather a blow, it must be confessed. The moment for action had arrived—I rapidly reviewed my position, notified myself that I was the Benevolent Public, and decided that the sick soldiers were, in some sort, the property of the B. P. Then I divulged *my* tactics. I informed the Bogies (how well that rhymes with Fogies) that I had ordered my carriage to return at such a hour, that the sun was hot, that I had no intention whatever of walking out in it, and that, in short, I had decided to remain. What there was in these simple facts, very quietly announced, to exorcise the demon, I am unable to say, but the gratifying result was that half an hour afterward Professional Etiquette made a most salutary repast off its own remarks; that I spent the remainder of the day where I was; that both the Bogies, singly, called the next morning to say—'Please, sir, it wasn't *me*, sir, —'twas the other boy, sir;' and from that time the wards were all before me."

J. S. W. to G. and E.

Dear Girls: Your full, interesting letters have come in and given great relief. G's of to-day is certainly altogether more cheerful in tone than Eliza's of Tuesday, and very naturally. We are beginning to "look up" a little, too. Your rebuff by Miss Dix has been the subject of great indignation, but we all devoutly hope you will not mind it in the least. . . . Whatever you do, go in and win. Outflank the Dix by any and every means in your power, remembering that prison visitors and hospital visitors and people who really desire to do good, have taken no notice of obstacles except to vanquish them, and as soon as one avenue was closed have turned with perfect persistence to another. We shall be very much disappointed if you do not establish some sort of relations with the hospitals, at least enough to give you free access, and to make a reliable channel for such things as we can send. You ought certainly to get those boxes to-day if not sooner. . . . All your details are very interesting. Pray, send any that you collect, and *make Joe write out* or *dictate* to one of you a connected story of what he saw and did from the time of the advance up to the Monday morning when he came in. It will be invaluable, and ought to be done while it is fresh. Your "*mémoires pour servir*" may immortalize you yet. . . . We have seen only a few people the last day or two, Mr. Denny, F. Bond, and Col. Perkins. All cheerful, hopeful and undaunted, say we can have ten men to every one lost now; that there is settled determination to use every resource to the uttermost. Uncle E. says, setting his teeth, "to the last drop of my blood!" Abby desponds. Thinks Scott to blame, that his tide of fortune is turning, or that he is childish, or, at best, that he let the cabinet have its way this time for the sake of saying, "I told you so." We begin to grin now when Abby begins to croak, but there is certainly something in what she says. Don't keep drumming about our going away. We should have been crazy if we had been in suspense in some small country place the last week or two. When things subside, and look *nearly* settled for the present, we will take our own time and go. . . . Frank Goddard is in the rebel army at Sewall's Point. "Hopes it will make no difference in our pleasant relations." Hm !!! perhaps it won't.

Why don't you come home? Now's your chance, if at all. The rebel army before Washington will melt away like a cloud and come down again suddenly in Kentucky, Missouri, Jeff knows where, where we are weak and unexpecting, and leave us sitting like fools behind our laborious entrenchments that nobody means to take. . . . How can you doubt Fremont? There has been *no positive* charge against him from any respectable source, only malevolent *rumors*, filling the air, coming no doubt from the Blairs and other malignant personal enemies who hate him, because they are slaveholders and he is just now the apostle of liberation. I announce my adhesion still and my painful anxiety that he should retrieve himself in Missouri against all the heavy odds of fortune. . . . It is pitiful to see how great and general a defection from him has grown out of absolutely nothing (so far) of any authority. . . . Take some measures to make Frank Bacon let his beard grow; tell him to go to Jericho with his "Victor Emmanuel." He is in the late fashion, by the bye; so much the worse. Why should a man who can look like a knight of the table of the blameless King voluntarily look like a Lynn shoemaker?

> "Yet, oh fair maid, thy mirth refrain,
> Thy hand is on a lion's mane."

Quote me to him; who's afraid? . . . Goodbye. I hope the highly accommodating Providence which directs, or rather acquiesces in all G.'s movements, will afford you both every facility for whatever you want to do. . . .

Hospital work in Washington and at home.

Having established our own position and made it clear that we had no intention of being bluffed off, we were accepted by the surgeons and Miss Dix at our own valuation (purposely made high!) and from that moment our path was as a shining light. All hospitals were open to us, and our relations with Miss Dix became most cordial and friendly, as the following notes, among many received from her (nearly all undated), show.

My dear Miss Woolsey: I am thankful you are going to the hospital. Express to the good nurses my kind regards and purpose of seeing them so soon as I am able. Thanks for the lovely flowers, with cordial regards to Mrs. H. I have very little strength; excuse brevity and abruptness. I must have some consultation with you so soon as I am *better*, concerning the position of the nurses. I fear they are over-tasked.

Very cordially yours,

D. L. DIX.

My dear Miss Woolsey: Will you give a little attention to the hospitals at Alexandria through next week for me if convenient? Any requisition on my stores will always be promptly met.

I still feel that all the nurses who are really conscientious are very heavily tasked.

Yours most cordially,

D. L. DIX.

Receiving the nurses, and seeing that they were safely started on their way to various hospitals, and reporting to the New York committees on their services therein were among our occupations in the first year of the war.

Dr. Elizabeth Blackwell to G. M. W.

NEW YORK, July 30th.

My dear Miss Woolsey: I was extremely glad to receive your excellent letter yesterday. Had I known that you were residing in Washington, I should have requested you some time before to collect information for our society. We had become extremely anxious about these women; we could not learn who had safely arrived, where they were, what they were doing, nor how they fared in any respect; and a check of considerable amount, sent to one of them, was unacknowledged. As we had pledged ourselves to protect these women, pay their expenses, their wages, etc., you may imagine that we felt extremely uneasy about them. . . .

I will ask you now, to find out for us where Miss E. H. and Mrs. M. S. are placed. They were sent from New York by the night train, July 25th, direct to Miss Dix, and should have reached Washington last Friday morning.

Will you also visit the Georgetown Hospital and report on two nurses whom we sent on last

Saturday. We should like some unprejudiced account of the management of this Hospital. . . .

I will see that any nurse going to Alexandria in future is furnished with a certificate signed by some proper authority here. We feel much obliged to you for all the trouble you have taken in this matter. . . .

As the government payment commences Aug. 5th, from that time our society hands the nurses over to the government.

I remain very truly yours,
E. BLACKWELL.

The nurses were required to take the oath of allegiance to the government, and to secure passes, in all of which G. helped them, also securing government ambulances to carry them to their destination :—

"Dr. Asch begs to inform Miss Woolsey that he has seen the officer in charge of the passes into Virginia. It will be impossible to procure them this evening as the office closes at 3 P. M., and in addition it will be necessary for the nurses to present themselves at General Porter's office for the purpose of making affirmation as to their loyalty,—when, on presenting the accompanying note, Dr. Asch trusts that there will be no delay in the accomplishment of their object."

SURG.-GENERAL'S OFFICE, Aug. 27, 1861.

Dr. Wood has requested Dr. Spencer to attend to the wishes of Miss Woolsey (in regard to the ambulances).

He very much regrets he is prevented from attending personally.

Government hospitals were multiplying in Washington, Georgetown, and Alexandria. As regiments were ordered forward extemporized camp hospitals were broken up, and patients were sent back to these large general ones in the rear.

By this time J. H. had ordered his horses and carriage sent on from Fishkill for our use and we were constantly driving about, seeing where the need was in camps and hospitals and supplying wants. In order to make our way to the many outlying hospitals about Washington and also to visit Joe's camp over the river, it was necessary for us to be provided with passes—not always an easy thing to procure. General Scott, however, came to the rescue and gave the following comprehensive one which was "good daily" during the rest of our stay in Washington:—

HEADQUARTERS OF THE ARMY,
WASHINGTON, Aug. 19, 1861.

Mrs. Joseph Howland (wife of the Adjutant of the New York 16th Regt.), sister Miss G. M. Woolsey, and man-servant (Stanislas Moritz) will be permitted to pass the Bridges to Alexandria (and return) and are commended to the courtesy of the troops.

Good daily.

WINFIELD SCOTT.

By command:
H. VAN RENSSELAER,
Col. and Aid de Camp.

Armed with this we constantly dashed over the Long-Bridge, the carriage filled with all sorts of supplies from the abundant and unfailing stores committed to us by the family and friends and societies at home. Warm woolen socks were always one item. Abby and many others never ceased knitting them during the war. Wherever we found a camp-hospital in need, there we thankfully left comforts from home, or arranged that the Sanitary Commission, whose general office was directly opposite to the Ebbitt House, should supply the want.

The Commission on its side was always glad to have our report and responded promptly to all our suggestions.

A few letters among very many will be enough to show the feeling on all sides.

SANITARY COMMISSION, WASHINGTON, D. C.
TREASURY BUILDING, Aug. 17th, 1861.

Miss Woolsey: In absence of Mr. Olmsted I answer your note in regard to supplies for the 25th N. Y. We will give immediate attention to this Regiment, and will gladly furnish them any supplies we have on hand for their comfort. There are now no beds or cases to fill with straw in the store-room of the Commission (but very few have ever been sent in). Mr. Olmsted, however, has sent for two hundred to be forwarded from New York as soon as possible, and when these arrive a supply shall be furnished to the 25th.

It has been the endeavor of the Secretary to send notice of the existence and objects of the Commission to the surgeon of each regiment: it may not have reached some, but the visits of the inspectors, now in progress, will ensure this notice to all.

Mr. Olmsted wishes to make the Regimental Hospital *comfortable*, but not to induce the regimental surgeons to retain patients who ought to be sent to the General Hospital.

I am glad to be able to add, that there is a reasonable prospect that a new General Hospital will be immediately established in or near

Alexandria for the sick of the regiments in that vicinity. Pardon haste,
With sincere regards,
Your obedient servant,
F. N. Knapp, for
Fred'k Law Olmsted.

Rev. Edward Walker to G. M. W.

Hdqrs. 4th Reg. C. V., Camp Ingalls.

Dear Miss Woolsey: Your kind note is just received.

A week ago our hospital was in wretched condition, but, thanks to the Sanitary Commission! we are at present provided with nearly everything we want. If anything is needed, it is a few more sheets, as we have some fever patients who require frequent change of bedclothes. The surgeon suggests that more pillows are needed and that a little Indian meal for gruel would be very acceptable.

There are 51 in the regimental hospital to-day—2 dangerously ill, and 30 on the sick list in the camp. . . . Should we find ourselves really in need of further aid from the Sanitary Commission I will let you know promptly, either by a note or by calling on you when I come in town.

Yours gratefully,
Edward Ashley Walker.
Chaplain 4th C. V.

CAMP TRENTON, 1861.

Miss Woolsey, Ebbitt House : I have the honor to acknowledge your favor of the 2nd inst., and would beg leave to say in reply, that the stores will be most acceptable, and in order that you may have no further trouble in the matter, an order signed by our Surgeon, Dr. Grant, will be presented you by our regimental wagoner, who will take charge of the goods for us.

With many thanks for your interest in behalf of the regiment, I have the honor to remain
 Your obedient servant,
  SAML. L. BUCK,
  Major 2nd Regt. N. J. V.

G. W. M. to Frederick Law Olmsted.

WASHINGTON, 1861.

My dear Mr. Olmsted : Can the Sanitary Commission do anything to prevent a repetition of the inhuman treatment the sick received last week, on their way from Jamestown to Alexandria? 150 men were packed in one canal boat between decks, stowed so closely together that they were literally unable to turn over: without mattresses, without food, without decent attention from the time they left till their arrival. Among them were three or four men with the worst kind of measles put in with all the rest: one of them died on the boat, and another on the way from the boat to the hospital, and it will be wonderful if the disease has not communicated itself to others among the 150. There was of course no ventilation, and the men say that they suffered greatly from bad air. A medical officer came down with the boat and is perhaps not responsible for the state of things on board; some one must be, however, and it may save further suffering if the affair could be made public. We heard this story through a friend who was in Alexandria when the boat arrived and has known all the facts of the case.

"Boston rockers" were an untold comfort to the men able to sit up. The first of the many sent to us were from Daniel Gilman's father and placed as follows:—

ALEXANDRIA HOSPITAL,
Aug. 14, 1861.

My dear Miss Woolsey: The eight chairs are very thankfully received and shall be disposed of precisely as you proposed.

Yours in haste,
Nurse in charge.

Miss L. L. Schuyler to G. M. W.
25 COOPER UNION, N. Y., August 7th, 1861.

My dear Miss Woolsey: Dr. Blackwell, at our last board meeting, read a very interesting letter from you, giving details about the hospitals. We should be very much obliged if you would be willing to write us a few incidents in regard to *hospital supplies.* Any little personal anecdote relative to the pleasure caused by the receipt of these delicacies and stores, any message from a wounded soldier, would go farther to interest our country contributors, than any figure-statements of what has been, and is to be, done. . . .

The response made to our appeals is grand, and it is a privilege to know and feel the noble spirit that animates the women of the loyal states. We have contributions not only from our own states, but from Conn., New Jersey, Massachusetts and Michigan. Within the last fortnight our receipts have amounted to over 7000 different articles of clothing and 860 of edibles. . . .

Our letters from the Sanitary Commission say that the hospitals near Washington are now well supplied.

A. H. W. to G. and E.
August, '61.

Dear Girls : Did you give the company captains my little books by Ordronneaux ? If not, please do so. They have much useful advice, and as each captain ought to be the father of his company, and look after its welfare in every respect, some such little manual might be useful to them.

In regard to your enquiry about sending the Tribune and Independent to the hospitals regularly from the publication office, I would say that I have already so ordered 10 copies of the Independent sent every week for the coming three months, beginning with this week's issue. It is prepaid and will be delivered free by Adams Express at the hospital. Charlie has gone down this morning to order the Semi-weekly World or Tribune sent in the same way. . . . You will receive 12 Independents which he has put up for the Columbia or any other hospital, and some packages for the chaplain of the 16th. . . .

The young men of the New York Christian Association who have been in Washington and Alexandria making the rounds of the hospitals, writing letters for the men and ministering generally, send word that they have never known a single chaplain of any regiment present himself to enquire for his sick or wounded, that there is no *resident* chaplain, and no one at hand to read or pray for a dying man, or to conduct the funeral services of the dead in the city hospitals. This must be especially the case with the Alexandria hospital—for in that town hardly any clergymen are left. . . . It would be encouraging to know that somebody was detailed in each hospital for special chaplain's duty. Cannot some arrangement be made? . . .

You must tell us something more about the men of the 16th. . . . How do they cook their food and how is it distributed? Is the camp kept drained and clean? What do the men sleep on? Have they chances for bathing, washing clothes, etc.? . . . Two-thirds of the New York regiments as examined by the Sanitary Commission are crowded too many in a tent—regardless of ventilation—and liable next month to some terrible pestilence. The only sign, so far, that I can see of God's mercy and the justice of our cause, is the absence as yet of any serious epidemic. . . . But as carelessness, bad habits, hot weather, etc., only sow *seeds* of sickness to ripen in autumn, we may yet have that plague too, overtake us.

Abby's informant was right. Up to this time there were no special chaplains in the Washington and Alexandria hospitals. G. and E. felt the need and wrote of it to Abby, who answers as follows: *Hospital Chaplains.*

A. H. W.

August, '61.

I think that the best you can do is to make your own private arrangement for missionary work two days a week, say, in the Columbia College and two in the Alexandria hospital. I mention these because I suppose they are the two you would be likely to have best access to, and where your suggestions would be best received. You would have to do it with the consent of, or knowledge of, the head physician, superintendent, or whatever Cerberus it is who guards the portals. . . . You need not wait to find out what anybody else is doing. You have a grand scheme on hand for making the hospitals military posts and so entitled to chaplains, but I hardly think you will succeed. . . .

Shall I not apply to Professor Smith for information about a graduate of Union Theological Seminary who would be glad of such an appointment and who has qualifications for such special missionary work?—some one who could be set to work at once, under the "young men's" auspices or your private patronage, and afterward get a government commission if such are granted. . . .

How strange some of the statements in Russel's last letter are! That there was no hand to hand fighting at Bull Run. No batteries charged and taken by the Federalists. No masked batteries at all on the side of the rebels, etc., and then that horrid, insulting, false editorial from the London Times in yesterday's Tribune! I am sure *that* is aiding and abetting our enemies if anything is, and Russell as the representative of such a paper ought not to be allowed within our lines again. . . .

Do you two ever refresh yourselves by a drive out into the country—for pleasure purely,—with your thoughts so busy always?

E. following up the Hospital Chaplain plan, wrote to General Van Rensselaer, of General Scott's staff and received the following note:

HEADQUARTERS OF THE ARMY,
WASHINGTON, Aug., 1861.

My dear Mrs. Howland: If you will send me the names of the persons you want appointed to act as Chaplains for the Hospitals, I will get the Lieutenant-General to give them (not a regular commission) but an authority to visit and have free access to the Hospital at all times.

This will invest with full authority, but no rank or emolument.

Yours very truly,
H. VAN RENSSELAER.

G. also wrote a private letter to President Lincoln asking that Hospital Chaplains should be appointed and handed it in herself at the back door of the White House; and, acting upon Abby's idea, E. wrote Prof. H. B. Smith of the Union Theological Seminary, asking him to suggest the right person, and soon received the following answer:

... I hope I have found the right man. Young Hopkins, son of President Mark Hopkins of Williams College, has just been in, and will think of it. If he can and will accept, he is as near being just the man as need be. He is not ordained, but I suppose can be, if necessary. Will you write me, if it is so? He is a Christian gentleman, every way, and a very able man intellectually. If you think well of him, and he agrees, when shall he come? Please write soon.

I have the most entire confidence in Mr. Hopkins' discretion and courtesy. He does not seek mere position, he only wants to do good.

Yours truly,
H. B. SMITH.

Mr. Henry Hopkins took the position, to our great and lasting pleasure, and the friendship so begun has remained one of the best things the war brought to us.

When he sent up his letter of introduction from Professor Smith to G. and E. in Washington, he expected to be descended upon in the Ebbitt House parlor by two elderly women all ready to superintend him. A year later he wrote to G. in acknowledging her photograph, "It is the very identical countenance which demolished so delightfully my ideal Miss Woolsey with iron grey curls, black silk dress and spectacle-case."

Mr. Hopkins did most admirable work in the voluntary unofficial position he consented to occupy at first. Later, wishing a more formal connection with the army service, he secured proper official recognition in the General Hospital, and still later he accepted an appointment in the field as regimental Chaplain.

C. C. W. to G. and E.

August, '61.

Dear Girls: I have wrenched this opportunity from Abby to take my turn in writing you. It is as good as a fight to attempt to do anything useful in this family. Each one considers it her peculiar province, and if I manage to tuck in a handkerchief or two in the next box of hospital supplies I shall consider myself successful beyond expectation—speaking of which, T. D. brought in a splended lot last night that we had commissioned him to get the night before. . . . Abby says, "would you like three or four hundred brown duck havelocks for any of the brigade?" They can be bought ready-made. If so, find out from the quartermaster of the *DeKalb* regiment which pattern he thinks best, and let us know. In this connection I would advise that you *answer* all questions that we ask, and don't suppose that they are put in to fill up. Mother and Charley are still in Astoria; they drove out in C's little wagon Tuesday evening. I think mother repented before she got to the corner. I arranged her toes under the iron bar of the dash-board so that she could have that at least to hold on by, in case the horse went off the slow walk which Charley promised to keep to. . . . We have been holding a family conclave down in Mother's room in which it has been decided,—that is, after bullying the girls into consent,—that Charley and I go up to Lenox on Monday, and engage rooms for the following Friday *somewhere*, if not in Lenox then in Lebanon. But go we must—the girls will slave themselves to death if we stay in town, and nothing short of heroic decision on our part will induce them to leave.

S. C. W. to E. W. H.

NEW HAVEN, August, '61.

The Second Connecticut Regiment returned on Monday and Willy and I rushed out to see them pass, poor, way-worn, tired fellows, as they were; and in their ranks we saw Dr. Bacon prance by, much to our surprise as well as pleasure. His family are all spending the summer in the country, and as the last duties of his place would detain him here for a few days, we offered him the shelter of our roof till they should be over, and so have had him to ourselves all the week—too tired and unwell to be as entertaining as usual, but still invaluable as a guide-book and interpreter to all the recent war movements.

I am hoping that a large blue pill which he swallowed publicly last night may make him even more graphic and interesting. . . . He gave me a charming description of his calls on you and Georgy and what you said and did, and what you meant to say and do. Oh, girls, don't I envy you, being so in the thick of everything!
. . . The reports from Lenox—(where Jenny and Harry Yardley, newly married, were settled) —are charming; the little house is just like a bower, transformed into such by all simple means and expedients. I am really getting appalled by the smartness of the girls. Dora and Lilly put carpets down themselves the other day in three rooms and did it as well as a professional. The last addition to the ornaments of the rooms was the pretty picture which Carry and Hatty brought from Rome for Jenny. Carry and Charley walked in upon them on Monday evening to their delight and surprise, having come up in search of rooms for the family—found at once quite near the Parsonage, and occupied by them to-day.

J. S. W. to a friend in Paris.

BREVOORT PLACE, August 8th, 1861.

Your response to my patriotic fervors gave me a sort of chill. We did not seem *en rapport.* . . . *We* are heartily ready to record our faith that the war is worth what it may cost, although the end may be only—*only!* the preservation of the Government, and not, just now, the liberation of the slaves. Perhaps you hold, with Mr. Phillips and Abby (I believe they comprise the entire party) that the war is not justifiable if it "means only stars and stripes." We think, or to resume the perpendicular pronoun, I think that is enough for it to mean or seem to mean at present. "The mills of the Gods grind slow," you know, or, if you will let me requote to you your own quotation, "you cannot hurry God." Don't you and Mr. Phillips want to hurry Him a little? I would rather, for my part, think with Mrs. Stowe, that the question of the existence of free society covers that other question, and that this war is Eternally Righteous even if it "means only the stars and stripes." . . . We are all getting bravely over the two or three dreadful days of a fortnight ago, and coming to think that our retreat under the circumstances was not such a bad thing after all. . . . Monday after Bull Run was a frightful day in Washington. Georgy says a thick gloom oppressed them which the knowledge of the safety of those nearest them could not lighten in the least, and that a sad procession of the wounded was passing through the streets all day under the heavy rain. . . . Many of the men are but slightly wounded, and all are perfectly patient, cheerful and only eager for "another chance." "Tell her about the wound in my hand preventing me from writing," one man said, for whom Georgy was writing home. "And the wound in your leg?" G. asked. "No, never mind about that." "And I shall say you fought bravely?" "Oh, no matter about that; she'd be *sure* of *that*." They have known two or three cases of Southern barbarity to our wounded. But the poor wretches expected the same thing at our hands. Dr. Bacon, an intimate friend who has just come home with his regiment, Connecticut 2nd, says in the battle on Sunday he came upon a piece of shade in which four or five wounded Georgians were lying, and what was very painful to him, every man believed that he had come to kill them, lying there disabled. One young fellow called out, "Don't hurt me, I'm hurt enough already," and the rest made a feeble show of defending themselves. Of course he dressed their wounds, and did what he could for them with more than usual care and gentleness, and I can bear witness how careful and gentle that must have been, but it was hard to tell which emotion was uppermost with them, gratitude or astonishment. Mr. Maclise, of the 71st, which has come home, says he found a wounded man under a tree, a Carolinian, he thinks, who begged for his life in the same way. "Bless your soul," Maclise said, "I wouldn't hurt you for the world; don't you want some water?" The poor fellow eagerly took the water from his enemy's canteen. "If I only had a cup I could give you some brandy," Mr. M. added. "Oh, just look in my knapsack and you'll find a cup." So Maclise opened the knapsack, took out a beautiful silver cup, mixed the draught, and made his patient as comfortable as he knew how, bringing home the silver cup, at the Carolinian's most urgent entreaty, as a souvenir of that sad day. He will try and return it one of these days. But what a blackness of darkness, of falsehood and misrepresentation lies behind all this. These perfectly intelligent men devoutly believed that we would kill them, unarmed, sick and helpless! . . . The "prevailing" Prince comes and goes, and nobody seems to care much about it. We have learned something, or it is that we have too many troubles of our own to care for the pleasures of princes. He overstayed his time at Mount Vernon the other day, and there was a splendid story that he had been captured, but he spoiled the bulletins and the joke by coming back to a soirée at two o'clock at night. . . . We are going, as much for duty as pleasure, to Lenox, to-morrow or Saturday, for a few weeks, to refresh ourselves for the winter. As long as McClellan keeps quiet we shall stay. He resigned one day last week. Col. Davies dined with us yesterday and told us so, from his uncle, General Mansfield, who had seen the letter. The administration attempted some interference in his reforms, and he sent in his resignation. It was immediately hushed up, refused, of course, and he was allowed to have his way.

E. W. H. to J. H.

EBBITT HOUSE, WASHINGTON, AUGUST 10, 1861.

Dear Joe: We had a very successful journey in from camp yesterday, for who should be on the boat but the Prince (called by the public "Captain Paris,") McDowell, and *McClellan* himself, whom Mrs. Franklin introduced to us, and who helped us all into the carriage when we reached Washington. He and General Franklin are old and dear friends. He is singularly young and boyish-looking for so important a position, but at the same time has a look and manner that inspire respect. The Prince is exactly like the picture of his uncle. We hoped they would all discuss secrets of state, but the topic was persistently the range of different kinds of cannon. . . . G. goes to Alexandria this morning to look up a hospital Mr. Vernon told her of and take them some comforts. . . . There is no news except the sad story of Lyon's death in Missouri, and the mutiny here in the 79th, which was put down summarily by the display of six cannon, three companies of cavalry and a good many infantry, which came down upon them yesterday afternoon. The ringleaders, about 26, were put under arrest last night and in irons, and the rest marched off into the darkness somewhere. The trouble was that they did not like their new Colonel, and would not serve under *Sickles* as Brigadier. In the latter we sympathize with them.

Letters from home report all well in Lenox. . . . I send one from Mary. We shan't think of going North at present.

M. W. H. to G. and E. in Washington.

Astoria, August 12th.

Dear Girls: If mother and the remaining three kept to the programme, they all left for Lenox on Saturday and are at last settled in their summer quarters, much to my relief. So long as they would not come to us, I think it was highly necessary for them to go somewhere, as the city grew hotter and *smellier* and more unbearable every day.

Knowing what New York is at this season, and inferring what Washington must be, I am sure you will consider my proposition reasonable when I beg that you will come on and freshen up a little here at Astoria "by the side of a river so clear." . . . When you come Robert will sail you up to Riker's Island, in order to make you feel more at home, where

<small>The family at Lenox and Astoria</small>

the Anderson Zouaves are encamped. We went up there the other day with some illustrated papers sent by Jane to the men, and were enthusiastically received by a company of bathers, who swam round the boat for whatever we had to offer, and whom we left seated on the rocks reading *Frank Leslie*, with not so much as a button or an epaulette on by way of dress.

A. H. W. to E.
LENOX, MASS., August 25, 1861.

My Dear Eliza: I don't believe you realize how interesting your letters always are. . . . Five nurses consigned to Georgy!—just think of it! I was going to ask you in my very next letter more particularly about the New York nurses—who they were obliged to report to on arriving in Washington, Surgeon-General Finley or Miss Dix, when lo and behold! I learn that they report to Georgy. . . . I see by the morning Tribune that the Sanitary Commission are said to have furnished light reading, as well as a quantity of little tables to stand on the beds with rests for the arms, etc., etc. I have thought of having some of those plain bookracks made for weak or armless men. It grieves me to the bottom of my heart to think of how many men are ruined for life by surgeons who with savage glee hurry to chop off arms and legs *ad libitum*. Many a brave New Eng-

land forester or craftsman will have to earn a sorry livelihood by stumping about at a toll-gate, or peddling candies, one-armed, at railroad stations, who might by a slower and more skillful process have been saved such humiliation.*
. . . I copied out Trench's sonnet on prayer for your young Lieut. Ferris. You know Mary has it in Trench's own handwriting given her by him with his autograph; and I also copied out a few of our least familiar hymns, thinking you could slip them among the newspapers now and then. I sent a package of *Boston* papers to Dr. Sheldon, at Alexandria, yesterday, and will do it again.

A. H. W. to G.

LENOX, Aug., 1861.

My dear Georgy: You need not speak so coolly of our staying here three months. Three weeks will give us enough, I guess. It is actually *tiresome* not to have anything to do, after being so busy in New York. We only take one paper too now—the Tribune, and that does not come in till four o'clock, so that our mornings are very blank. There is a newsboy here however —think of that! who sells the New York and Boston papers every day on the hotel steps,

---

[*Dear Abby's gloom, and her low opinion of army officers generally, kept the family in cheerful mood on many a doleful day.]

after the arrival of the stage. And there is a brick store and a telegraph office, connecting with the telegraph in Springfield. Messages come over the wires in the short space of three days, I am told! . . . Is there not some newsstand or book-store on Pennsylvania Avenue where Moritz can buy you the illustrated papers for the hospitals? I hope so, as we cannot send anything now except perhaps a stray Boston paper which everybody here has finished. I sent word to Edward Gilman, who has been in New York, when he goes home to Maine to mail you every now and then a Bangor paper for some sick Maine volunteers. . . . When we go back, we will constitute *ourselves* into a society, and do things more systematically and thoroughly. . . .

Our letters must be few and stupid. Your last to us was Eliza's, written last Monday in camp. What scenes you must have gone through there, in the arrest and examination of those women spies! What strange romance history will be, by and bye, to May and Bertha. Gay ladies and courtly gentlemen, and ragged rebel volunteers, and city brokers, and wily politicians, all assigned their respective cells side by side, perhaps, in Fort Lafayette. You wonder what "horse-cakes" are, which the old woman declared her packets of letters to be, when found between her shoulders. They are gingerbread of the "round heart" consistency, cut in the flat, rude shape of a prancing horse with very prominent ears and very stubbed legs, sold in various small shops in Alexandria, along with candy balls, penny whistles and fly-specked ballads. "Horse-cakes" are an Alexandria institution. You should buy a few for lunch some day in the bakery. . . . We live in the newspapers and in your letters. It is impossible to think of anything else. I have tried on successive afternoons to get interested in Motley's Netherlands, and give it up as a bad job. One reads a sentence over and over without getting the sense of it. And then, I remembered, that I *couldn't* remember a name, or fact, or date in the three volumes of Motley's other work; so what's the use of reading anything? "Fort Sumter" is ancient history enough for me. To-day we have quite a budget of news—the details of Butler's expedition to Fort Hatteras, which of course had to be successful. They went against the weakest point of the coast, with an overwhelming force. Little as it is, it serves for a subject of brag for us, and the newspapers glory over it as a splendid naval victory in the style of true *Southern* reports. We have the text of Fremont's proclamation. It is all very well in itself, but I don't see the object of setting slaves free in Missouri, and setting soldiers to catch them in Virginia;—shooting rebels out west and letting them off with "a mild dose of oath of allegiance" in Washington. . . . It is my growing conviction that nothing would be worse for the country than to be let off *easy* in this war. We should learn to think lightly of Divine guidance and Divine judgments. Providence means to humble and punish us thoroughly before full success is granted, and it is best so.

M. W. H. to G.

ASTORIA, MONDAY, Sept. 2nd.

Dear Georgy: Your interesting letter was highly appreciated by little May, as well as by her parents, who thought it very kind of you to elaborate so nice a little story out of the materials. May's artistic efforts were revived by it and all her inspirations lately breathe of camp life and army movements. I enclose the last one, "Recollections of what I saw on Riker's Island when passing in the boat," which is really not bad for a fancy sketch. You would have been amused to hear her reading the newspapers aloud to little Bertha the other day. I was writing at the time and took down verbatim one sentence. "We are sorry to state that General Brigade, a contraband of war, was taken prisoner last night at Fort Schuyler: he was on his way to visit the navy-yard at Bulls Run and was brought home dead and very severely wounded."

The children and nurses have just driven off with a carriage full of little pails and spades to spend the afternoon digging in the sand at Bowery Bay. You know the bliss, especially if the tide admits of rolling up their pantalettes and wading in. We are having lovely weather, which I wish you were sharing. Indeed, I am greatly disappointed that you will not come on while things are comparatively quiet and stay awhile with us. Robert and I have had some delicious sails in the boat, for which I have taken a great liking, and we are having a quiet but delightful summer. To-day the Astoria flags are out in great numbers for our naval capture; a little victory which is refreshing after so many defeats. Abby and Cousin William are very blue up in Lenox and write desponding notes in the *Toots* style. The Micawber mood will probably follow, in which Abby will be "inscribing her name with a rusty nail" on the walls of some southern dungeon. Indeed I begin to think she must be in the confidence of the rebel leaders, from the entire assurance with which she looks for an attack by sea upon some northern port, while the land army meantime marches triumphantly to Washington.

We are looking for Sarah Woolsey this week to make a little visit, and were in hopes that Rose Terry, who was with her, would come too.

I sent your two letters to Mother, who will enjoy them as much as May did. When you write again tell us more about Joe,—how he is looking after the summer's campaign, how he really is, etc. It seems strange to think that autumn is already here and the dreaded hot weather for the troops nearly over, I suppose. If we can get anything for you in New York while the girls are away, or do any of the things for which you have depended upon them, be sure to let me know. . . . I wonder if a season will ever come when for once we can all spend it together without the need of ink and paper. Some large, generally satisfactory Utopian farmhouse, where, as in Pomfret days, one vehicle and one horse (alas, poor beast!) and Mother to drive, would be ample accommodation and style for all. Give our love and a God-speed to Joe when you see him next, and insist upon his taking good care of himself when out of your sight.

Affectionately yours,

MARY.

M. W. H. to A.

ASTORIA, Sept., '61.

Dear Abby: Sarah and I have been all the morning arranging flowers. . . . Our roses are most luxuriant this year, and just now we have outside the front door two large orange trees from the greenhouse which are one mass of blossom and perfume the whole place. We have been quite on the *qui vive* yesterday and to-day at the expected arrival of the Great Eastern at Port Morris which is that cluster of buildings, you may remember, next to Casina dock, on the opposite side of the river. The vessel comes consigned to Howland & Aspinwall. The English agents sent them word at the last minute that she would come in by the Sound, so we have been constantly on the look-out. It would be very pleasant to have her lying in sight of the windows for some days. On Saturday we had a fine view of the imperial yacht which passed up the river with royalty on board, and looked beautifully with its gold prow and the gold line running round the sides. Sarah particularly enjoys the river, bathes every day in a highly ornamental costume brought for the purpose, and floats round on the surface like a cork. We have had some charming sails too, and indeed divide our time about equally between the water and the carriage, with occasional short digressions among the rose bushes. Tell Carry that Mr Stagg spent Saturday evening with us, and brought up the package of handkerchiefs which he promised her. They are a dozen of large, fine, colored-bordered ones, very much in the style of those I brought Ned from Paris, and such as I should not at all object to crib for private use. He must have intended them in case of a cold-in-the-head of the War

Dept., they are on such a grand scale. However, I thanked him on behalf of the national nose, and will take charge of them for Carry.

S. C. W. writes during her visit to Astoria at this time:

"The children are my delight all day, especially Bertha, whose little flower of a face tempts me to continual kisses. Dear little puss, she grows sweeter every day. Una, too, develops continually powers and talents undreamed of. She has learned to say 'R-r-ra,' which means Hurrah! and she says it with great enthusiasm whenever a steamer passes full of troops and we all rush out to the bank to wave our handkerchiefs to them,—the children held up by Ann and Maria, and solemnly gesturing with their little hands, and May waving one flag and the gardener's boy another. The group is so very patriotic that we are generally saluted by cheers from the boats."

The home letters, full of sweet air and peaceful views, were delightful to get in the dust and confusion of Washington, which, however, with all its discomforts, nothing would have induced us to leave. Among the letters of introduction which made our way simple and pleasant were those from

Cousin Wm. Aspinwall to Senator Dixon and General Ripley ("a fine, blunt old gentleman") of Connecticut, and to Generals Hamilton and Van Rensselaer, on the staff of the Commanding General Scott. Also to Generals Wool, Dix and McDowell, Admiral Wilkes and family, and the household of Mr. Hodge, a cousin of our good Dr. Hodge of Philadelphia. We imagined that our unctuous way to the good graces of the Commanding General was made by the gift from J. H. of a number of very fine hams. These, cast upon the water, came home to us later in an invitation to dinner, which seemed rather to have the nature of a military summons, delivered as it was by a Colonel on the staff. We accepted with the mixed feeling which one must have who receives the "Queen's Command" to an interview.

The hams appear in the following note:

HEADQUARTERS OF THE ARMY, WASHINGTON.

Dear Mrs. Howland: The Lieutenant General desires me to send his thanks for the hams sent to him by Mr. Howland. He considers them very fine indeed, to which opinion I beg leave to add my own.

Yours very truly,
H. VAN RENSSELAER.

E. to J. H. in Camp.
EBBITT HOUSE, Sept. 5.

I hope you are not entirely without starch this damp, sticky day, and that you have kept "Manassas"* busy all the morning bringing wood for the fire. Since my note we have had the confirmation of Jeff. Davis' death, reported yesterday. If he is really gone, I suppose we mustn't abuse him, but the fate is much too good for him.

We won't go down to camp again till we hear from you, as you ask, but meantime I am anxious to know what your plans and prospects are, and what the order to be "ready for instant action" meant. . . .

We had a charming dinner with General Scott yesterday, and shall value the remembrance of it all our lives. We are the only ladies except Mrs. Thomas Davies whom he has entertained at his table during the war. We ought to feel highly honored, and we do. There were only the three aides present, and it was all very social and pleasant, but they didn't tell any state secrets. The General looked very well indeed, but showed his feebleness when he attempted to leave his chair. He spoke in high praise of the hams, which we suppose to be the humble cause of the politeness to us, and toasted the "absent Adjutant" in a bumper of sherry.

---

* A "contraband of war" freed by the 16th N. Y.

G. takes exceptions to the word "charming" in connection with that dinner, and perfectly recalls it as a fearful joy, where none of the aides dared speak unless spoken to, and she and E. hardly then. J. S. W., however, writing from Lenox and rising to the occasion, said: "Georgy's letter received last night with its gorgeous item of your dinner at General Scott's was very interesting. You are lucky to be so honored above all other women, and will consequently be able to brag to your posterity to the third and fourth generation of them that hate you."

Mother to G. and E.

LENOX, September.

My dear Girls: Abby, as usual, is writing away vigorously, and I am very sure her letters to you are better far than mine would be, therefore I always give place to her; but do not think me *indifferent* to you or to any little circumstance whatever connected with you in the most remote way, for I assure you every word relating to Washington has a deeper interest than I can express to you, and in all my reading of news I turn with indifference from other parts of the country and items of other regiments, to seek eagerly for some word of those immediately about Alexandria and Washington, and we look with more desire than ever for your letters. The "expected attack" dwells upon our minds and hearts, and our sympathies and fears are all alive. When will the *end* come? In God's own time, and we must only wait in patience and faith, looking to God for strength to help us in this time of need. . . . Ask counsel of some of your *wise* friends in Washington as to the prudence of your remaining for the present there. Do you not think in case of an attack upon the city you would be better elsewhere? I scarcely know where either, south of Philadelphia. Had you not better take the chance, before communication is cut off, of coming north? I should fear your being in Baltimore more than staying in Washington. I hope you will call on Mrs. McClellan and her mother, if the latter is with her. I knew them both, you recollect, in North Conway, and I would like you to make their acquaintance. You might consult with your familiar, General Scott, as to the propriety and safety of your being in Washington in case of an attack. What a nice thing for you to have dined so socially with the General. It will come in as a pleasing little incident in that history which I hope you are writing for coming generations.

A. H. W. to Harriet Gilman.

LENOX, Sept. 12, 1861.

To-day has been very beautiful. Such floating clouds and corresponding shadows, such liquid blue on the distant hills and such gold green on the nearer meadows! We saw it to advantage at sunset, from Mrs. Sedgwick's house. Only Miss Catherine was at home, and we saw her in her own little parlor, hung with photographs and engravings and one or two old choice portraits. But the picture from the window was best of all. . . . We had a charming drive one day with the Warners (of the " Wide, Wide World ") to Tyringham, the Shaker settlement below Lee, which name reminds me of the story we heard of the loyalty of *that* little village. It had already sent its full proportion to the army. But that dreadful night when the news of disaster at Bull Run came, the baker told the Warners " Nobody couldn't eat nothin' and nobody couldn't sleep none." That very midnight *sixty* men of Lee started in the cars for New York and enlisted for the war. . . . I had a chance of seeing Mrs. Kemble to-day as she drove by, silks and lace and birds of paradise, several I should think by the size. She is the great woman of the place here. Her daughter, Mrs. Wistar, was with her—strikingly like her, and yet young, fair, simple and beautiful. She came back yesterday from New York with

Julia Butler the sister. They had been down to see their father in Fort Lafayette.

In consequence of complaints made of the treatment of the political prisoners, Dr. Bellows, the President of the Sanitary Commission, inspected Fort Lafayette and reported to the Secretary of State Oct. 31, 1861 —" Every man has his own cot, plenty of blankets and abundance of food. They were in better condition in all respects than our own men in the field. They have many acres for play-ground. They complained of nothing though I gave them abundant opportunity."

S. C. W., writing from Lenox, says;

· · · I was highly diverted by a story Mrs. Kane told Jenny Yardley of Mrs. Kemble. She was playing whist the other night with Mrs. Ellery Sedgwick as a partner, and became really furious because Mrs. Sedgwick played so badly. Finally, just as her rage had reached its height, Mrs. Sedgwick remarked, " I do not know what is the matter with me! somehow I can't play well, or talk straight, or do anything right this evening, and it is strange, for I certainly do know how to play whist." Whereupon the majestic Fanny exploded : " Well, I am glad to hear that. It is a comfort to know that one has for a partner an inattentive genius and not a *born fool!*"

Mrs. Kemble was most friendly with the various members of the family, though unexpected at times, as for instance when she remarked to Harry Yardley, while Lilly Woolsey was his guest, "Mr. Yardley, you have a very handsome young woman at your house; I do not refer to Mrs. Yardley." However, the people in Lenox seemed used to these little bursts. They never resented them and only made a good story of it all, which they enjoyed.

CHAPTER IV.

E. W. H. to J. H.

Sept. 11th, 1861.

Where do you think I am writing? In the Patent Office, where we heard the other day that a large number of sick men had been brought from the 19th Indiana regiment. We found them in a dirty and forlorn condition and have come to do what we can. The whole regiment, nearly, is down with sickness from great exposure when they first arrived, they say. The assistant-surgeon of the regiment and the matron are here all the time, and a number of Washington women come in to help every day. <small>Patent Office Hospital.</small>

From G's letter to the Sanitary Commission Fair's paper this account of the hospital is taken:—

"One of the first extemporized hospitals of the war was in the top story of the Patent Office, where the 19th Indiana regiment was brought, nearly every man of them. The great, unfinished lumber room was set aside for their use, and rough tables—I can't call them beds—were knocked together from pieces of the scaffolding. These beds were so high that it was impossible to reach them, and we had to make them up with brooms, sweeping off the mattresses, and jerking the sheets as smooth as we could. About six men could be accommodated on one table. These ran the whole length of the long room, while on the stacks of marble slabs, which were some day to be the floor, we spread mattresses, and put the sickest men. As the number increased, camp-beds were set up between the glass cases in the outer room, and we alternated —typhoid fever, cog-wheels and patent churns —typhoid fever, balloons and mouse-traps (how *many* ways of catching mice there are!)—typhoid fever, locomotives, water-wheels, clocks,—and a general nightmare of machinery.

Here, for weeks, went on a sort of hospital pic-nic. We scrambled through with what we had to do. The floors were covered with lime dust, shavings, nails, and carpenters' scraps. We had the rubbish taken up with shovels, and stacked in barrels at one end of the ward. The men were crowded in upon us; the whole regiment soaked with a malignant, malarial fever, from exposure, night after night, to drenching rains, without tents. There was so much of this murderous, blundering want of prevision and provision, in the first few months of the war—and is *now*, for that matter.

Gradually, out of the confusion came some system and order. Climbing up to the top of the Patent Office with each loaf of bread was found not to be an amusing occupation, and an arrangement of pulleys was made out of one of the windows, and any time through the day, barrels of water, baskets of vegetables and great pieces of army beef, might be seen crawling slowly up the marble face of the building.

Here, for weeks, we worked among these men, cooking for them, feeding them, washing them, sliding them along on their tables, while we climbed up on something and made up their beds with brooms, putting the same powders down their throats with the same spoon, all up and down what seemed half a mile of uneven floor;—coaxing back to life some of the most unpromising,—watching the youngest and best die.

I remember rushing about from apothecary to apothecary, in the lower part of the city, one Sunday afternoon, to get, in a great hurry, mustard, to help bring life into a poor Irishman, who called me Betty in his delirium, and, to our surprise, got well, went home, and at once married the Betty we had saved him for.

By-and-by the regiment got through with the fever, improvements came into the long ward, cots took the place of the tables, and matting covered the little hills of the floor. The hospital for the 19th Indiana became the "U. S. General Hospital at the Patent Office," and the "volunteers for emergencies" took up their saucepans and retired."

A. H. W.

LENOX, Sept. 15, 1861.

Charley talks of going down to-morrow to be inspected and mustered into State service with the regiment—the Home-Guard. He thinks his fine for non-attendance will about equal his railroad fare down and up. He is to stay over night and will see Mary at Astoria.

C. C. W.
Sept. 18.

Charley left on Monday to be with his regiment, which has been drafted into the U. S. Service—the first step towards Washington. The members singly can resign at any time, and Charley will do this when called upon to leave the city.

The family took this consoling view of Charley's duty to his country, and saw him leave Lenox without anxiety. Charley's private views developed later, when, after valuable service with the Sanitary Commission at the front, he entered the 164th N. Y. regiment and was immediately assigned as aide de camp to very active duty at Army Headquarters.

Rev. Henry Hopkins to E. W. H.
CITY HOTEL HOSPITAL,
ALEXANDRIA, Oct., 1861.

My dear Mrs. Howland: I want to tell you how I am coming on here in my new field, for at Washington I received the impression, which it will take a long time to wear away, that you and Miss Woolsey are cordially interested in all that concerns me in this work.

Dr. Sheldon is entirely propitious thus far. . . . Those who are religious women among the nurses hail my coming with real joy. The very first one whom I encountered was such a woman, and as I sat down in her cheerful ward before the bright fire on the hearth, talking with the men, a poor emaciated creature who was sitting wrapped in blankets, with his feet upon a pillow, asked me—"Are you a physician?" "No," I told him, "I am a clergyman." He stretched out his lean hand to me, and said—"Oh, sir, I am *so* glad to see you. I have been very sick, so that they gave me up, and now I am getting well, and I am not a Christian, and I *must* be." Could the most trembling faith ask more than this?

I have just come from attending the funeral of a soldier of the 27th N. Y. regiment, who died last evening of typhoid fever. It was severely simple in all its accompaniments, only a little gathering in the hospital dining room, and a simple exercise; while a corporal's guard were the only ones to attend the body to the grave, to hear the last sad words spoken. But in the very simplicity of it, and in the peculiar circumstances of those concerned, and especially from being the first time that I had ever officiated on such an occasion, it was to me very impressive. Had I not been here it is unlikely that he would have received a Christian burial.

... Dr. Sheldon called me *Mr. Woolsey* this morning, and as long as that association of ideas continues I am sure of most excellent treatment.

E. W. H. to J. H.

Oct. 1, '61.

Very little to tell you about except a few calls, including one from Mrs. General Franklin to ask us to take tea with her to-night. Lieutenant Lusk of the 79th, whom we used to know as "Willy" Lusk, also came. He seems to have grown up into a very fine young fellow, handsome and gentlemanly, and with the same sweet expression he had as a child. He was studying medicine in Europe when the war broke out, but came home at once and enlisted as Lieutenant in the 79th, where he is now Acting Captain—so many of the regiment were either killed or taken prisoners at Bull Run. Dr. E. also came again and Captain Gibson and Col. Montgomery of Philadelphia, so we had quite a levee.

Oct. 2. G. and I are just going up to Columbian College to cover and arrange a nice box of books Hatty Gilman has sent on at our suggestion to form the nucleus of a hospital library —an excellent selection of books, histories, biographies, etc.; half worn, but the covering and labeling we mean to put them through will make them highly respectable and attractive.

We took tea last night with Mrs. Franklin and met five or six other people, among them Major and Mrs. Webb—he on General Barry's staff. Dr. Bacon has brought G. some splendid bunches of roses this week, the finest I ever saw. He expects to be ordered off with his new regiment, the 7th Connecticut, within a few days, probably to join the Coast Expedition, but this is a secret.

We have been with Captain Gibson all through the Corcoran Art Building, now used as a government warehouse and filled with clothing and camp equipage of every kind, one item being twenty thousand tents. From the roof, to which we mounted, we had a fine view over the city and environs, the river, the opposite heights and an army balloon.

E. W. H. to J. H.

Oct. 6.

After dinner yesterday we drove out to the camp of the Rhode Island 2nd, to see the friend of our infancy and of hay-loft and cow-stall memory—Col. Frank Wheaton, son of Dr. Wheaton of Pomfret, Connecticut, to whose farm-house Mother took us all to board, the summer after Father's death. It is about twenty years (!) since we all played together. You know it was for him that Mary got that ugly scar across her nose, in her anxiety to reach him through a glass window, and they two at the age of about seven were married in state and went to housekeeping in the cow-stall on apples and flagroot. He says he remembers it all most distinctly and still claims Mary as "his wife by right" though he has had one, and is engaged to a second.

He was very much pleased to find that he had met you too, for he was mustering-in officer at Albany when you were there, and swore in, part of the 16th. He and the others were "delighted with Adjutant Howland, who used to come to their office nearly every day and *always had his muster rolls right.*"

I was sorry to hear that the mare "Lady Jane" was so sick and I send George Carr out to camp to see if he can do anything for her. As he has known her from early youth he may understand her insides better than others do. You may be surprised at my being able to get a pass for George, but not more than I was! A mere statement of the case dissolved all the adamantine walls round the Provost Marshal, and is only another proof of our being "noble-hearted women of *luck.*"

A. H. W. writes:

How funny it is that you should have met the Wheatons again. It is one of the queer ways in which people turn up. I wonder if they remember the little school which Mother held for us every day in the porch of their father's house in Pomfret, and the yellow hymn book, and the tunes of

and
> "Our Father in Heaven
> We hallow Thy name,"
>
> "God is in Heaven, would He hear
> If I should tell a lie?"

—and then how at times we used to see who could eat the most ears of corn! And the *skeleton* in his father's office, what a corner of horrors that was!

E. to J. H.
WASHINGTON, Oct. 7.

After dinner to-day we said good-bye to Dr. Bacon, now Surgeon of the 7th Connecticut, and he left in the night we suppose, with the regiment, to join the second great land and naval expedition for the southern coast. F. B. with the Port Royal Expedition.

Oct. 9, '61. As I told you, Dr. Bacon left either Monday night or early yesterday for Annapolis with the 7th Connecticut. They seem to have been the first ones dispatched, for yesterday others went, and, as I write, a long train of baggage and men equipped for a journey is passing down the street. We think of sending Moritz on to Annapolis this afternoon with a basket of sea-stores for the Doctor, and he can bring us back accounts of the number of vessels, etc. Moritz is anxious to know before leaving if the troops—including the 7th Connecticut! are Union ones!

Oct. 14. Moritz got back from Annapolis all right. Found Dr. Bacon and delivered the basket. There was no prospect of their going before next week. All the 15,000 had not yet arrived and only one transport was ready. The railroad was blocked all the way by immense trains of stores, ammunition, etc., and Moritz was from half-past two till eleven o'clock getting there.

F. B. to G. M. W.

CAMP WALTON, ANNAPOLIS, Oct. 18th, '61.

Pardon a wretched notelet, written on camp stationery with the very dregs of the day's ration of nervous energy. Everybody is both tired and busy to-night with this embarkation business. . . .

You will readily believe they are sober enough, these long, undulating files of honest brown faces, as they pour down upon the wharves, but there are good, rousing cheers, too, as the tenders swing out into the stream and go scuttling away to the great motionless ships in the roads.

I notice with surprise, and with some apprehension as well, that the 6th and 7th Connecticut, green as I have thought them, are farther advanced in the military art than any other troops I have seen here. This is not brag, you will please consider, it is very reluctant conviction. But still, as for me, turning more sadly than ever before from the loyal North, I feel an exultation in helping to strike, as we are hoping, the heaviest blow at the great crime that it has yet felt.

Your basket is such a miracle of packing that I have hesitated to thoroughly ransack it, fearing that the attempt to restore its contents to their normal condition might reduce me to a state of hopeless idiocy, like a Chinese puzzle, or a book on political economy.

Moritz delicately hinted at French rolls as being the only things that could not defy the ravages of time, and so, one terribly stormy evening, being the second after the arrival of the basket, Chaplain Wayland, my brother the Captain and I, having our rival teapots all in a row, each singing over her own spirit-lamp, I removed the stratum of rolls and disposed of them to the immense satisfaction of the tea-party. This gave me a glimpse of the blue and gold Tennyson lying lapped among the balmy bolognas. Ever since, I have been longing for the golden moment to come when I could sit, or, more properly, lie down to my own individual, personal, particular, blue and gold Tennyson. This may probably be when every soul in the regiment except myself is helplessly, hopelessly seasick, and nobody can "come a botherin' me."

F. B. to G. M. W.

HAMPTON ROADS, Oct. 27th.

We still loiter here in a seeming imbecile way, waiting now for weather and now for nobody knows what. Meanwhile patience and strength are ebbing in twelve thousand men. The condition of some of the regiments on shipboard is said to be very bad. Ours is fortunate in its ship, and they say is in better order than any other. A villain of a division-commissary, supplied fifteen days' rations of pork and no beef, for the entire expedition! Finding this out just as we were leaving Annapolis, I felt that we could never stand it, and we have behaved so cantankerously about it, that we have secured beef enough, fresh and salt, to greatly mitigate the Sahara of pork, for this regiment. God help the others! Oh to have a Division-commissary's head in a lemon-squeezer!

Leave of absence. J. H. got a week's furlough about the middle of October and we all went North together. Just before leaving Washington E. writes:

We did a few errands, went to see the Indiana boys at the Patent Office again, and to the Columbian College Hospital, and also to call on Will Winthrop, now Lieutenant of the Berdan

Sharp Shooters. He entertained us in his tent, a nice neat one, full of contrivances—painted table, book shelves and a *wash-stand*. Captain Hastings* of his company received us too ; and when we left, Will begged us to walk down the color-line with them as "it would increase their importance to be seen with two *rather* good-looking women. And if one of the field officers would *only* come by and ask who we were!"

On Sunday (the 13th) we went to St. John's Church and shook hands with General Scott and asked him in fun for leave of absence. He "thought we couldn't be spared!"

E. and J. H. went at once to their own home at Fishkill.

Mother to E. W. H. at Fishkill.

NEW YORK, Thursday, Oct. 17th.

My dear Eliza : I must write a line to you this afternoon, not only to congratulate you and dear Joe upon being together again in your own pleasant home but to tell you how charmed I am at the prospect of seeing you here. We began to pack up immediately on the receipt of our last letter from Washington and came down from Lenox as soon as possible, reaching home yesterday in time for a six o'clock dinner. I

---

* He died insane, at the close of the war.

wrote to old William we were coming and he had everything very nice and clean. . . . Mary received our letter last night, telling her we should be in town, so that this morning the first thing, Georgy—who had gone right out to Mary—and Carry rushed in upon us, and right glad were we to see Georgy again, and to find her looking so well; not entirely grey-headed and wrinkled with age from the cares and anxieties of her Washington campaign, as we expected! but really looking better and certainly fatter, than when she left home. It is delightful to hear her account of things, and it will be very charming when you are here with us too, to join in the pow-wows. We are all eager listeners to Washington doings, and I cannot bear to be out of the room a minute while Georgy is talking. . . .

Do give my kind remembrance to Thomson and his wife; I have a great respect for him. I hope you will come to us as soon as you can. We shall be all ready for you, except the "nicknacks," and I don't mean to take any of them out. I found William had opened Joe's likeness, and set it out, as a delicate little attention to the family! Hatty waits to take my note.

          Ever affectionately yours,
                    MOTHER.

E. writes:

On reaching home we found everything in the nicest order, gas lighted, bright fires, plenty of flowers, a delicious supper, and Thomson and his whole family, and Mechie (the gardener) with his arms full of pears and grapes, waiting to welcome us. They were all glad to have us back, and seemed unable to do enough for us. Mrs. Thomson and the gardener's niece helped Moritz, and we lived like princes for the few days on the products of the place without lifting our hands.

Joe went back to the army at the end of his week's furlough, G. and E. staying in New York a fortnight longer with Mother. On returning to Washington they found that General Scott had just resigned from the head of the army, Nov. 1, '61, and General McClellan had been appointed commander-in-chief. They began work again at once. E. writes home the next day:—

"We have been up to Columbian College Hospital and have helped Miss Dix cover a lot of books; were most affectionately welcomed by her on the field of our old conflict. Joe is in a new camp near Leesburg Pike and very comfortable. We took a lot of things to the Alexandria Hospital and to Slocum's brigade, including a number of bright prints Mother and Hatty sent on."

E. to J. H.

EBBITT HOUSE, WASHINGTON, Nov. 11.

It is very late, but I scribble a line before going to bed to say we got over safely from camp, stopping on the way for Mr. Hopkins, who is going to Poolesville with us to-morrow. We got in at six o'clock and since then we have been in a blaze of glory, for there has been a splendid torchlight procession in honor of McClellan, with rockets and blue lights and all sorts of fine things. Of course we followed it with Chaplain Hopkins, bringing up at Mrs. Hodge's in H street, next door to McClellan's own house, where the procession halted and called out Seward and Lincoln and Cameron and McClellan himself, and there were several little speeches, the best of which was General Blenker's, who said: "Citizens and soldiers, when I shtand on de battle field with your thousands volunteers I will fight de enemy better as I shpeak your noble language." Then on tiptoe he patted McClellan on the back and I think kissed him! Seward's speech was highly vague and promiscuous.

We came home at midnight, just now, with our patriotic noses smutty from the torches.

At 9 this morning we start for Poolesville and have the prospect of a fine day.

The battle of Ball's Bluff near Pooles- *Ball's Bluff.*
ville had taken place while we were on
"leave of absence" at home, and on our return to Washington, Major Potter, U. S. paymaster, and his wife, starting on an expedition to pay the troops up the Potomac, invited Chaplain Hopkins and ourselves to join the party, which we did with great delight, though it involved a three days' journey in our own carriage—a formidable thing at that time. It gave us an opportunity of visiting the scene of the desperate fight at the Bluff and the encampments at Poolesville and Darnestown and of taking supplies to these distant hospitals.

From E's Journal.

... "The officers told us the whole story of the battle and described terrible scenes to us of cold, suffering and death by drowning which we hope to forget. . . .

While standing on the dreadful bank where our poor wounded were dragged up (and from which we plainly saw the rebel pickets across the river gathering in a little group), we understood fully and bitterly the wicked incompetency of whoever is responsible for this blunder. . . .

Bright and early next morning we left for Darnestown on the return drive. There Captain Best, of Battery F, 4th Regular Artillery, was our host, and a most kind and attentive one, he and the other officers turning out of their tents for us and treating us like queens. Frank Crosby turned up there as Senior 1st Lieutenant, a position, Captain Best told us quietly, *he* worked fourteen years for in the regular service. Our tent was the *salon* and round our little fire that evening gathered Captain Best, General Hamilton of Wisconsin, Major Crane, Lieutenant Hazzard of Battery A, R. I. Artillery, Colonel Stiles of the 9th N. Y., Captain Perkins, Lieutenants Muhlenberg and Crosby, Dr. Wier of the Battery and others. They all came laden with refreshments from the sutler's, and all seemed to enjoy the fun. . . . Next day we called at Fort Muggins, lunched with the General, dined with Lieutenant Hazzard of Battery A, and left for Washington. We were stopped on the way for lack of countersign and marched to Tenallytown between files of soldiers! but managed to establish our innocence, and finally reached the Ebbitt house at 8 P. M.

At Darnestown we received the first official confirmation of the success of the great expedition and the capture of Port Royal. Captain Rodgers of the navy was selected by the Commodore as the first man to go on shore and run up the Stars and Stripes; and Dr. Bacon, who was one of the party, was sent inland with General T. W. Sherman's proclamation, issued on his own responsibility, to the citizens of South Carolina, exhorting them to "pause and reflect upon the tenor and consequences of their acts," etc. So deserted was the whole neighborhood of all but slaves that they had to go twelve miles to find a white man to hand the proclamation to, and *he* took it with oaths and under protest."

A. H. W. to G. E.
8 BREVOORT PL., Thursday.

The details of the landing of the fleet at Port Royal fill all minds and mouths. I hope Georgy will have, from "our own correspondent" with the expedition, a full account of the landing of the 7th Connecticut, which seems to have been the first on shore. The sight of those vessels rounding to and sailing past, with sails spread, and the bands playing, and the men crying, instead of cheering, for joy! must all have been wonderful. The poor blacks coming down to the shore, with their little bundles in their hands, is the most touching of all. Every one asks me what I think *now* of the state of the country, and I say—the results of the expedition are good, as *far as they go*. We must have something more than a Hatteras fizzle this time.

Flags are shown from all the private houses today. Our's is out again, and I dare say Broadway will be quite a sight.

F. B. to G.

TYBEE ISLAND.

The 7th was the first regiment ashore in South Carolina. It made the first reconnoissance in force; a detachment of five companies occupied Braddock's Point and its batteries, and was the first to reconnoitre Daufuskie and neighboring islands. The greater part of the regiment now holds this position, with a fragmentary German one. If you have ever wondered how I could be accessory to Sherman's proclamation in any way, let me suggest in the faintest possible whisper that I improved the occasion to issue on my own account a considerable number of small proclamations "to the loyal people of South Carolina of various shades of black and yellow scattered over the country from Beaufort to Port Royal Ferry."

C. C. W. to E.

Nov. 18th.

H. and C. meet Major Anderson.

Dear Eliza: Your most delightful letter has just been read aloud amid the cheers of the assembled family. What a splendid time you are having with your brigadiers and serenades. How I should like to sacrifice myself and join you in a few of your "noble" sprees, and become acquainted with some of your suffering generals. We, meantime, have been devoting *ourselves*, giving all our time and energy to the work of soothing and captivating a poor nervous soldier, Major Anderson. I suppose you heard that we started on our Christian enterprise the day after you left again for the same work. When we reached Tarrytown, the scene of our labors, we were received, as such heroines should be, with a great deal of state, and as we found a dinner-party of some twenty awaiting us we rushed up stairs to dress in our red silk and our mauve. . . . The whole regiment of us encamped in the house for the night and we had a jolly time.

On Wednesday, General Anderson, wife and son arrived. Mrs. A. is a great invalid and did not appear for the first two days, and when at last she was announced I looked to see a pale shadow glide in, and was astonished by the sight of a little, fat, plumpy woman with big bare arms and a good deal of jet jewelry; quite a talkative, frisky person. The General is lovely, quiet and gentlemanly and devoted to young ladies—a very important requisite in a hero. His health is very much shattered but his loyalty is unshaken. We were speaking of a lady who was engaged to a Southerner. "Break it off," he said, "break it at once, he is a lunatic;

I would as lief go into an insane asylum and argue with a man who calls himself Christ, as reason with a secessionist." Mrs. Anderson said she never saw such a change as being up in Tarrytown made in her husband. In town he was worn out by callers and indifferent people who came to see the hero and ask him why he did not do this and that and the other at Sumter; and propound their own theories as to how he should have acted. . . . We told General Anderson you were in Washington doing what you could, etc., and he said "God bless them, it is a good work they are doing." . . . We were sorry to come home on Tuesday, but had to, as I had invited the ———s and Mr. ——— to dinner. When we got home about an hour before dinner not a soul was here, Mother and Abby gone to Sing Sing for the day, Jane dodging a procession on Broadway, and one dish of chops ordered for dinner! We sent William out for jelly-cake, beef, etc., and with a spread of linen and glass, which fortunately was not in the closet of which Mother had the key, we set out quite a nice little table. . . . Cousin Mary Greene, Gardiner, and little Gardy arrived yesterday; the two last are still here. Gardy cuts into every conversation, asking innumerable and unanswerable questions: is now reading Ferdinand Second as pastime! aged ten.

Lenox Hodge (Hugh's father) was ready to give us all the help in his power, and we depended upon him often to fill our commissions for the hospitals. He writes from Philadelphia, Nov. '61.

Dear Georgy: I hope that you will duly receive the six air-beds, which agreeably to your request I have ordered. The cost was eleven dollars apiece and one dollar for express. I send also 100 pairs of slippers and 100 palm-leaf fans.

J. S. W. to G. and E.
NEW YORK, November, 1861.

Dear Girls: I went to the provisional Hospital here to see if the volunteers wanted anything. Mrs. Darragh took me all over, and said she wanted woolen shirts and socks *very much*. So I sent the requisition to the society and she will get all she wants there. . . . Mrs. D. also suggests slates for the men to scribble on, cypher on, do puzzles, etc.; thought they would be very nice, in which I agree. Perhaps the idea may be useful to you. . . . Do you remember Peck, the man all twisted with rheumatism? He is getting well, and is a great gourmand. They let him have anything he wants. While we were there he remarked sentimentally, "I say, send we some more of that *roast pig*, won't you." I shall adopt the New York volunteers to the mild extent of taking them some papers occasionally. . . . Mrs. Bennett, poor old soul, called yesterday to tell of the death of her son with typhoid dysentery in the camp, and, what with her grief and childish elation at having news to tell and being an object of sympathy, was most pathetically comic,—" dead and gone! dear, dead and gone! and this is his picter that he sent home to his mar," was her greeting to everyone that came down stairs; "and I hope you'll all be ready in time, my dears. It's bad enough to be *left by the cars*, but worse not to be ready when you come to die." Her great desire seemed to be to see and thank a drummer boy, who in the last few days of her son's life walked a mile and a half every day to get him a canteen of spring water. He was consumed with thirst and could not drink the river water. . . . Do the surgeons know that you can have money at your disposal for delicacies, as well as clothes, etc.? Let them know it, if you have not, and *spend, spend* indefinitely. I say to myself often, "fifty or sixty thousand dollars would give quite a lift, why do I cumber the ground?" So if you don't want to see me dead and the ducats in my coffin directed to the Sanitary Commission, say what I can do or send.

A. H. W. to G. and E.

November.

Bessie Wolcott's wedding came off very brilliantly. Carry went out to Astoria the day before. Mother and Hatty drove out together. Mary is said to have looked very handsome in white silk trimmed with black lace and white silk ruches. Hatty wore her crimson silk with white valencienne spencer or waist, and mother was very resplendent in velvet and feathers, stone cameos and black lace shawl. . . Charley drove out and back with his pony as rapidly as possible, as they had to drill for evacuation day, Charley's first appearance in a procession. We all stood on the curbstone and we winked, and he winked, and Captain Ben Butler and others twinkled and winked, not daring to do more, so precise and martial was their array. . . . Have you received a large brown bale that you didn't know what to make of? It is black curled hair. Eliza said *whole pillows* were much needed—underscoring the words. I don't know what she means, unless that mere empty tickings to be filled with straw don't answer. I have thought that the best way was to send you the hair, as it can be packed far closer than any number of ready-made pillows would be. The tickings are all made and will be along in Washington soon.

J. S. W. to J. H. in camp.

November 25.

We have been evacuating the British with great zest to-day; good weather, clean streets, and many praises for the 22nd, Charley's regiment, among other battalions—praises, that is, with the exception of some vile youths of the street, near Stuart's, who shouted "hurrah for the never go 'ways!" . . . We had a very interesting meeting of the Bible Society last night, second meeting of the army branch, many excellent speeches; Dr. Roswell Hitchcock, of course, who *apropos* of the slavery question, said, "Patience; we need not be hurrying matters—*that* cause, like the soul of old John Brown, is 'marching on,' and the chorus is 'Glory, Hallelujah!'" The allusion was charged with electricity, and the audience responded appropriately. A gentleman, I forget his name, had been to visit the Hatteras rebel prisoners and described the scene; a sad, sorry six hundred as you could well find. He made them an address on repentance (of the gospel sort), and begged them to sing, to "start something"—"Pray, sing my brothers; it will do your hearts good." So some one began "All hail the power of Jesus' name." Then followed "Jesus, lover of my soul," and last "There is rest for the weary." He said they sang well, and it was a strange and even touching sight. He said they were comfortably cared for, and he saw a lot of underclothes sent them in a wrapper marked, "from a father and mother whose son (a Union soldier) is in prison in Richmond." ...

How are you going to spend your Thanksgiving, and what are you going specially to give thanks for? The question will rather be what to leave out, than what to put in the *action de grace*. Did you read Governor Andrews' proclamation? if you didn't, do! It is like a blast out of one of the old trumpets that blew about the walls of the strong city till they tumbled down. Have you read the Confederate President's message, in which he has contrived to out-Herod Herod? ...

Tell the girls to get F. L. Olmsted's "Cotton Kingdom" if they want anything to read. He labors a little with his conscientiously faithful statistics, but when he breaks into his story his style runs smooth and clear, and there are few prettier pieces of travel-telling than his ride through the pine forests with the filly "Jane," for instance.

The Governors of all the loyal states issued in these dark days their annual proclamation of a day of Thanksgiving. Governor Andrews' of Massachusetts was dated Nov. 21, '61, " the anniversary of the day on which the Pilgrims of Massachusetts on board the

Thanksgiving Day.

Mayflower united themselves in a solemn compact of government:

'Sing aloud unto God our Strength.'"

The proclamation proposes to "give thanks for the privilege of living unselfishly, and dying nobly in a great and righteous cause."

These state proclamations came, heartening and sustaining a people sorely in need.

E's Journal.

November 28, THANKSGIVING.

We have kept the day with J. in camp. He commissioned us to ask Mrs. Franklin to meet the General, unbeknown to him. So we sent the carriage for her by half-past eight, and started a little after nine, hoping to reach camp in time for service with the regiment. The roads were very bad, however, and we were too late. We stopped at the Brigade Hospital on the way, to leave oysters, jelly, oranges, etc., keeping some for the regimental "sick in quarters." Our camp looked very neat and comfortable, tents all raised three or four feet on logs and clay, and nearly every one with a fire-place or stove. J. had arranged everything nicely for us, and his little fire and General Slocum's were running races. General Franklin soon arrived, and we all sat round the firesides till dinner time. The dining-room was the Sibley tent, charmingly ornamented with evergreens, and the dinner was a great victory in its way; for out of the little tent-kitchen appeared successively, oyster soup, roast turkey, cranberry sauce, canvas-back ducks, vegetables, and a genuine and delicious plum pudding that would do justice to any New England housekeeper. Cake, pies and ice cream were also among the good things. The whole day was delightful, ending with a visit to General Franklin's camp and the return to town with outriders.

E. to J. H.
EBBITT HOUSE, December 1, '61.

We saw yesterday a nice dodge for enlarging your tent and making the back one more private. It is pitching the two tents three or four feet apart and spreading the fly over the intermediate vestibule. Chaplain Edward Walker of the 4th Connecticut, whom we went to see yesterday, had his two tents arranged so, and the effect was very pretty. In the front one he had the regimental library (a very nice one) and the back one was his own, and between them was the little vestibule floored like the others and boarded at the sides to keep out the cold, and in it he had his stove and washing apparatus, and from its ceiling hung a pretty wire basket filled with moss and wild flowers! a charming little bit of New England country life in the midst of civil war. He is a nice fellow, one of Dr. Leonard Bacon's Congregational boys and just the one for an army Chaplain—so cheerful and strong, and honest and kind-hearted. . . . He went with us through the camp and to the hospital, where we left them some supplies, including a lot of hair pillows which we had made from Abby's material.

G. lately drove Chaplain Wrage's wife out to her husband's camp, carrying socks, pillows, comforters, farina, etc. to the hospital. The camp was very German and dirty; no New England faculty shown in keeping *it* warm and clean, and the little German bowers looked dreary in the freezing weather. The Colonel, who addresses us as "my ladies" in a polite note, is under arrest for stealing; the Lieutenant-Colonel and Quartermaster are fools, and the men suffer in consequence.

Mother to G. and E.

THURSDAY EVENING, December 5.

My dear Girls: This will be a little Sunday greeting to you, probably, as I write it merely to give you my love, and your address to Mr. Charles Johnson of Norwich. He is now here spending the evening, and, as usual, very entertaining. He leaves to-morrow for Washington. He goes to secure, if possible, a paymaster's position in one of the Connecticut regiments, and has Governor Buckingham, Mr. Foster and others interested for him. Jane has told him that perhaps you can "pull the wires" for him in some quarters! I fear we are beginning to feel proud of you, as we hear your praises sounded in various quarters, and read paragraphs in the papers of your doings. At the wedding last night, Mrs. Colby told me all she had heard from your French widow nurse, who, it seems, has told her all about your visits to the hospital, etc., and what a "sunbeam" Georgy is, and how much comfort you have both been to her, and to all the other nurses. . . . The largest box yet, stands all nailed up and marked, ready for the express, in the front hall, and when Mr. Johnson said he was going on and would take anything for us, we told him we had a small parcel which he probably saw as he came in; the poor man looked aghast at the idea! . . . How very pleasant Mr. Hopkins is, but I think he must have been quizzing you in his very flattering remark about me. I do not like this in him. You poor, dear, little girls! I wish I could place a tray before you every day or two with something relishing. A large dish has come up to-night of jumbles, which I should like to empty on your table. . . . Charley has just come in from drill, with his new military overcoat, which is quite becoming. . . . Many kisses and lots of love.

A. H. W. to G. and E.

December 6th.

If Mr. Craney thought the bundle of hair was a feather-bed, he will certainly think that the stocking box, when it arrives, is the bedstead following on. . . . Let me describe its contents. In the first place, E's cheque bought seven dozen and a half pairs of socks. . . . We have added as many more dozen as our own purchase, and friends sent in nearly two dozen knitted ones, so that the whole number is sixteen dozen. The pair of Mackinaw blankets looked like very heavy and handsome ones, from one of Robert's parishioners. We added two pairs more of less expensive ones, and in the folds of one are a couple of little framed pictures, out of a lot Charley brought down to be sent, but I thought two were enough to run the risk of breakage. . . . Of woolen gloves there are five dozen—Jane's purchase, etc., etc. . . . Lastly, after the box was all nailed up, came Dorus with a dozen of "country-knit socks" from the store in Friendsville, near where Annie Woolsey lives. We had the middle plank of the box taken off and stuffed them in. . . . It is unpardonable that Wrage's men, or any men, should be badly off for socks. The dishonest quartermasters are a curse to our army and our cause. . . . Mother thinks the best part of all this is to be able to put the pillows *yourselves* under the sick men's heads. What a scene your room must be with its boxes and bags! . . . We are amused to think that you admire the President's message. . . . What do you think of his muddle about the slavery question? about Government taking slaves at so much a lump for taxes? expatriating a man from the soil he was born on and loves, because he is loyal to the government and of dark complexion.

C. C. W. to G. and E.
December 1st.

L. came in a few evenings ago. He was at Conway last summer, and able to contradict an absurd story that was going the rounds,—that Charley and Joe having joined the army, Mother had given up housekeeping and gone into the hospitals, and all the daughters were children of the regiment!

Dr. Carmalt called too. He is very quiet, but good-looking, and ready to laugh at poor jokes, which is much in his favor. . . . I never told you what a nice dressing-gown the one you left for Abby was; and though she was immensely disgusted at your having given it, she wears it every night and looks comfortable and warm, which is what she did not look, with her flannel petticoat over her shoulders.

Abby would not spend a penny that could be helped, on herself, during the war. She casually mentioned one day with modest pride that she had spent only $300 for herself this year. Jane looked at her with surprise and remarked, "I can't imagine where you've put it!"

F. B. to G. M. W.

TYBEE ISLAND, Dec. 24, '61.

Tybee Island. You speak of our hospital as a matter of course; and we are, by and by, to have one, as yet uncommenced; but we owe the medical department no thanks for this when we get it. Dr. Cooper, Medical Director of the expedition, a sensible man, urged the necessity of a hospital; Surgeon-General Finley thought otherwise —"in this mild southern climate tents would do very well for men to have fevers in." It would suit my views of the fitness of things to have Surgeon-General Finley exposed in scanty apparel to a three days' Texas norther, by way of enlarging his views of southern climates. . . .

I was just laying the foundations of a log hospital for our men at Port Royal when we were ordered here, and, as I have no compunction about committing any crime short of high treason for a hospital, I had effected a neat little larceny of a lot of windows and sawn lumber which were to work in so sweetly. It was a sad reverse to abandon it!

One great trouble has been to keep our sick men, with their lowered vitality, warm in tents. There is a popular prejudice against cannon balls which I assure you is wholly unfounded. My experience is that there are few pleasanter things to have in the family than hot shot. It would raise the cockles of your heart some of these wretchedly cold nights, to walk between the two long rows of men in my large hospital-tent just after they have been put to bed, each with his cup of hot tea and his warm thirty-two pound shot at his feet, and to see and feel the radiant stack of cherry-red balls in the middle of the floor. This is troublesome and laborious to manage, however, and we greatly need some little sheet-iron stoves. I sent for some a good while since, which should be here shortly. Your inquiry about medicines is a sagacious one, and shows that you have not neglected your hospital-walking opportunities. My dear unsophisticated friend, permit me to indoctrinate you in a dainty device whereof the mind of undepartmental man hath not conceived. Know that there is one supply-table of medicines for hospital use and another for field use. Some very important, almost essential, medicines are not furnished for field service; when your patient needs them he is to go to the hospital. Very good—where is the hospital for us? Now, before we left Washington, with a perfectly clear notion of what was likely to befall us in the way of fevers, and out of the way of hospitals, I made a special requisition for some things not in the field supply table, such as serpentaria, and some of the salts of iron, and went in person to urge it through the purveyor's office. No use.

Ask any sensible, steady-going old doctor how he would feel with a lively fever *clientele* upon his hands, and no serpentaria or its equivalent.

I declare, it seemed to me like a special providence that in my pretty extensive "perusings" about these parts, I picked up, here and there, from rebel batteries and deserted houses, both serpentaria and many other needed medicines which have turned to the best account. . . .

If you should hear some day that some rebel Major-General had been rescued from impending death by hemorrhage by the application of Liq. Ferri Persulphat. in the hands of the surgeon of the 7th C. V., you may lay it all to that little bottle which was not the least wonderful content of that wonderful basket sent to Annapolis. The Tennyson and Barber inspired me with emotions too various and complicated here to describe; the bologna cheered and invigorated; the Castile soothed and tranquilized my soul; but at the sight of the Liquor Ferri Persulphatis! — — — what shall I say, except to repeat the words of our own Royston—"a halloo of smothered shouts ran through every vein!"

and whenever since, I have started upon any expedition giving promise of bullets, I have popped the bottle into my pocket, hoping to use it upon some damaged rebel.

Our tents, flimsy speculator's ware at best, are now in a most deplorable state. I am distressed to think of the possibility of a long rainy season overtaking us with no other shelter. . . .

This island upon which we are now encamped, though a lonely wilderness enough and several days farther from home than that which we have left, is on the whole more interesting, as it seems to offer "a right smart chance" of a fight. At any time we can, and often we do, get ourselves shelled from Pulaski by walking upon a certain stretch of the beach. This afternoon a rifled shell came squealing along in its odd way and plumped into the ground without exploding, a few yards from where my brother and I stood. The rascals seem to have defective fuses, and as yet they have hurt no one. By creeping along under bushes we get within Sharps' rifle range of the great grim fort, and look right into its embrasures. Don't mention that fact just now. . . . . Every day, about the time Pulaski begins her afternoon shelling, "Old Tatnal"* runs down

---

* "Old Tatnal" originated the expression, "Blood is thicker than water," when as flag officer of the U. S. squadron in '57, he came to the assistance of the English commander in Chinese waters. In 1861 he turned traitor to his flag.

his fleet and gnashes his teeth at us from a safe distance, but doesn't come within range of our new battery or the gunboats. We hear cannon practice at Savannah occasionally, and from one quarter or another great guns growl every few hours. On the whole, a lively place. . . .

Our jolly German neighbors have begun upon their Christmas eve with such rolling choruses right behind my tent, that I must step out to see. . . . —I find that they have a row of Christmas trees through their camp, all a-twinkle with candles, and hung with "hard-tack" curiously cut into confectionary shapes, and with slices of salt pork and beef. Sedate, heavy-bearded Teutons are sedulously making these arrangements, retiring a few paces to observe through severely studious spectacles the effect of each new pendant.

We have all the foliage orthodox for Christmas here, including holly and mistletoe with berries of scarlet and white wax. The jungly unscarred forest of this island is superb. . . . The purple grey depths of the wood all flicker with scarlet grosbeaks like flames of fire, and quaint grey and brown northern birds flit in and out with the knowing air of travelled birds, and plan the nests they will build next summer, in spite of bombs and bayonets, in New England elms and alders. . . .

I owe something to Captain Howland for keeping up my spirits, for, sometimes when I think how utterly these wretched Carolinians throw their best and their all into their bad cause as if they believed in and loved it, and then see, with a sort of dismay, how few, comparatively, of our first-rate men have come personally to the fight with self-sacrifice and out of pure love of the cause, I think of Captain Howland and take comfort of him at least.

The Trent affair, to which the next letters refer, was the capture by Captain (afterwards Admiral) Wilkes, of Messrs. Mason and Slidell, rebel emissaries, making their way to England via Havana, on board an English vessel, the Trent, with their secretaries and families. They were afterwards surrendered by the U. S. Government without an apology to England.

A. H. W. to G. and E.

December.

My dear Girls: The news of Mason and Slidell's release has arrived since you wrote. It was generally known here about 11 A. M. Saturday. I am quite satisfied with the release and with the grounds of it. In making the claim, England runs counter to all her preced-

The Trent Affair.

ing history in the matter of maritime laws. In holding the men, we should contradict our own previous course. Is it not far better to put *England* in the wrong, by yielding to her claim and so negatively securing her assent to what America has so long contended for—the rights of neutrals? As the Washington Intelligencer said, Mason and Slidell are for a day, Maritime Law is for all nations and all time. For my part, I think our position more assured, more dignified, more honorable to us since the surrender than ever before. Of course it will not satisfy England. Their peremptory demand, and Lord Lyons' laconic acceptance, are in contrast with Mr. Seward's wordy, sauve, argumentative letters. They have got in part what they asked—possession of the men; they have not got what they asked—an apology for the "insult to their flag" and the violation of rights of asylum. The Manchester Guardian even says plainly that "whether Mason and Slidell are returned or not, war preparation on the part of England must go on, the day being not far distant when the Southern Confederacy must be recognized, and England must be prepared to support her policy." Mr. Seward, too, you know, says very plainly that recognition of the South would instantly be the signal of war between ourselves and all the recognizing powers.

J. S. W. to G. and E.

December '61.

Dear Girls: "We are in the midst of stirring times," as the newspapers say—or rather, stirring times are in our midst, as well as all around us. I am prepared to be astonished at nothing, and to regard all events with stoicism bordering on a fiendish glee. New York was sizzling on Monday and Tuesday; shops, omnibuses and everything, full of "don't give 'em up" and "come on, Britain." Wm. Bond was here on Monday evening and said he never saw such a state of things down town. In their office they had drawn up a subscription paper among themselves for *one privateer, with two rifled guns; to sail from New London.*—" But I thought privateering was a sort of barbarism, Mr. Bond?" —" Oh, no. It is a *relic* of a *bygone* age; that is all."—Mr. B. brought invitations to the breakfast at the Astor House to Gov. Buckingham and the officers of the 11th Conn. Mother, Abby and Charley went yesterday and had a very nice time. . . . The young line officers munched and crunched and giggled and clapped with the keenest enjoyment. The remarks about England were the same in tone that most sensible people make—"*prove* us wrong and we will apologize like gentlemen; if otherwise then otherwise." . . . For my part, as to war with England; I do not see it where I stand. Infinite are the resources of diplomacy, and Mr. Seward and Mr. Lincoln are cool hands.—What a horribly satisfactory thing the burning of Charleston is — retribution from within; — Sumter avenged without our responsibility. There is something quite dramatic in the denouement. "As the captain of the Illinois came by, the whole sky was one red glare, with the outlines of Fort Sumter black against it." . . . A note from Sarah Woolsey says she will be here to-night. I shall take her round to some of the fairs and things of which there is no end. The Union Bazaar is the biggest. Stewart gives a shawl—$1,500—to be raffled for; Dr. Hughes a bronze statue, ditto; Miss King a doll bride with trousseau, trunks, French maid, etc., all complete, ditto; and so on. They took in $3,000 the first night. We have just sent off a lot of old party dresses to the Tracys for doll finery, everything we could find; you may miss something familiar when you come back. . . . I observe that when *you* write two sheets you speak of it as a letter. When *I do* it becomes a note.—We had a lot of little things already collected for F. B. and shall send them on as a little Christmas box without waiting to hear. I am going to put "Spare Hours," by author of Rab, in the box, and the jolliest tin canister of bonbons "as ever you see." . . . Anna Rockwell read us a lot of interesting letters from Charles. He is "head-ing home" now; he belongs to the 7th; the 7th may have to turn out yet to garrison the forts. If there is war with England Robert says he shall enlist. . . .

Mother to G. and E.
MONDAY, December 24, 1861.

My dear Girls: Col. D. is a godsend! I was in despair at the thought of not getting some little Christmas box off so as to reach you to-morrow, when lo! he appeared, like an angel of mercy and offered to take anything we might have to send. So of course we gathered together our duds, which we had set aside as an impossibility as Christmas gifts, to take their chance in reaching you for New Year, and have just sent off the bonnet box filled with love and best wishes in all the chinks, mixed in with the sugar-plums and covering over everything, to make all acceptable to our noble-hearted girls, who are "extending their benevolence to all within their reach." . . . I have sent Joe a cake, which you must dress with its wreath and flag, for him to take down to camp. . . . We are going to give little May a Christmas tree and have a beauty now standing in the middle parlor ready to be decorated. It is a very large one, and will take the whole of a box of one hundred colored candles which I have been arranging in little colored tin candlesticks with sharp points which fasten on to the branches. We have also a number of small colored lanterns and a great variety of beautiful and cunning toys. This is to be my Christmas gift to the children. . . .

E's Journal:

Christmas Day we spent with J. again in camp, going round by Alexandria to pick up Chaplain Hopkins and take him with us. We had taken some goodies and little traps with us for the men in the hospitals in Alexandria and were glad to find the nice arrangements that had already been made by Madame M. She had got Col. Davies to detail some of the 16th men to bring her Christmas greens, and had dressed all the wards with festoons and garlands, little flags, mottoes, etc., besides arranging for a grand Christmas dinner for her "boys."

The Mansion House Hospital too was resplendent with bright tissue papers and evergreens and Dr. Sheldon showed us with great pride his kitchen and store-room arrangements, which are excellent in every respect. Fifty roast turkeys were preparing for the Christmas feast, sixteen large loaf-cakes iced to perfection and decorated with the most approved filigree work, pies without number, cream puffs, cranberry sauce, puddings of all sorts, etc., etc.—altogether the most Christmas-like scene we have looked upon, and all arranged with the greatest order and cleanliness.

Among the little things we took out were Mother's and Jane's socks, which we gave to men likely to go back soon to their regiments. The only boy without mittens got Mrs. Smith's.

After our own camp dinner, at which the Colonel and the Doctor joined us, we sat round the last and best chimney yet built, and talked about old times five or six months ago, which now seem like so many years. J. says his Christmas Eve was dreary enough in his tent, and they all agreed that our coming was the only thing that prevented their Christmas Day from being so too.

A. H. W. to G. and E.

December 26.

Dear Girls: We had a great day yesterday. *Of course*, Mother and the girls and Charley broke through the rule we had prescribed for ourselves, not to give Christmas presents, and launched upon Jane and me wholly unprepared, a flood of pretty and useful things. . . . We dined at Mary's, and there Mother was made happy by a superb dish of moss, growing and trailing over, and set in a carved walnut table or stand which Mary brought from Germany. . . . Our children's "Christmas tree" went off very successfully. Little May came over early and did the honors as nicely as could be to the arriving guests, introducing them all to each other and providing amusement. There were the three little Howlands and their mamma, the Prentisses and theirs, Mally and Willy Smith and theirs, little Kernochan, little Parker boy, and Mary and Helen Skinner with the Rhinelander children. The tree was in the back parlor with the doors closed and windows darkened, and the effect was very pretty when the candles and the lanterns were all ready and the doors were thrown open, and the tree blazed out in its own light. Each child had half a dozen little things and was delighted, choosing, when left to him or herself, the most hideous Chinese toys only intended as decorations. Then there were ice cream and jelly, which the older people helped eat, and Mr. Prentiss came in, and the children gradually went away—and we subsided into quiet.

And so, the first year of the war closed with at least a happy time for the children.

SECOND YEAR OF THE WAR
1862

CHAPTER V.

E's Journal.

January 1862.

... Sunday evening James Gillette came up to our room to tell us his story. He is one of the two hundred and forty Union soldiers just released from Richmond prisons in exchange for an equal number of rebel prisoners from Fort Warren. He was with the 71st N. Y., a three months' regiment, and his time was out before the battle in which he was taken prisoner. These five months of prison life have turned him from a dapper little fellow into a sad-looking, care-worn, sick man. He and his fellows were in Prison No. 2, a tobacco factory, dirty and uncomfortable beyond description— 170 men in a room 40 feet by 60. They immediately organized themselves, however, into a little military community under strict discipline. A detail of men was made every day to police the place, and all *unnecessary* uncleanliness was punished by the court they instituted for the trial of offenders. They had plenty of water but no soap or towels. Their rations were about

<small>A New Year's call on G. and E.</small>

eleven ounces of bread daily and one ration of beef or pork, and the water in which this was boiled was served at night as soup—"Confederate swill" they called it. They had no clothing given or sent them except what came to the Massachusetts and Rhode Island men, and an occasional little bundle handed in secretly by some sympathizing citizen. . . . The principal suffering was from the ignorance and brutality of the prison guards, who treated them roughly and often shot at them. Several were killed in that way; and yet these same sentinels would let the prisoners stand guard in their places, and go off and get them whiskey; and when they themselves were drunk, our men would pass them and take an airing in the city. The sick suffered and still suffer for want of decent care and medicine. One building is given up to cases of gangrene—a sufficient commentary on the condition of things. As a rule the prisoners kept up their spirits well and used all sorts of means for entertaining themselves; a debating club, a court, menagerie exhibitions, carving in beef-bones, etc. I have a little ring cut from part of their rations. Some men, though, have grown simple, almost idiotic, from the confinement; some have gone insane; and some of good standing at home will now wrangle pitifully over a bit of cracker or meat. About one hundred of our men, he says, have already died in Richmond of sickness, besides those dying from their wounds.

Among these released Richmond prisoners were twenty-one men of the 27th N. Y., a regiment brigaded with our 16th.

E's Journal, Jan. 11, '62, says:

Joe told us of the pretty reception they had given the returned Richmond prisoners of the 27th. It was a shockingly muddy day or the whole brigade would have marched down to meet them. As it was, the General and Staff and the 27th marched as far as the Brigade Hospital, where they met the poor fellows trudging up the hill, each with his little bundle. They gave them a grand greeting with band-playing and hand-shaking and then the procession was formed: first the band, then the prisoners at the head of the column, then the rest of the regiment, and the General and Staff bringing up the rear. As they marched through the different camps there was a perfect ovation, friends and strangers alike smothering them with hugs, cheering them, slapping them on the back and "old-fellowing" them. The regimental bands were *all* out in force and the camp of the 27th was dressed festively for the occasion, the procession entering it by an archway over which hung the words "Welcome, Comrades! Your wounds bleed afresh in our hearts.." They were all more or less wounded but are now in pretty good condition and all are to have a furlough of thirty days.

J. S. W. to J. H.

SATURDAY EVENING, January, '62.

I received yesterday from Mr. Stephen Williams thirty dollars, on the part of Mr. Alexander Van Rensselaer, "for a soldiers' library." Stephen, good old soul, said, "Oh! I've got this commission; now won't you help me? *I* don't know about libraries; you can consult Howland," etc., etc. . . . It will buy about forty plain books for a hospital or regiment. Would the 16th or any regiment in the brigade like one? . . .

Lizzie Greene sent a box of flannel shirts to a Connecticut regiment lately, and put a dozen cigars and a paper of tobacco in a pocket in each—"true Christian philanthropy," William Bond says;—"send them something they ought not to have." . . . We have been trying to persuade Mother to go down to Washington with Hatty and Charley, and take a look at things, but she is not to be prevailed on, I am afraid. Charley's lame hand will prevent him from going for a while, but I think he and H. will go on while Carry is in Boston. Carry goes on Wednesday to Mrs. Huntington Wolcott's and afterwards to Miss Parsons', (lately engaged to a tall Captain Stackpole in a Massachusetts regiment now at Annapolis, expecting to go up the York river with Burnside's expedition). Abby saw Mrs. George Betts to-day, who says her husband (in Hawkins' Zouaves) expects to join the same expedition immediately. Transports are to take them at once from Hatteras to the rendezvous at Fortress Monroe. They have suffered severely at Hatteras; the mortality in George Betts' regiment has been very great. . . .

Malvina Williams says she hears G. and E. are known in Washington as the "Angels!" . . .

Mr. Prentiss came in just now for a little call, cheery and bright, asking for your photograph to put in a book he had given him for Christmas. So you can send him one. It's a good book to be in, Mr. Prentiss' good book. . . .

William Wheeler, who has been very ill with camp fever, writes home that he has received great kindness from Miss *Jane Woolsey*, meaning G., and "was delighted with her." I *begged* his friends not to mention it; it was but little I could do! But tell Georgy. . . .

Would you like three or four dozen more gloves for your men, lonely and cold sentinels, for instance? Spake the wurred. Mr. Gibson sends a lot of London papers all deep-edged with black for the Prince Consort (rest his soul) and their own sins (bad luck to them) I should hope. The "whirligig of time will no doubt bring in its revenges." . . .

I had a vision of you to-day, as might be a year ago, sitting on the box seat of a sleigh, with a fur cap with ears, and, shall I say it, a roseate nose, visible when you turned around, skirrying over the crusty roads with the blue bloomy hills lifting, and the white fields rolling away, with the wonderful sparkling rime on everything and the heavy snow breaking down the fir-branches. The vision passed, as Cobb would say, and I tried to make another out of your present circumstances and didn't succeed at all, which proves that your normal state is not war-like.

Young people at home could not be kept on the nervous strain all the time, and an occasional festivity served as a breathing place, though the regular occupation of the family followed hard upon it.

M. W. H. to G. and E.
January.

Dear Girls: I have only been waiting for the New Year to come fairly in and shut the door, before sitting down quietly to wish you all the traditionary compliments of the season. . . . We all spent Christmas day together as usual in London Terrace. . . . The prettiest feature of the season was Mother's Christmas tree for the children, who were in ecstasies of delight, and insisted even upon perching on the branches to get as near to it as possible. Night before last was devoted to a brilliant little party for the children Hatty and Carry,—a very handsome and successful affair. I did not go, my wardrobe presenting only the alternative of bogy or bride, either black silk or a too dressy white silk, but Robert and I feasted on some of the remains last night, on our roundabout way home from Mr. Everett's lecture at the Academy of Music, and had a near and satisfactory view of the spun sugar beehives and candy castles surmounted by nougat cherubim, which graced the occasion.

A. H. W. to G. and E.

8 BREVOORT PLACE, January 7.

My Dear Girls: I have only time before mailing hour for a short letter, but must tell you how pleasantly Hatty's and Carry's little party went off last night. . . . Maillard sent up at eleven a very handsome little supper. . . . Bessie and Mr. Merchant came in the afternoon to dinner, which was hardly over and our dresses pitched on when the company came. Miss Tilly Dawson was the prettiest girl here, and Charley Johnson was made happy all the evening by an introduction to her. I think Zenie Smith* was the next prettiest. She came with two young friends staying with her, and Minnie Worthington brought the sweet young fellow she is engaged to ; and there were the McCurdy girls and Helen Skinner, and Lilly Lusk and Tom Perkins, and Frank Bond, and Mr. Stagg, and the Cryders and McKeevers, and Bucks, etc., etc. Supper was so delayed that I don't know how we should have got on if it hadn't been for the man Charley had engaged to play the piano, and they all danced, and you can imagine that it was not a slow time when I tell you that I! figured in a Virginia reel. Some of Charley's chums were agreeable young fellows, young Marsh, the son of G. P. Marsh, and others. Charley himself had been on the bed all day with a sick headache, but brightened up when the evening was half over, and in spite of his lame hand, dressed himself quite elaborately with a roman scarf for a sling and came down. . . . Chaplain Wrage goes to Washington to-night and will take you a hundred hymn books in German, which I bought at the Methodist book concern. They will do to give away when you come across a German soldier in the hospitals. . . . Did you know that the Boston Tract Society has an agent and a depository in the Post Office Building, Washington?

---

* Arixene Southgate Smith, now your Aunt Zenie.

... The box of books for Joe, directed to Alexandria, Va., went off yesterday. Cousin Sarah Coit has sent us her one pair of stockings, her giant pair, that she says she has knit, and knit, and knit on, and seemed to make no progress.
... Young Crosby begged, the other night, for whatever mittens we or our friends might have this week, to make up 120 pairs for Frank's artillery company of regulars. Did you know how many of the Crosby family are in the army? You saw Frank Stevens, who has a Lieutenancy at last, in Pratt's Ulster Guard. Then Schuyler Crosby is in the Regular Artillery at Fort Pickens. Floyd Clarkson is Major in a cavalry regiment at York, Pa. Rutgers is somewhere else, etc., etc. Charles Wainwright is Captain of a battery in General Cooper's Division on the Lower Potomac.

Little May has been fairly launched in school life, and Mary says she doesn't know which has raised her in her own importance most—going to school or going to the dentist's, to have ever so many fillings put into her little back grinders.
... We have had intelligence of Aunt Adela Newton, who tried to go through the lines to protect her property in Charleston. Somebody told Amelia Bailey that they had seen a lady from Richmond, who had lately seen Mrs. Newton and daughters in that city. They had passed our lines at some point not stated, had

travelled by private conveyance and reached Richmond after every hardship and difficulty, wandering at one time three days in the woods —lost. I want Mother to write a few lines to Aunt A. to go by Fort Monroe and flag of truce. It would get South in course of time if it was short and not treasonable. . . . Dr. Buck came in last night and re-vaccinated Hatty and me. He says if Georgy wants to be vaccinated he can send on a little quill with pure virus (Union virus, as Joe says) from here. There is much small-pox and considerable alarm about it here as well as in Washington.

Mother to G. and E.
8 BREVOORT PLACE, TUESDAY EVE.

My Dear Girls: The question of my going on to Washington has been agitated for some time past, yet I do not seem to come to any decision about it; not but that I would dearly love to look upon your faces again, and enjoy ever so much being with you, and seeing for myself all your goings and doings. Independent of all this, however, I confess I have no desire to visit Washington, and unless I could make myself useful there, and in every way a comfort to you, I think I am more in my place at home. Your uncle Edward was here this morning, and threw cold water on the movement, said it would be *madness* to run any such risk, as Washington was full of small-pox and typhoid fever. Now I write this evening to ask you what *you* think of our going on at present; whether there is really so much sickness as to cause any alarm. Do you want us? will it be a comfort to you to have a little visit from me? I do not ask these questions because I have any fears myself, but I am not willing, after your uncle's remarks this morning, to run any risk in Charley's or Hatty's going. I feel now that it will all rest upon what you say about it. . . . The report here this morning said twenty-five hundred cases of small-pox in Washington! This evening it has come down to eighty. . . . My eyes failing last night, I left my scrawl to finish to you this morning. We have had our breakfast, cold turkey (not boned), hot biscuits, and fish-balls, and the girls are gathered round the front parlor fire with the newspapers, reading items, and discussing the times; Charley is directing Elizabeth about his cushions for the chair he has carved and made, and I am scribbling this in the dining-room, feeling an occasional pang when I look up and see a horrid stranger, John by name, in the pantry, instead of the old faithful servant, William. You don't know how much I miss him in a thousand little things. This fellow is a perfect snail, never gets through with anything, and of course half is not done at all;—an Irish drone and tobacco chewer.

Poor William's occasional spree was really preferable. . . . I have nothing to say to begin another sheet with, but to send you my love and a Mother's blessing. Give Joe his share in both.
Yours lovingly.

Small pox was more or less prevalent about Washington at this time, and one of the sad cases, entirely characteristic of war, was that of G. R., a private in the 19th Indiana, cared for earlier by G. and E. in the Patent Office Hospital. He went safely through camp fever, measles and rheumatism, to die at last of small-pox in a lonely camp hospital in the outskirts of Washington, among strangers.

C. C. W. to G. and E.

BOSTON, January 13th.

Dear Girls: I dare say you will expect a letter from me while I am in Boston. . . . I find it exactly as I left it three years ago, only warmer. It used to be the coldest place imaginable, but the heated term seems to be on, so there is no skating and no talk of it. The Sanitary Commission occupies all the ladies, and in the spare time they work for the contrabands. Mrs. Huntington Wolcott is entirely devoted to it. She keeps thirty poor women in sewing and runs I don't know how many machines. Mattie

Parsons, too, has come out in an entirely new character and fairly slaves for the cause, besides taking care of two families of volunteers in Mr. Stackpole's regiment, left destitute. They say she recruited a fourth of his company and knows every man in it. They are all devoted to the "Captain's lady," and swear to bring him safely home to her. . . . I went out to Cambridge on Saturday to review the scenes of my youth—three years ago—at the Prof. Agassiz' School. Alas! the former familiar faces that were wont to flatten their noses against the law school windows no longer beam upon my path; they are married and gone, and I am sorry to say the best are in the rebel army. The undergraduates look very small and the college grounds don't seem as classic as of yore.

E. to J. H.

WASHINGTON, '62.

We have made an engagement with Rev. Mr. Kennard, a young Baptist clergyman here, to visit the jail with him, where the poor contrabands are imprisoned on suspicion of being runaway slaves, or for debt. We have the Marshal's permit, secured through a friend. . . . We made our visit; it is a wretched place, but the contrabands are better off than the convicts, though many of the poor creatures are almost naked. There are twenty men and boys and a

_{Washington Jail.}

few women, all runaway slaves. We gave them socks, shirts, drawers, etc. and shall go again. The women were very glad to get the sewing we had arranged for them.

Mrs. Gibbons.
Mrs. Thomas Gibbons, mentioned in the following letters, was one of the distinguished Hopper family of "Friends"—strong abolitionists and managers of what was called the "underground railroad." Through their efforts many wretched hunted colored people were landed safely in Canada. Mrs. Gibbons was busy in the war from the beginning, and all her life long, with serene determination, waged her own war against evil wherever she encountered it.

From A. H. W.
J. C. called here yesterday bringing Mrs. Thomas Gibbons to see us. She told me much that was interesting, and disgusting too, about her experience at Fall's Church; the brutality of the regimental surgeon, etc. She and her daughter go on again the 24th of this month, and unless they hear something to the contrary will go to the same regiment, the 23d New York Volunteers. She had thought of writing to Georgy; wished I would do so, and see if she could learn from any of the assistant-surgeons, at

the office, from the Commission, or from the army officers, where she would be most needed. They want to go where people are least liable to help, and where there is most to do. We are to have some towels, little books, etc., ready for her. . . . Mrs. Gibbons said that Horace Greeley was greatly distressed at the course of the Tribune; he was sick at *her house* three weeks with brain fever, this autumn, the result of disappointment, etc., etc., in the paper.

E. W. H. to J. H. in Camp.
January, '62.

To-day we are going out to look up some nurses for Will Winthrop's regiment, and then to the Senate. I forgot to tell you a pretty story we heard the other day from Mrs. Gibbons, our Quaker lady friend. She is a very sweet, kind old lady, and she and her daughter have been out at Fall's Church getting the hospital there into working order, and showing them how to nurse and cook for the sick, and, thanks to them, one poor fellow who was dying was nursed back into the right road and is now nearly well enough to go home with his father, who, meantime, had been sent for. He, a plain well-to-do farmer from Western New York, was so overcome with gratitude to Mrs. G. and her daughter, that he entreated the young girl to go home with him and be his daughter! "He would do all in the world for her and she should be an equal sharer with his son in the farm of 300 acres," and it was said (Mrs. Gibbons told us) in the most delicate, genuine way, without any allusion to the young Lieutenant and probably without the least idea of "making a match." Of course the young girl declined, and then he went to the mother to ask if she hadn't other daughters like herself for whom he could do something to show his gratitude. Isn't it like some old ballad? . . .

The management of the jail was before the Senate yesterday and we heard the discussion, and left just before the bill was passed, requiring the release of all persons not committed for crime, which means, principally, the contrabands. Mr. Grimes, the chairman of the Committee on District affairs, abused Marshal Lamon roundly for his bad management and his insolent exclusion of congressmen from one of the institutions which it is their duty to supervise. G. sent Senator Dixon a note asking if, while the subject is before Congress, something can't be done about separating children committed for petty crimes, from hardened criminals. . . . There ought to be a reformatory school attached to every jail.

E. to J. H.

January 28.

My only letter by the mail last night was from Major Crane, about some of the patients of his Division who came down the Potomac in a wretched condition on a canal boat some time ago. He is going to do his best to find out who is responsible and prefer charges, and he wants us to help. Don't mention this, as we shall do it as quietly as possible, but also as thoroughly. . . . We hear every now and then of some new abuse among the surgeons, regular and volunteer,—for instance: Mr. Hopkins told us of one poor fellow of a Vermont regiment who was brought to the hospital in Alexandria with typhoid fever, having *both feet frozen* and one of them eaten by rats! It is too horrible to think of, but I tell you that you may understand why we feel so strongly on the subject. Good old Dixie hearing of the story went at once to McClellan and told him, and he sent an officer to find out all the facts and bring the responsible person to justice. . . .

The Miss Schuylers went down with us to Alexandria to-day and we showed them through the Hospitals, much to the delight of the nurses.

We have gone into the pension business too! and are going over to Mr. Wrage's camp to arrange about getting the necessary papers for a poor woman who is applying for a pension and wrote to G. about it. We knew her and her husband here in one of the hospitals and she has the most implicit faith in G's power and influence.

Mother goes to Washington.

The end of January Mother and Hatty went on to Washington under Charley's escort for "two or three weeks," which lengthened out into three months with G. and E., and proved a great delight to all.

E. writes Jan. 29, '62:

Mother, Hatty and Charley arrived last night in the middle of the storm and mud. Mother is now writing at the table with me, while H. is gazing admiringly at a group of Irish Brigadiers at the door. Charley is out somewhere, and is to meet the rest of us in the Senate Chamber at noon. We are cosily settled and having a very nice time. The roads are almost impassable owing to melting snow and frost and incessant rain. J.'s last ride back to camp the other day was very hard. He and the General floundered about in mud "like unfathomable chewed molasses candy," and stumbled against the stumps till darkness overtook them before they reached camp. Reports are brought in of private carriages abandoned along the road, and one—Mrs. Judge Little's—was fairly dragged in two by a government team which tried to haul it out of a hole. J. says we must not think of coming out to camp.

E. W. H. to J. H.

Jan. 30th.

The only thing of interest I have to tell you is of a very nice call we had last evening from General Williams (your friend Seth). He got Miss Wilkes to bring him round and introduce him, and told us he had long wanted to call on us and offer his services. He hoped we would call on him for anything he could do for us, and said if I would send my letters to you up to Army Headquarters he would send them out at once by the orderly who comes in every day. So I will begin to-day by sending this one. They say that General Williams is as good as gold, and as modest as he is good. Miss Wilkes, who came with him, asked us all to spend Friday evening with them to meet a small party of Washington people and a few strangers. "Mrs. McClellan would be there and they hoped to see the General too," and I suppose the Franklins and Porters, and our friend General Williams and other "officers of note." Don't you want to come in? We shall go, as it will be a nice chance for Mother and Hatty to see the notabilities and will be pleasant for all. . . . How dismal it is again and how wretched the camp must be!

[margin: General Seth Williams.]

Our pleasant acquaintance with General Williams—the Adjutant-General of the Army of the Potomac throughout the war—lasted all his life. A year later than this first call Charley was assigned to duty on his staff as his personal aide, at Headquarters of the Army. General Williams held a position of immense responsibility through all the fearful years of the war, and died insane, at its close.

E's Journal.

February 1.

We all went to the Wilkes's Friday evening—a very pleasant little party. General McClellan could not come, but there were five other generals, FitzJohn Porter, Stoneman, Barry and Butterfield; also Commodore Shubrick, Commodore Wilkes, Judge Loring and family, the Prussian minister and family, and a good many lesser lights. General Seth Williams was the most modest man in the room, in plain skimpy citizen's clothes.

Feb. 4th. Mother and all of us went down to Alexandria to visit the hospitals,—Charley provided with camp bed, blankets, etc. to go out and make Joe a visit. Joe met us in Alexandria with the General, and a spare horse for Charley. . . . Saturday afternoon Joe came in from camp riding "Lady Jane," but, poor creature, she took cold again on the boat, was dangerously ill all Sunday and died early Monday morning, kneeling on her fore-knees "as though saying her prayers," George Carr said. He and J. and the doctor were with her all Sunday, but could not save her. Joe had brought her from her comfortable stable at home to carry him through the war.

One of the alleviations of the situation at the Ebbitt House just at this time was the coming in now and then of the family cousin William Winthrop, from his camp near Washington, or an occasional jolly, not to say audacious, note from him.

William Winthrop to G.
   HEADQUARTERS BERDAN'S U. S. SHARPSHOOTERS,
        February.

Dear Mrs. Brigadier: For why should we not say so, when we know it will be so? Why this timidity of expression in time of war? . . . What is age, time, aeons, space, blood, prejudice, quite-another-arrangement-made-by-your-mother, or any other triviality? . . .

I LOVE wedding cake. . . .

P. S. THE NIGHT CAPS. Doctor Snelling had just come up from the hospital tent, after making his evening rounds, anxious and disturbed because of the want of *just such!* On account of the gale, the fires couldn't be well kept up; but the patients could keep warm in bed *as to bodies. Heads*, however, were unprotected; and the Doctor had instructed the nurses to capitate the men with their stockings, in want of night caps. Just then I entered the tent with your caps. All was gladness. You quieted minds, warmed heads, perhaps saved lives! I say there is a singular patness, appositeness in your composition. . . . Even the woman to whom my affections are irrevocably pledged might learn a thing or two from you. What more can I say?

This from a tent and with coldest fingers. I don't repine. Yesterday half the tents were blown down, but the cherub left mine standing. . . . Having immediate use for blankets for sick men, I send down *Burr* of my Company for the three or four which you said last evening I could have. Our surgeon says that the colored women nurses will be welcome. You say *you* will "send them out." If you can't, please inform bearer to that effect. When they come let them report to Dr. Marshall, Surgeon of the 1st Regiment Sharpshooters. Trusting you are blithe, I am, etc.

P. S. I address the envelope to you by your maiden name

E. to J. H.
                                February 13.

I have nothing more than the usual "all right" to tell you, but you must always have that. We ought to congratulate each other on the good news from Roanoke Island and Tennessee, which quite thrilled us all yesterday. We were out at Will Winthrop's camp when the boys cried the "Star" and the victory, and we heard the particulars first from Mrs. Captain Rodgers, who came here directly from Mrs. General McClellan's. Mrs. McClellan described to her, her husband's delight when the news came. He flung his arms over his head, and, fairly radiant with glee, pronounced himself the happiest man in Washington, "and the General, you know," his wife says, "is such a quiet man usually. I have seldom seen him more excited." . . .

We managed to get out to Will Winthrop's camp yesterday without an upset, but (so Mother thought) at the peril of our lives! What will she say to the Virginia roads on the way to *your* camp? She is overwhelmed with pity for the poor men and officers. When we left, Will tramped some distance through the mud to show us a better way out, and we were immensely entertained at his manifesting his tongue in his cheek (behind Mother's back) when he found the road worse than he thought, remarking, "Why! this is quite a godsend. I had no idea of finding such a good highway."

... This morning George Carr has been out on horseback to take Will some cake and candy from Mother, to make up for a well meant but bad cake we took him when we went ourselves.

... We hear New York is overflowing with cheers and jubilees for the victories, and in Philadelphia the celebration was the best of all, for they took steps at once to raise a fund for the orphans of the soldiers killed in that battle and to found a "Soldiers' Home" for all maimed and helpless volunteers when the war is over.

E. W. H. to J. H.

February 18th.

C. C. W. goes to Roanoke Island.

We have just packed and despatched Charley for Baltimore and Fortress Monroe, and are now writing notes of introduction for Mr. Vincent Colyer, who is to join him at the Fortress, and if possible take him with him to Roanoke and Port Royal. I have given him a note to Mr. Withers, and G. will write one to Dr. Bacon, and I only wish we had some jolly little things to slip into the envelopes too. Mr. Colyer is to take down a quantity of stores for the hospitals. Charley also has a large trunk full. We hear from private sources that the sick of the Burnside expedition have suffered terribly for actual necessities—water to wash with, and food to eat, and this six weeks after the expedition had started! . . .

Charley was at the War Department yesterday just after the news came of Grant's success at Fort Donelson and Mr. McClure described McClellan as coming in "pale with excitement" to rejoice over the victory a moment with Stanton before going to work again. . . .

Feb. 21. We went yesterday to the Navy Yard and were very much interested in all we saw. They make 15,000 Enfield rifle and musket balls in every twelve hours, or 30,000 while (as now) they work day and night! They also turn out 800 rifled and other cannon balls a day, and three rifled brass cannons a week, besides the ordinary work of a ship-yard and naval station. Our usual luck attended us, for we fell in, by mere chance, with a young naval officer whom Hatty had met in Rome, and he took us about and, best of all, showed us all the *rebel flags* which are to be presented to Congress, so we had an opportunity, which probably no other outsiders have had, of trampling them privately under foot. The flags of Fort Donelson and Fort Henry were there—fresh and new and without the trace of a bullet hole—those taken from Roanoke and Hatteras, and the famous *palmetto* one which was replaced by the Stars and Stripes at Hilton Head. There was also a pretty little company flag made of choice silk and embroidered by ladies' hands.

. . . Later. . . . News from Charley. "Inside of Hatteras inlet, just going up to Roanoke Island." The voyage had been rough and wretched but he was well and happy. . . .

We had no letters of interest yesterday except one from Carry, which Mother enclosed to Charley at Roanoke Island. She gave a very funny account of a wretched swollen face she has had. The Doctor recommended a leech, so they sent for one, but were completely at a loss to tell its head from its tail, and finally with many pokes from a hairpin (a new use) they wriggled it into the tube and trusted to Providence to turn it right end up! During the process, however, she was foolish enough to faint dead away, and no sooner had she revived than Miss Parsons did the same. And Carry wanted to go as army nurse!

E's Journal.
WEDNESDAY, February 26.

Encouraged by several windy days, which were likely to dry the roads, we ventured out to J's camp for the first time since early in January, to show it to Mother and Hatty. The roads were unexpectedly good, the only really bad places being near the camp. J. had dined, but gave us a nice and hearty after-lunch, and

Mother enjoyed the experience very much. While we were there the general order arrived placing the army in readiness to march at very short notice. Four wagons are allowed to each regiment, and quartermasters are to see that they are not heavily loaded: the men to carry knapsacks and blankets and the little shelter-tents large enough for three or four men to creep under. The order cast a gloom over our little visit, but the effect on the troops was very different. As we sat in J's tent we could hear the cheers ringing through the camps as the order was read—three times three and a tiger.

Just before this J. H. had mailed a little box of trailing arbutus "from camp" to J. S. W. and this acknowledgment came back.

Arbutus from Camp, near Alexandria.
Sent by Capt. J. H., 1862.

"Thank God for Spring!" I said;
While no one watches, through the gloomy hours
She walks the weary earth with noiseless tread
    And fills the graves with flowers.

    And, holding in my hand
My Soldier's message, in its leaves I read
Through winter-sorrows of a weeping land
    A dawn of Spring indeed!

> Dull, sodden leaves o'er-strown,
> Then, tears of rain, and then, these flowers for me.
> The wild war horses tread the blossoms down
>   And set the sweetness free.
>
> So get me flowers again
> Dear Soldier;—not alone of Hope and Spring,
> Flowers of full Summer, through the crimson rain
> And battle thunder of the stormy plain,
>   Close on their blossoming!
>
> Red roses, flushed and bold,
> Red victor-roses,—sea-blue bells wide blown
> That ring for joy the river-edges down,
> And white Peace-lilies with the spike of gold
>   That clasp the perfect crown.

J. S. W.

A. H. W. to G. and E.

March.

Dear Girls: May is busy concocting things for a fair she and Bertha hold to-day, for the benefit of our "BRAVE VOLUNTEERS." Papa and mamma and aunties are to buy the things, and May is to spend the money in little books, the first day she is well enough to come over. Robert asked me to say that he sent a box of books to Eliza's address, Ebbitt House, for some hospital library. They were chiefly English reviews, which were too good reading to give to any of the recruiting camps here, and he thought in a general hospital there would always be *somebody* who could appreciate them. I was glad to get Charley's second letter and wish he could hear from us. . . .

Perhaps these winds will dry the roads and enable you to go comfortably at least to Joe's camp. It is too bad to have Mother leave Washington just as March winds prepare the way for McClellan's advance. I am ready, mind you, Georgy, to wait for McClellan just as long as he desires. Only I think unless he *threatens* the enemy in some way, and thus keeps them cooped up, he may wake up some morning and find them all flown southward and he left, stuck in the mud. I don't see why he couldn't have done on the Potomac last December what Halleck has just done on the Tennessee.

. . . I shall take great interest in the working of the educational and industrial movements among the blacks at Port Royal. A large party of teachers, with supplies of various kinds, seeds and sewing machines, etc., went out in the Atlantic. Some of the lady teachers are known to us through friends, and though the whole arrangement has been matured very rapidly, it seems to be under judicious oversight. Jane has a venture in it. She went into the office to collect information and to offer help, and was levied on for eight neat bed-spreads, which she purchased at Paton's. We can imagine the lady teachers reposing on their camp cots, in those distant islands, under Jane's quilts. . . .

I wish I could feel that the end of the war will see, (as Prof. Hitchcock said on Sunday), in all this wide country "not a master, not a slave, only all Christ's Freemen." . . .

Jane and I get along famously, as independent as two old maids. We are not even troubled with evening callers, but sit each in our arm-chair with a foot-stool, a cup o' tea and a newspaper, and shall be very much "put out of the way" if Mother comes home from Washington. We write begging her not to think of it again. Her duty and pleasure are both to be with you, and I don't want her to have a moment's uneasiness about the thought of separation, even if she stays months.

J. S. W. to G.
March 10, '62.

Theodore Bronson has just called to say that he saw Mr. Woolsey (Charley) in Baltimore last night all well. He saw his name in the papers as bearer of despatches and wondered whether he really had any, or if it was a sort of passport. I am glad if he has been able to do any service, but I should not like him to go into the army.

E. to J. H.
March 12, '62.

Charley has come back safe and sound via Baltimore from Roanoke, with rebel bowie knives, "shin-plasters," etc. He is ready to keep with us or go South when we go. He brought up parcels and letters from General Burnside for friends in New York, and took them on personally at once.

Mother, or "Moremamma" as all the grandchildren called her, and Hatty, were still with G. and E. in Washington, having a most interesting inner view of the city's daily war life. Mother kept up with the advance of the war in all parts of the country, and her little journal of events, as she wrote it from day to day, is kept among the family papers as a precious possession.

CHAPTER VI.

E's Journal.

Saturday, March 8th.

J. H. becomes Colonel of the 16th N. Y.

The item this morning is that Colonel Davies was confirmed yesterday by the Senate as Brigadier General, so J. is now Colonel of the 16th by unanimous choice of the officers, and will take command at once.* He writes by the orderly that he has been with General Slocum to see the regiment pitch their new tents in the valley of Four Mile Run.

March 9. A day of great excitement, for beside the news of the evacuation of Leesburg and the capture of Cockpit Point battery, we have the great naval fight at Fortress Monroe.

---

* *Mr. Robert S. Hone to E. W. H.*

NEW YORK, March, 1862.

Dear Mrs. Howland: Mr. Russell has just been in my office and wishes me to say that he has just left Governor Morgan, who informed him that he had to-day signed Joe's commission as Colonel of the 16th Regiment, and that he was delighted to hear the very high terms in which the Governor spoke of Joe.

With congratulations, I am, etc

The great demon ship, the Merrimac, came down from Norfolk toward Newport News and attacked our ships Congress and Cumberland, destroying both. She split the latter in two and sank her, and burned the Congress to the water's edge. The Minnesota meantime was aground and perfectly useless, as well as several others of our vessels.

This ended the first day's fight—a victory for the rebels and a terrible disaster for us; but early this Sunday morning, when the Merrimac came out again, expecting to finish her little affair by defeating the Minnesota and then running out to sea, she found the new Ericsson iron-plated steamer, the "Monitor," all ready to receive her. From 8 A. M. till noon the two fought hand to hand, their sides touching, and then the Merrimac was towed off towards Norfolk, supposed to be in a sinking condition, while the "Monitor" was unhurt. The submarine cable from Fortress Monroe was laid just in time to bring the news. The cable was finished at 4 P. M. and the news flashed over it at 7.

G's Journal.
March 10.

All strange rumors come on Sunday. Josepha Crosby, Hatty and I went down to spend the afternoon at the Patent Office Hospital. During the week the camps had been emptied of convalescents, sent north to recover, and their places in the hospitals were occupied by others. The Patent Office is full again; four rows of beds and very sick men in them. I stooped down between two 8th New York Cavalry men in their little cots while they told me that their regiment had moved off silently on Saturday night. Coming away, I hurried up to Mrs. Captain Rodgers' house and heard the story of the Merrimac fight. The first intimation they had of it was in church on Sunday morning, when, during service, a messenger came in and was seen to whisper something to General Meigs, who immediately left the church. A little while later General Totten was summoned, and then a Commodore somebody, by which time the congregation was in a state of suppressed excitement miserable to bear. Dr. Pine preached an unusually long sermon, and finally the people rushed out and heard the bad news.

Manassas evacuated by the rebels.

While I was talking at the door with Mrs. Rodgers a four-horse ambulance was standing at McClellan's door, and we sat down on the steps intending to see who got into it, and which way it went, a determination shared by plenty of other people on their way from church. At last a servant brought blankets, and McClellan and Franklin got in and started on their way over the Potomac; and then I came home, and presently

Colonel McClure came in and told us that Heintzelmann, with whom he had been sitting an hour, expects to move in the morning and that Manassas was reported evacuated. Contrabands brought word of it to Kearney's quarters; he made an armed reconnaissance and discovered the truth; word was sent to McClellan, and his ride on Sunday P. M. was in consequence. Mrs. Rodgers came in as we were in our petticoats, getting ready for bed, and confirmed it all.

E's Journal.

We went to bed in a state of great excitement and were awakened early Monday morning by a knock from George and a note from Joe saying it was all true. He wrote at 2 A. M., having been up all night. They had just received their marching orders—the brigade to leave at 5 A. M., the rest of the corps at 9. I sent George over at once with a note to J., and he found him on horseback just starting, the regiments formed and ready, and the General and staff in their saddles, all off for Fairfax Court House, which they reached, J. writes me, at 5 P. M., all in good spirits, having borne the march well. The rebs have abandoned both Centreville and Manassas, falling back, the "Star" says, as far as the Rapidan and Gordonsville—whether by panic or by a preconcerted plan, is unknown.

J. writes the climate at Fairfax C. H. is lovely and the air dry, pure and very sweet, but the country is utterly desolate, houses burnt or pulled to pieces, fences gone, and the inhabitants, except a few miserable negroes, fled.

G's Journal.

March 11.

The Peninsular campaign begun. So the great move was made, the thing we had been looking forward to for so many months. The entire army was in motion, troops on the other side the river advancing, troops on this side taking their place. All day Monday and far into the night regiments marched over the bridges into Virginia,—50,000 over the Long bridge, they say, and to-day we drove up to the Chain bridge, and they told us 15,000 crossed there yesterday. We walked down towards the Long bridge to-day; crowds of people were collected on 14th street to see the move. As we crossed the canal, mother, Charley and I, swinging along with the rest, three large army wagons brought up the rear, marked T. E., carrying the telegraphic apparatus for the Engineers, and the wires must have been laid last night, for this morning General Williams had the announcement from McClellan (who slept at Fairfax Court House), that our troops are in possession at Manassas.

G's Journal.

March 12.

The most extraordinary movements are taking place. While I write the 85th Pennsylvania is scattered about at rest on 14th street, having just marched back from the other side of the river. The 14th New York Cavalry, dismounted and serving as infantry, marched up before them; wagons filled with baggage, blankets, canteens, etc., have followed them. It is reported now that all the regiments are ordered *back again*, and Edward Walker tells us that the roads on the other side of the river are all lined with them returning.

March 13. While we were cooking some arrowroot in our parlor for a Vermont private, sick in this hotel, Joe came in, back from Fairfax for a ride. The officers had been all over the old battlefield at Bull Run, McDowell crying, and all of them serious enough. The rebel works at Centreville, Joe says, are splendid, as formidable as any of ours about Washington. Their winter quarters were capital log houses, enough to accommodate 100,000 men. The burial ground was near at hand, and not far away a field of hundreds of dead horses. The works at Manassas were very slight, mounted in the most conspicuous places with logs of wood painted black. The rebels had been evacuating for some time, but, at the last, left in a sort of panic, leaving dead bodies lying beside coffins, and quantities of food, clothing and baggage of all kinds, some of it fired.

E's Journal.

March 14.

One of General Franklin's aids has been in to say that his Division is now marching into Alexandria and is to *embark* on Saturday or Sunday, down the Potomac. . . . We went down to Alexandria and took lodgings at Mrs. Dyson's, on Water street, over Sunday, and two more wretched or longer days I never passed. Through a drenching storm McDowell's corps was marched back from Centreville, 35 miles, and arrived at dusk, cold, hungry, wet to the skin, to find no transports ready and no provision made for their shelter or comfort. The city was filled with the wretched men, many crowded into the market stalls and empty churches, others finding shelter in lofts or under sheds and porches, and some, we know, sleeping in the open streets. In the market they had large fires, but with soaking knapsacks, no dry clothing to put on. In one place, the loft of a foundry, where Chaplain Hopkins found shelter for one company, the steam which rushed out as he opened the door was as that of a laundry on washing day. The poor fellows suffered from hunger as well as cold and fatigue, for on Sunday all the stores were closed. Whiskey could be had, which Moritz and G. and H. distributed among tired and wet volunteers on cellar doors. Some of them actually begged for bread or offered to sell their rings and trinkets for food. It was a wretched and heart-sickening day and shook our confidence in McClellan or McDowell, or whoever the responsible person may be. We sent Moritz up to Washington for a half barrel of socks Aunt E. had just sent on and took them to the churches where the soldiers were quartered, and distributed them among the eager and grateful men. The men were lying on the benches and floors, and in the baptistry of the "Beulah Particular Baptist" and the Presbyterian secesh churches, and we stumbled about, holding the end of a candle for light, distributing socks. All ours were soon gone, and Chaplain Hopkins went back to the hospital, and telling the steward to *protest*, so that *he* might be shielded from blame, deliberately took ten dozen pairs from the store-closet and distributed them. The two long useless marches with nothing accomplished, no shelter and no food, have shaken the unbounded faith in McClellan. Congress has been debating a bill displacing him; the Star says it was withdrawn to-day. *Our* soldier, Joe, and the 16th, were not in that wretched plight but were kept in bivouac out of the town. Joe took final command of the regiment that Sunday morning.

E's Journal.

March 21.

A damp, drizzly day, but I wanted to see Joe in camp once more, and we went down to Alexandria, where Mother and Hatty distributed a lot of sweet flowers to the poor fingerless, one-armed and broken-legged fellows in the hospital, while I went on.

Joe has only had command of the regiment these few days and I found him extremely busy reorganizing and getting it into condition for the advance. Each man has been thoroughly inspected and all deficiencies in clothing, etc., are being filled. He keeps the officers busy, has an informal class of instruction for some of them, and has been issuing orders for arrangements on the transports, precautions against fire, etc. I only stayed a very little while. On our return boat from Alexandria we had a chance to see *eleven* of the transports start down the river crowded with troops, the men cheering and tossing their hats. It was a fine and striking sight as the boats, densely packed with volunteers, moved out from the docks, the sun lighting up the sails and colors of the schooners and steamboats, the signal flags nodding and bobbing, and the bands playing lively tunes, while the crowds on shore cheered in response.

We met the Berdan sharpshooters marching down to embark, and shook hands with Will

Winthrop and Capt. Hastings. As we drove into town, McClellan (looking old and careworn) and Franklin passed us, going out to the army.

G's Journal.
March 20.

We have been getting some stores to-day for Will Winthrop. They are at last delighted by the order to join Heintzelman. Twenty to thirty thousand men have gone in the transports already. Will's black mess-boy came in to us and took out a basket with enough for the voyage. Have been up to see Charles Bradford, son of Captain Woolsey Hopkins' sister, at Columbian Hospital, and have sent him jelly, oysters, etc. Nice young fellow and pleased to see us.

From Mother's Journal.
SATURDAY, March 29.

To camp again. Snow-storm. Stayed at Mrs. Bright's cottage Saturday night and drove up to camp on Sunday. Service in hospital tent, Dr. Miller, of the 16th, and Dr. Adams, of the 5th Maine, officiating. Communion—about thirty soldiers and several officers partaking. Heavy and continual thunder, with everything outside covered with snow—a singular combination of summer and winter, and rendering this interesting occasion still more strange and impressive.

Stopped Sunday night again at the Brights', a clean and comfortable cottage at the head of Cameron Lane. All around us were the tents *d'abri* and other tents, and hundreds of men without any tents at all, bivouacking on the hills and in the fields and swamps everywhere; one cavalry regiment had arrived and their tents were pitched while we were out at the 16th. The camp fires at night were a new feature to me, and strangely did they loom up in the darkness, bringing to view groups of soldiers gathered round them;—hundreds of these fires in all directions.

E. W. H. to Chaplain Hopkins.
WASHINGTON, D. C., April 1st, 1862.

Dear Mr. Hopkins: I send some Independents with the "Rainy day" in them. We mentioned that you liked the verses, and Abby sent these on for you to distribute among your patients.

We spent last Sunday near Alexandria ... glad to be storm-stayed on many accounts, one of which was the opportunity it gave us of going to service in the 16th, the first communion service since Mr. Howland took command. It was pleasant to see the little "church" assemble in a hospital tent in a Virginia field.

Chaplain Hopkins to E.

ALEXANDRIA HOSPITAL, April 5th.

My Dear Mrs. Howland: Yesterday was one of the brightest, pleasantest days I have known for a long time. The wards were more inviting, and the men more cordial than usual. All day I seemed to be in the right place at the right time, and by a glad intuition, to discover the avenues which were unfortified and the doors which were unbarred. I have told you this because I am fully convinced that it was owing wholly to the good start that you gave me by that early morning visit. By some skillful adjustment, which I failed to notice at the time, you left me in tune. . . .

Please thank your sister Abby for the bundle of Independents. They were very welcome and I gave them away, each with the charge: "Be sure and read the Rainy Day in Camp." Did I tell you that I read it after each of my services last Sabbath? and I think that it did more good than all that went before it. The men listened in perfect quiet. I feel sure that, if I could have looked up myself, I should have seen tears in the eyes of more than one who had been "skulking in the rear."

Mary had written a number of verses for the soldiers, and they had been printed as leaflets, each one floated over by the flag in red and blue, and distributed widely among the enlisted men. The first of these was

A Rainy Day in Camp.

It's a cheerless, lonesome evening,
    When the soaking, sodden ground
Will not echo to the footfall
    Of the sentinel's dull round.

God's blue star-spangled banner
    To-night is not unfurled;
Surely *He* has not deserted
    This weary, warring world.

I peer into the darkness,
    And the crowding fancies come:
The night wind, blowing northward,
    Carries all my heart toward home.

For I 'listed in this army
    Not exactly to my mind;
But my country called for helpers,
    And I couldn't stay behind.

So, I've had a sight of drilling,
    And have roughed it many ways,
And death has nearly had me;—
    Yet I think the service pays.

It's a blessed sort of feeling—
    Whether you live or die—
You helped your country in her need,
    And fought right loyally.

But I can't help thinking sometimes,
   When a wet day's leisure comes,
And I hear the old home voices
   Talking louder than the drums,—

And the far, familiar faces
   Peep in at my tent door,
And the little children's footsteps
   Go pit-pat on the floor,—

I can't help thinking, somehow,
   Of all the parson reads
About that other soldier-life
   Which every true man leads.

And wife, soft-hearted creature,
   Seems a-saying in my ear,
"I'd rather have you in *those* ranks
   Than to see you brigadier."

I call myself a brave one,
   But in my heart I lie!
For my country, and her honor,
   I am fiercely free to die;

But when the Lord, who bought me,
   Asks for my service here
To "fight the good fight" faithfully,
   I'm skulking in the rear.

And yet I know this Captain
   All love and care to be:
He would never get impatient
   With a raw recruit like me.

And I know he'd not forget me;
   When the day of peace appears,
I should share with Him the victory
   Of all His volunteers.

And it's kind of cheerful, thinking,
    Beside the dull tent fire,
About that big promotion,
    When He says, "Come up higher."

And though it's dismal—rainy—
    Even now, with thoughts of Him,
Camp life looks extra cheery,
    And death a deal less grim.

For I seem to see Him waiting,
    Where a gathered heaven greets
A great victorious army,
    Marching up the golden streets.

And I hear Him read the roll-call,
    And my heart is all a-flame,
When the dear, recording angel
    Writes down my happy name!

—But my fire is dead white ashes,
    And the tent is chilling cold,
And I'm playing *win the battle*,
    When I've never been enrolled!

E's Journal tells of a quiet day in camp before another advance by the regiment:

HEADQUARTERS OF THE 16TH REGIMENT,
In the field, April 3.

We were on the point of driving out here yesterday when a telegram came from J. saying he was coming in. It was with his camp wagon this time, to carry out various things—new guide colors for the regiment, stationery, etc., and his new Colonel's uniform "with the birds on it," as Moritz says. Suddenly it occurred to me to come out to camp too. So I put up my things hastily and J. drove me out, sending James ahead on "Scott" to order another mess tent put up for me and have the fire made. It was our first drive together since Joe entered the service nearly a year ago. "Fairfax," the pony, jogged along at his ease and we didn't reach here till after dark. Camp-fires along the road and over the hill-sides burned brightly and picturesque groups of men gathered round them, cooking and smoking. The 16th, when we reached it, seemed like a little village of lighted and well-kept streets. James soon got supper for us and when the fire was burning we felt as serene and comfortable as possible. The "Evening Star" and the printing of a lot of postmarks with the new regimental stamp, filled the evening, and then, building up a good fire and getting under the piles of blankets Surgeon Crandall had sent in, I slept soundly and warm till "reveille" just after sunrise. After reveille came roll-call, then the sick-call on the bugle, then breakfast for the men, then guard-mounting at eight, then our breakfast. After this J. went out to drill the battalion and I wrote letters, had a call from General Slocum, and sent General Franklin the flowers I had brought him; by which time the drill was over. The day was delicious, warm, soft, spring-like, and fires were oppressive. The evening parade was an uncommonly nice one. General Slocum, Colonel Bartlett and J. reviewed them and the men looked finely. The white gloves and gaiters Joe has given them greatly increase the neat appearance, and the band is quite another thing. "Coming through the rye" is no longer played as a dirge.

The new colors were all brought out and the effect was very pretty, as they were escorted out and back and saluted by all the officers and men. After parade came a game of base-ball for the captains and other officers, and in the sweet evening air and early moonlight we heard cheerful sounds all about us as the men sang patriotic songs, laughed and chatted, or danced jigs to the sound of a violin. There is a nice little band of stringed instruments in the regiment, and Joe sent for them to come and play for me in the tent, and then it was proposed to adjourn to General Franklin's Headquarters and give him a serenade. This with a call on Col. Bartlett in his patriotic tent, hung with American flags, finished the evening. We went to bed, tired, but as peaceful and unwarlike as could possibly be. . . . At 3 A. M. we were suddenly roused. The brigade was again under marching orders, to leave at ten o'clock for

Manassas once more! This was the meaning of the vague rumors we had heard that our division was not *to sail* after all.

I built up the fire and dressed and after a cup of tea at 5.30 said good-bye. Our peaceful little time was over.

April 7. A note from J. tells of the regiment's safe arrival at Manassas, where they are camped. The General had complimented J. on moving his regiment better than any of the others.

G. and E. had "enlisted for the war," which they did not understand to mean staying comfortably housed in Washington, while the army marched to danger and death. So when the orders came for the advance of the Army of the Potomac, they definitely determined to go too, in some way or other, and not to allow themselves to be kept back even by dear J. H.'s concern for their comfort and safety, feeling sure of his consent when the right moment came. G. writes to him: *[G. and E. plan to follow the Army.]*

Will you, dear Joe, seriously think about our going when and where you go. . . . The distress of having you away and in the greatest danger—hours and hours, probably days—beyond our reach, would be infinitely harder to stand than any amount of cold, hunger, or annoyance, and the knowledge that Eliza was in such a state of mind would make you quite as unhappy as the thought that she might be hungry and cold. . . . We want to be within one hour's ride, at most, of the battlefield, and to be there ready for the battle if it must come. When it is all over what possible use would there be in our coming on? There will always be some roof of a barn at any rate that would give us shelter enough, and where we could stay if there was fighting. It was enough to go through Bull Run here in Washington. Nothing can be more miserable than a second such experience. . . . You only laugh when I talk to you, so I am obliged to write.

E. to J. H.

. . . I feel it to be my right and privilege to follow you, not only for my own satisfaction in being near you, but because we know we can be of great use among the troops in case of sickness and danger. We can follow you in the carriage, keeping within reach of you in case of need, and with George and Moritz we can be sufficiently protected anywhere in the rear of our army. I trust to you, dear, to do all you can to forward our plan, and I am sure you will not leave us in doubt and indecision longer than you can help. . . .

The impression seems to be that a great battle will take place in the neighborhood of Yorktown very soon. In view of this, think of the criminal neglect of the medical department in not having any hospital arrangements made there or at Fortress Monroe which begin to be sufficient! One of the doctors of the Sanitary Commission writes that on his arrival there he found already 500 sick men without beds to lie on. The Commission have fitted up one large hospital on their own account, and have sent for supplies to be forwarded immediately, and we have this morning set a large amount of sewing going—bedticks, etc., to be forwarded to Old Point as soon as possible. There are so many sick and so few to take care of them that Dr. Robert Ware of the Sanitary Commission has had to undress and wash the men himself. And this is *before* a battle.

A. H. W. to G.

NEW YORK, April, '62.

I notice what you say of bed sacks. The Sanitary Commission furnished thousands to the Burnside Division for its hospitals at Roanoke. Charley says not one of these was ever filled or used, there not being a wisp of hay or straw or moss or anything, except what was brought there for forage. The men all lay on the board floors. At Fort Monroe it *might* be easy to send down from Baltimore ready-made mattresses, or the material for filling, but I question whether anyone on the spot would take the trouble of seeing them applied. You could mention the instance of Roanoke to the Sanitary Commission to prove to them that mere *sacks* are not enough. . . .

Yesterday when I came in from Mary's, I found "Robert Anderson, U. S. A."'s card on the table again. John said he bade him say General Anderson called in person to thank Miss Carry Woolsey for the flowers. . . . James Gibson writes from Belfast that "England did not want war with America, and special prayer meetings for peace were held"; but wasn't it Earl Shaftesbury who refused to attend, saying such an act would place him in hostility to his government? If England did not mean war, why did she fly to arms in that indignant and indecent haste! Why did Lord Palmerston suppress the nature of the despatch from Seward, read to him by Mr. Adams, and even allow it to be contradicted in his organ the Post? No; *two things* will always stand on record as showing the hostility of the governing class in England toward America in its life and death struggle;—this hurry to make a *casus belli* of what ought to have been a question for diplomacy to settle; and that first great wrong done us in the outset, when the English ministry, while Adams was on the railway train, the very day he was on his way from Liverpool to London, last May, hastened to declare the North and South equal belligerents. They confound the law-power and the law-breaker; they call the police and the burglar brother-rogues. . . .

It is just as Mr. Scharff's father said at the very beginning of the war, "Well, John, I don't know what part England will take in this matter, but I am very sure of one thing, it will be the *meanest* part, possible." . . .

Eliza's lovely home at Fishkill was all this time shut up and desolate, but the grounds were in the hands of their neighbor, Mr. Henry W. Sargent, who kindly undertook the work Joe had to give up for the war. He planted the place, selecting trees and superintending the work day after day. The little rise in the lawn north of the house he named Mars Hill, and there Mr. Thomson, the farmer-in-charge, set up a flag-pole and kept the colors flying, though the house stood empty.

C. C. W. to E.

April 9th.

Dear Eliza: We have made our little visit to the W's at Fishkill, and the first thing after dinner drove over to your place. . . . Every one says it is very much improved, and the trees that are being set out are very fine ones and add to the general air of elegance. . . . I must tell you how beautiful too your greenhouses looked, lots of flowers and very beautiful ones, and two large boxes have come down this week for Mother, and been arranged in rustic baskets, etc., and make us look very popular to the seven usual evening callers; last night they were admired by Messrs. Beekman, Shepherd, Goddard, Denny, Bronson, Frothingham and Dorus W., and each gentleman tried to look conscious to the others, while I looked so to all. . . . Returning from Fishkill we found Sarah Woolsey here, and she is now sitting on the sofa reading the news. Uncle Edward has just gone, and Jane and Hatty are off at the hospital. Abby is very down in her mind about the Merrimac, and thanks fortune (secretly) there is always something to be melancholy over. . . .

Sarah drove out one morning to see Aunt E., who entertained her with abusing Abby for her political opinions! She said the Tribune was not a paper for Christian people, particularly *females*, to take, and that as long ago as Rutgers Place times Uncle E. had warned us against it. "I read it myself, it is true," she said, "but then the curious eye and ear must be satisfied!" Capital reason for doing what a Christian "female" should not do!

J. S. W. to Mother in Washington.

THURSDAY EVENING.

Dear Mother: Your letter, or rather G.'s, E.'s check, etc., arrived this morning, with the important item inscribed, as usual, on the flap and disfigured in opening. We are very sorry to hear that Hatty doesn't get on faster. Perhaps if, instead of a " good old soul " of a doctor, she had an enlightened young one, she might get sooner rid of her sore throat. I believe much more devoutly in modern than in ancient doctors . . .

Sarah, Abby, Carry, Miss Parsons, Charley and Robert have all gone to the " Reception " of the Cumberland's men to-night. It was time to show some interest in them. The Chamber of Commerce has got this up. I hope it will be a success. You remember the officer calling to the half-drowning men, " Shall we give her another broadside, boys?" and the "Aye, aye, sir," and the final volley, as the water rushed in at the portholes. We have had two visits lately from Prof. Hitchcock on the subject of a ladies' committee of visiting ; auxiliary to the gentlemen's committee of the New England Soldiers Relief Association. He asked us to collect some names of ladies willing to serve (visiting only), and we have enrolled six or eight : Mrs. Gurden Buck, Mrs. H. B. Smith,

Miss Annie Potts, Margaret Post, etc., etc. I fancy there will be little to do really, as there is a resident superintendent and wife, and, I believe, nurses, in the house corner of John st. and Broadway. You will see the details of the arrangement in the papers. . . .

All the flags are out again for the Western victories and the Western heroes. Col. Bissell, the officer who *made a river* 12 miles long to flank the rebel position, is Mrs. Dr. Parker's brother, a man of extraordinary energy and perseverance. . . .

Mrs. Bacon told Sarah that Frank had 700 sick men under his care and made a point of seeing every man every day, so never wrote, leaving that business to Theodore. We sent, him and Mr. Withers each, another bundle of papers by the last mail.

Sarah Woolsey to G.

NEW HAVEN, April.

J. S. W. at work in New York.

I spent one delightful day in New York with Jane at the New England rooms, where everything is nicely prepared for 300 men. The superintendent has time during intervals to rush down stairs and compose puffs on Jane, which he publishes in the newspapers next morning! The day we went down, we had the luck to fall upon the first wounded soldier of the season, and, though he was not very sick, Jane went to work in the most approved way, and you should have seen her with her bonnet off, her camel's-hair shawl swung gracefully from her shoulders and a great-pocketed white apron on, making tea over a spirit-lamp and enjoying it all so thoroughly. The Newbern hero was fed with sardines and oysters and all sorts of good things, and face and hands washed by Jane's little paws so nicely. . . . Don't say anything when you write home, for Jane is rather huffy when we talk too much about it, since her appearance in the public prints. Did you see the letter from a soldier in the hospital, describing Jane, and using the celebrated sentence which, as she says, leaves no doubt as to the identity: "I dare not mention her name, but she is beautiful."

William Winthrop to G.

BERDAN'S SHARPSHOOTERS,
CAMP BEFORE YORKTOWN, April 11, 1862.

Dear Cousin: Your welcome and full letter brought joy and facts. . . . As for us, we are sitting down before Yorktown, as yet untaken. The enemy retreated before us, first from Great Bethel, then from the extensive entrenchments at Smithville, two miles beyond. Yorktown is their stronghold; the works are understood to extend pretty much all the way across the Peninsula to the James. They have some forty guns on the works now facing us.

On the 5th, we saw something like war. As the head of Porter's Column—*we* are that head—emerged from the wood and rose upon the open land which forms a gradual natural glacis to the batteries, we were saluted with shell after shell, and all day the shell and round shot and rifle bullets cracked and boomed and whizzed about us. *We*, as usual, skimmed the *crême de la crême*, being posted as skirmishers, as well under cover as we could get, about three-fourths of a mile in advance of the main army, and one-half mile in advance of our own artillery. We lost two and had four wounded during the day, and it is most unaccountable that our loss was not twenty times as great; for the horrid, detestable music of shot and shell and ball was almost continually tingling our ears. One of the killed was in my own company—Phelps. I had him buried next day—a sweet Sunday—and laid the green turf neatly over the mound. . . . By the way, I think of you and Eliza as I see the little hospital flags hung out from all the more respectable farmhouses. . . . General Porter said in a note of commendation on our regiment, read on parade, that the enemy "by their own admissions had begun to fear *us* and provide against us as far as possible." This praise has rather turned the head of our Colonel. *Moi*, I have been too cold, too weary, too wet, too unslept, too unwashed, to feel conceited or proud. Further, our teams have not yet come up with the officer's baggage, so I am without mutations of raiment, or have to depend on strangers for the same ; also am only one-half blanketed. But these are minor ills, for which, no doubt, our lovers are pitying us more than we deserve as they sit in their boudoirs far away.

The brandy and things which you sent me, just before going off, were very valuable. I had a few swallows of the liquor left in my flask a few nights since on picket, and it proved worth more than so much liquid gold. A soldier of the 2nd Maine, on picket with my men, was struck by a ball which broke his leg. He crawled through the rain and cold of that miserable night, half a mile, on his hands and knees, to the reserve picket, and was just fainting when I came in with your brandy, treasured up for just such a moment.

The weather is now fair and warm and delicious. I walked through the woods this A. M. before reveille, to the sandy beach of York River, and saw the sun come up out of the sea ; and watched our gunboats, which are ready to co-operate when the right moment comes. I hope we shall not be cheated out of a good battle.

Since the sailing of the great expedition from Annapolis, F. B. had been on active duty with the troops on the coast of South

Carolina and Georgia, and at the reduction of the two forts at Port Royal, and of Fort Pulaski, April 11th. At the siege of the latter he was on duty with the battery nearest the fort, and was requested by General Gilmore to keep an account of the shots fired from our batteries and from the rebel guns within the fort. Here he stood in a scarlet-lined cloak with Gilmore's long, shining, double-barrelled field-glass in his hand for two days,—a fine mark for the enemy. After the fight he went about the fort with the rebel officer who surrendered it, and who said, as they came to a big gun, "I commanded here, and sent a large number of shots at a man who stood at the corner of that cistern, and wore a cloak, and had some long shining thing in his hand. I wonder if I hit him!"

General Franklin's wife to E.

April 12.

My dear Mrs. Howland: Last night (late) I was informed as a *great secret* that General Franklin's Division *was* to go to General McClellan after all! I was wondering when I awoke this morning if I might not go and tell *you.* . . . General Meigs was one of the authorities given for the truth of the report—so I think we may believe the good news. . . .

I have a favor to ask, which is, if you decide to go down to Alexandria to try and see your husband on his way through, will you let me know? as I would like very much to go too.

I feel as if it would be a great comfort to see them before they start South.

Love to your mother and sisters. It is truly a mercy from above to have the Division relieved from the *false position* they were placed in, and now we have only to pray for their safety.

Yours aff'ly,
ANNA L. FRANKLIN.

G's Journal.

ALEXANDRIA, April 15, '62.

Saturday morning we had private information that Franklin's Division was shipping down the river, and we packed our bags at once and with Mrs. Franklin came down to the Dysons' Cottage, Alexandria. . . . Dyson's two slaves, Harriet and her mother, have run away, for which I sing songs of thanksgiving. . . . The 16th and all the others have arrived and are camping under Fort Elsworth, their old ground.

At the street corner coming down here, we found ten men struggling with one of their comrades of the 5th Maine, who had just fallen in a fit; about a hundred had collected to shut off the air and double him up, with his knapsack still strapped on his back. We asked the crowd to do what they ought to do for him, till we were tired ; and then we pushed them aside and went in ourselves, had a strong sergeant keep the crowd off, put the man on his back with his clothes loose, bathed his head and poured brandy down his throat. E. went to a near hospital, but they would not take him in. So we put him in his blanket for stretcher, and started him off with bearers to the Mansion House, while the crowd dispersed, one woman saying, "Poor fellow, he is fighting in a good cause, and ought to have a dose of ipecac."

Mother to G. and E. in Alexandria.

EBBITT HOUSE,
MONDAY EVENING, April 15 or 16, 62.

Dear Girls: We have just had a call and salute from Joe's manservant James, who wished to know if we had any "word for Mrs. Howland in the morning." What with your three devoted "Mercuries" we seem to keep up a pretty constant intercourse, which is very cheering. . . . I was at my lonely tea this evening when suddenly I heard a sepulchral voice at my shoulder saying, "How is Miss Woolsey, Madam, this evening?" It was "me" young Augustus on his way out from the table behind me, where I had not noticed him. "You seem to be quite alone. I will be happy to take my breakfast with you, if you will permit me!" I was horror-stricken at the idea of having either of your chairs occupied by anyone to whom I should feel called upon to do the agreeable. . . .

I shall be *very late* unavoidably to-morrow, so that he will eat and go before I get down. This seems to be a favorite little attention with our gentlemen friends here—"taking breakfast with you!" . . . Only think of my missing another call from Mrs. McClellan and her mother. I had ventured out on a stroll by myself, to get my cap, which I didn't get, and to bring Hatty a tumbler of ice cream, which I *did* get, and she enjoyed it very much with some fresh lady-fingers. This woman is not to be relied on, the cap was not done, and I shouldn't wonder if she is taking the pattern instead of clear-starching it. I continued on to the avenue, bought Hatty a pair of gloves, looked in at one or two stores for something extremely pretty and cheap for a spring dress, but was not successful in finding it. The sun was very hot, and I was glad to get back again. . . . How in the world are you all accommodated in that small house? . . . So, after all, you mean to go, if you can, to Fortress Monroe. I am sorry for one thing—you will be so much more inaccessible to your family, almost beyond our reach, as *only* those belonging to the army will be permitted to go there. Nevertheless, I will make all the enquiries you name, and although *my* heart will break, will speed you on your way. Plague take this war! Hatty is better, but misses her other two nurses, and I do not believe has any confidence in my cooking; she acknowledges, however, grudgingly, that the beef-tea "tasted good," and the arrowroot was excellent, though I saw her afterwards pouring in a double quantity of port wine, I having already seasoned it with sherry.

AFTER TEA.

I have seen Mr. —— by particular desire in the parlor,—waylaid him, tied him down and pelted him with questions—as to the facilities, etc., of reaching Fortress Monroe at this present time. He gave no encouragement whatever as to your getting there; said he was quite sure that no passengers were allowed to that point and none on the Baltimore boat. . . . You had better not set your hearts upon such a plan. Would you not be quite as near, and hear as readily, in New York? We should be so glad to have you there with us. But I do not urge anything; all I can say is take care of yourselves, as you are very precious to your

MOTHER.

We were pulling every possible wire to get permission to go to Fortress Monroe, and Mother was aiding us. General Franklin lent a hand too, but all failed.

General Franklin to Brigadier General Thomas.
HEADQUARTERS 1ST DIVISION, 1ST CORPS,
ARMY OF THE POTOMAC.

My dear General: Mrs. Howland, the wife of Colonel Howland, of the New York 16th Regiment, desires to be presented to you in order that she may get permission to join her husband, who is in my Division. I beg that if you can do anything to assist her in obtaining her very natural wish, you will do it, and I will consider it as a favor done to me.

Mrs. Howland is by no means an idler when she is with the soldiers, but has really done more than any other lady of my acquaintance in adding to the comfort of the sick as well as those in health. I therefore believe that it will be for the interests of the service that she should have the permission for which she asks.

Very respectfully yours,
W. B. FRANKLIN,
Brig.-Gen. Com. Div.
Brig. Gen. L. Thomas,
Adjutant General U. S. Army,
Washington, D. C.

General Thomas, however, failed us: his general orders prohibited all passes.

C. W. W. to G. M. W.

NEW YORK, April, 62.

Dear Georgy: Your letter to me came this morning about the facilities for (or rather the hindrances to) getting from Baltimore to Fortress Monroe. . . . Cousin William A. tells me all authority on General Dix's part to grant passes to anyone has been suspended. . . . he has refused all—the Vice-President's son among others. . . . If *he* cannot give us passes *no one can* unless we can be smuggled through on one of the transports from Alexandria down the Potomac. . . . Fortress Monroe is crowded to overflowing, though I know you would be satisfied with a square inch per man if you could only get there (minus hoops). . . . If I get letters that *will* take us by the transport to-morrow morning, I will telegraph you and come on immediately.

Cousin Margaret Hodge to G.

PHILADELPHIA, April, 62.

H. L. H. goes to the front.

My dear Georgy: I feel a great interest in dear Eliza and yourself, and also in your dear mother, and all the family, knowing how anxious you must all be about Joe. I do wish you could get to Fortress Monroe, or, as you say, to the Hygiea Hotel. . . . We had a letter this morning from Lenox, dated from on board the steamer Welden, which Dr. Smith has chartered to fit up as a hospital ship for the Pennsylvania wounded. You know we have 50,000 at Yorktown, at least so say the papers.

Lenox seems much pleased that they have the steamer, as it makes them so independent, and enables them to go where they may be most needed, without troubling any one. Dr. Smith's plan is to have a building on shore for a hospital, and the steamer can convey the wounded to it. Some of the doctors are to attend to their removal from the field, while some are to take charge of them on the steamer, and the remainder to receive them at the hospital. . . . Lenox was just going off to Cheesman's landing. He is very much interested in all he sees ; has visited the Monitor and been all over it, and also he had been over the fortress and visited several camps.

It is a great trial to part with him, but he has wanted so long to do what he could for the cause that it is a great gratification that he can go now without interfering with his duty to his father. The lectures are over, and he can spare him better than he could before, though even now Lenox is a great loss to his father. . . .

My love to your dear mother and Hatty, and say I am still looking for their promised visit, and shall count on their coming here on their way home. We have Lottie and baby here now, for a little visit, but I have plenty of room for all.

From H. L. Hodge.

FORTRESS MONROE, April 19th, 1862.

Dear Georgy: We were summoned to Yorktown, and about twenty of us left Philadelphia yesterday morning. We passed on the Bay this morning many transports bearing, as I suppose, Franklin's Division. I presume that Joe and myself were not far apart. He goes, however, if report be true, to the opposite side of York River. They brought down here some wounded yesterday; they are under the care of Surgeon Cuyler and are comfortably located.

We have come only in anticipation that we may be needed, and may therefore remain a short time or for a long while, according to circumstances. . . .

<small>J. H. leaves for the Peninsula.</small>

On April 17th the 16th had finally started from Alexandria on the steamer Daniel Webster. No. 2, with Franklin's Division, to join McClellan on the Peninsula.

J. H. to E. W. H.

STEAMER DANIEL WEBSTER, April 18.

I have a chance to send a boat ashore to get a mail and so can say good morning to you. All the steamers are lying in the stream two or three miles below Alexandria receiving their "tows." There are about a hundred schooners and barges to take down. We tow four. All's well. The boat is very crowded, but the men are more comfortable than I supposed they would be and are behaving admirably. The work of getting them well on board was a hard one. I have 820 officers and men on this boat and the four schooners. The sick are doing well; the change of air and rest are curing the dysentery. I do not know where we are going.

NEAR FORTRESS MONROE, SUNDAY, April 20.

No orders. The boat is becoming very dirty and cannot be cleaned as she is so crowded that there is no place to put any number of the men while cleaning is being done. The decks are swept and *shoveled* once or twice a day, but need washing. The regiment is behaving well. I have had to punish only one man since we left Alexandria, but have made an example of him for smuggling and selling liquor.

We had a nice little service a short time ago and the chaplain is repeating it in different parts of the boat, as it is not safe to assemble the men in any one part where even a couple of hundred could hear. The men were very attentive. The more I see of the regiment the more highly I think of it. I am sure the old 16th will always behave creditably.

YORK RIVER, April 22.

Here we still lie awaiting orders, without a word of news and nothing to do. The boat is so crowded and dirty that life is becoming intensely disgusting, yet there does not appear any prospect of getting away. Last night there was heavy firing towards Yorktown and we could see the flashing of the guns; but we do not know what it was.

April 24. Yesterday, at last, I landed the regiment, having asked permission to do so and have the boat thoroughly cleaned. Having picked out a piece of level ground at the head of a little bay where there are lots of oysters, I got a stern-wheeler and sent the regiment ashore by companies, and got all fairly into camp before sunset. I put the major in command on shore, keeping my headquarters on the steamer, and had the work of purification begun as soon as the hold was cleared.

I saw Franklin yesterday, and he asked after you and ours. I took the steamer's quarter-boat last evening and serenaded the old chap with our stringed band. He seemed pleased and the music sounded very sweetly on the quiet water.

I suspect Commander Rodgers is the right sort of man for the Galena. I heard a story of him to-day. Some one said to him, "Your iron plates are too thin; their thickness should be at least four inches." His reply (somewhat profane) was, "What to h—— do I care about their thickness,—my business is to go up York River and shell the enemy."

J. S. W. to G.
NEW YORK, April 25, '62.

... I always have a little talk with Col. Betts coming out of church, he keeps out such a sharp eye. He predicted all that business of the sub-division of McClellan's command and the Rappahannock department exactly as it fell out. He predicts now—(he laughs and says of course he only guesses)—*no* desperate fighting at Yorktown. He thinks there will be some bombarding but *no* storming of the works; that the great battle at Corinth, now imminent, will occur before a battle at Yorktown, and will probably greatly demoralize the rebel cause. . . . Cousin William Aspinwall has just sent us in an interesting letter from Lieutenant Greene, giving his experience on the Monitor in the voyage and fight. He is only 18, and was in command for a little while after Worden was blinded. I have been down several days this week to the New England Association, and have succeeded in doing nothing with considerable *éclat*. We have had only eight or ten transient lodgers, have had some droll incidents, have made a few beds and a few cups of tea, got great glory in the newspapers, and that is all. Don't think I am going into a minute account, for I have no idea of it. Indeed there is none to go into. The ladies' committee does not work altogether smoothly, and I think there will be some further attempt at organization with a responsible head. W—— B—— looks in occasionally and does nothing. M—— P—— tries to come the heavy patronizing over me with entire want of success. . . . The house is admirable, and the patients (if there are any) will be splendidly taken care of. If you know any New England men coming home invalided, and who want to rest over a night or two (most of them will not do it), send them to us.

A. H. W. to Mother.

NEW YORK, April 26th.

My Dear Mother: We are all bright and well this fine morning. Jane and Charley have gone to the Philharmonic rehearsal and Carry is practicing some of her old music on the piano, in a way to make you, who love to hear it, happy. Mr. Prentiss came in last night to see us, looking well, but queer, as he always does in a black stock. He had been hard at work moving his books, and did not intend to go to prayer meeting, and evidently didn't suppose *we* had gone, or he wouldn't have come to spend the evening with us. He told us much that was pleasant and funny about his visit in Washington, which, short as it was, paid him well, he thought, for going. . . . He hopes E. and G. will get their wishes and go to Fort Monroe, as they are in a state of mind to be fretted and troubled if they don't. . . .

Very few of the wounded brought by the Cossack from Newbern were landed here. . . . All were crazy to get home, all full of spirits and fun. The five or six who were carried to the N. E. Relief only fretted at having to spend a night longer on the road. The man with both legs gone smoked his pipe and read his newspaper. His chief anxiety was to go into New Jersey by a certain train. . . . Five or six ladies were at the rooms, Jane among them, yesterday, a lady apiece and several men to each volunteer. . . . No wonder it dazed an Irishman just released from four months imprisonment in Richmond. "Begor," he said, "I can't pay for all this!" . . . Jane says there is nothing much for the present set of ladies to do, except to rearrange the piles of shirts, etc., on the closet shelves—changing them about from the way she had fixed them! They immediately proceeded to that work, and each new set of ladies will have *that*, at least, to occupy them. As for the Park Barracks, a portion of them have been scrubbed and whitewashed, the bunks taken down, neat iron beds all made and put up. Mrs. Mack is to live there as Matron, and, for the purpose of a mere halting place and infirmary, it is as good an one as they could have, though too many ladies were on hand, switching things over with their hoops, giving unlimited oranges to men with the dysentery, and making the surgeons mad. There were, beside, half the medical students in the city, all staring and eager for jobs;—no difficulty in the men's having all, and more than all, the attention they want. One good thing Mrs. Woodruff did, at Mrs. Buck's suggestion,—sent over to the Astor House for a steward, and through him ordered a good dinner brought in of tender beef, fresh eggs, etc., for the twenty or thirty New York and New Jersey men who were resting there. It will be charged to New York State, which supports the Barracks. . . . We have Lloyd's map of Virginia hung under the front parlor picture of the Virgin, along the back of the sofa, and we sit there and read the papers and study it.

E. to J. H.

WASHINGTON, April 26.

Mr. Knapp, of the Sanitary Commission, has just been over and offers to take a note for me when he goes to Yorktown to morrow. We like him so much, and shall be in communication with him all summer if we succeed in going down, *and we are very likely to go!* Mr. Knapp said the Commission had been speaking of us and hoping we might be able to go, and that, if they found women would be allowed, they themselves would be very glad to have us under their charge, and would manage to get us there. We mustn't call it "our luck." It is something far better, and I for one shall be truly grateful to God—and the Commission. Mr. Knapp asks as a special favor that we will keep him informed of our movements.

A smiling providence opened the door wide for us at last.

CHAPTER VII.

E. W. H. to J. H.

MONDAY MORNING, April 28.

<small>The floating Hospital service. G. and E. nurses at large.</small>

Where do you think I am? On the "Daniel Webster No. 1," which the Sanitary Commission has taken as a hospital ship. We are now on the way down to Cheeseman's Creek, near Ship Point, and when you receive this we shall be lying just there. Saturday afternoon the gentlemen of the Commission, Mr. Olmsted and Mr. Knapp, came over to see us, and to our great surprise and pleasure proposed to us to come down with them in the ship as "nurses at large," or matrons, or what not—to do of course all we can for the sick and wounded men in the approaching battle. They had telegraphed to Mrs. William P. Griffin and Mrs. Lane of New York to come on at once, and go too. We only had one night's notice, as they were to leave early Sunday morning, but we accepted the offer at once, and here we are! We four are the only women on board except a colored chambermaid, but there are 30 or 40 men nurses and hospital dressers, and several members of the Commission—Mr. Olmsted, Mr. Knapp, Mr.

Lewis Rutherford, Mr. Strong, Dr. Agnew, Dr. Grymes, etc. They have two boats, this and the Elm City. The latter is to be a receiving ship and permanent floating hospital, and this one the transporting one, in which the wounded will be carried at once by sea to New York, Philadelphia, or Baltimore and Washington, as the case may be. It is an old ocean steamship, and used to run on the Aspinwall route ; is stanch and seaworthy, but now wretchedly dirty. A dozen stout contrabands are at work night and day scrubbing and cleaning, and, as they finish, the whitewashers and carpenters succeed them, and by degrees it will be put in good condition. . . . I saw Mrs. Franklin the night before we started and have a note for the General. We left our little dog Mopsey with her. . . . If you are still off Ship Point we shall be very near each other. . . . There is a P. O. station at *Cheeseman's Creek* to which please direct your letters to me, care of Fred. Law Olmsted, Hospital Ship of Sanitary Commission.

G. to Mother.

FLOATING HOSPITAL, DANIEL WEBSTER.
CHEESEMAN'S CREEK, April 30, '61.

The sail down the Potomac to Acquia Creek, where we anchored for the night, was extremely pretty. Just as we started the little gunboat " Yankee " passed up, bringing, all on a string, five rebel craft she had just taken in the Rappahannock.

Late in the afternoon we passed the stone fleet, eight boats all ready to sink in the channel, in case the Merrimac should try to run up the Potomac. The rebels having taken up all the buoys, we had to come to anchor at dark. Sunday, the first day, was gone. As for us, we had spent it sitting on deck, sewing upon a Hospital flag fifteen by eight, and singing hymns to take the edge off this secular occupation. It is to be run up at once in case we encounter the Merrimac. Just as we anchored, a chaplain was discovered among the fifty or sixty soldiers on board—men returning to their regiments, and in half an hour we got together for service and an unprepared discourse exhorting the Sanitary Commission to works of charity! The contrabands all came in and stood in a row, so black, at the dark end of the cabin, that I could see nothing but eyes and teeth; but they sang heartily and everybody followed them.

H. R. W. to G.

EBBITT HOUSE, April 27.

<small>Mother and Hatty wind up affairs in Washington.</small> Everybody was delighted with what you left in Washington for the hospitals. Some of the jellies and wine (I found a whole box of it left without orders), and some shoes, I took over to Georgetown to Mrs. Russell, who was just out

of all. Mother is going about the room indignant still at the Bank, and "expects to have every policeman in the city tapping her on the shoulder to know the facts of the case." We try not to miss you, but yesterday was *very* like Sunday, much more quiet and Sabbath-like than when you were here; to-day we have had the bank excitement to keep us busy.

The "bank excitement" is the little incident recounted in the Evening Star as follows:

A Cool Operation.—This morning, Mrs. C. W. Woolsey went to the Bank of the Metropolis to draw the money for two checks of a hundred dollars each. Unacquainted, apparently, with business of the sort, she stepped into the bank, and instead of applying at the counter, presented them to a person who was standing at a desk outside, and returned to her coach. This person presented the checks to the paying teller, who refused to pay because they lacked Mrs. Woolsey's endorsement. He took a pen and went out to the coach and returned with the checks properly endorsed. They were paid, and the fellow made off with the money, leaving the lady minus.

The man had just the right business manner, not too polite—stepped out without his hat as if he had left his desk to oblige a lady. He was thanked for his courtesy, and left "right sudden" with the funds.

It was hardly fair in us to run Mother on this winding up of her triumphant career in Washington, which city, as she indignantly said, she "left, under the full recognition of several of the Metropolitan police?"

A. H. W. to G. and E.
NEW YORK, April 28.

My dear Sisters: Mother's letter of Sunday morning, giving the startling intelligence of your having gone off suddenly to Fort Monroe, came before breakfast. Since it was your very earnest wish, and, as Mr. Prentiss tells us, you might have chafed at being held back—why I am glad you have gone. But it seems to me a very trying position for you: you will work yourselves sick. Joe will be the *most* surprised person, and I don't believe he will approve of your being on a hospital boat. It is very satisfactory that Mrs. Griffin is on board; as long as she stays you will not need either man or woman protector. . . . Georgy's letter to Charley came with Mother's. He will see to the wire camp-beds, and we will put the other stores, your hats, etc., etc., all in a trunk and have them ready for the first opportunity. If you write for Charley he will take them on at once. . . . It is strange that Mr. Olmsted should have had you in mind, without having known of your desire to go. It shows that, as Georgy says, "Heaven had opened the door." . . . Our best love to you two dear brave girls; you are doing what you love to do, and I hope will take care of yourselves as well as of the soldiers.

A. H. W. to J. H.
April 30.

. . . We had a very pleasant visit the other night from Charles Johnson, of Norwich, just returned from Port Royal. He went down as Allotment Commissioner from Connecticut and had pretty good success. He was particularly indignant about the chaplain of the Connecticut —th who had made a "handsome thing" all along out of the men whose money he received for being forwarded to their homes. He charged them a commission, and then by buying drafts on New York, which are at a premium in Bridgeport, Conn., managed to make his one per cent. net. Charles J. arrived out the day of the bombardment of Fort Pulaski and was among the first visitors after its surrender. It was curious, he said, to see the extra defenses prepared by the rebels; heavy timber blindages against the casemates and quarters, all round the fort inside, sodded six feet deep with earth dug from trenches with which the whole parade was crisscrossed. These ditches were already two feet deep with the green, slimy water which had oozed upward through the soil. . . . He said that the 7th Connecticut, now garrisoning the fort, were a pale, peaked, sick-looking set, but every man of them as proud as Lucifer, and he came home with a higher idea than ever of the energy and spirit of our troops. One night he and Colonel Terry and Dr. Bacon couldn't sleep on account of the mosquitoes and heat, and they agreed to bring out the letters left behind by the rebel prisoners, which had to be examined and sent some day to Savannah by flag of truce. There were more than a hundred; some very laughable specimens of course, but some well written and sensible. About thirty were written in one hand, by some officer for his different privates I suppose, and every one of them began, "We have met the enemy and we are theirs!" always winding up with the earnest advice to their friends, to quit Savannah. . . . Mr. Prentiss has lately spent a week in Washington, in company with Dr. Stearns and Professor Schaff. Everywhere they went, of every great man, Professor Schaff asked his stock question—whether the social and political conquest of the South was not to be more difficult than its military conquest. He received very characteristic answers. President Lincoln thought "perhaps, yes—but it wouldn't cost so much money!" Mr. Seward said, decidedly, "No!" and then trotted himself out, most obligingly, in a dainty little sort of oration, using one of his fine figures in illustration. "You are like President King," he said, "who was greatly concerned here, last week, about the dome of the Capitol, how it was ever to be finished, and whether it would bear the weight of the figure of Liberty that is to be placed on it, and how the figure was to be got up there, etc. I don't *know* how it is to be done, but the engineers know. The plans were all made to accomplish just that result. The dome was built for the figure, and this figure cast to be in harmony and size with it, and the pulleys and ropes are all agreed upon; and though it is a long way from the ground, where the statue lies now, to the top of the finished dome, I *know* that the work will be done, and *the figure of Liberty shall yet stand on the top of the Capitol.*" . . . Mr. Chase was not so eloquent or philosophic. He thought we ought to "do our present duty and leave the future to Providence," which perhaps was the best answer of all; and putting the three together Professor Schaff was well satisfied with the argument and quite willing to be laughed at by his friends for his pertinacity in asking the question.

From E's Journal.
S. S. DANIEL WEBSTER.

Just before sunset, last night, we passed the mouth of the York River, and could see our gunboats and a fleet of some four hundred sloops and schooners lying a little way up it—among them *our* fleet, Franklin's Division, still lying off Ship Point. We made our way in among them and dropped anchor just off the Point within a stone's throw of the rebel barracks, now used as a hospital for our men. After dark we could see the lights of the fleet all around us like the lamps of a great city on the shores of a harbor, and these, with the camp-fires on shore lighting up the horizon, and the little row-boats darting about, dashing up phosphorescence at every stroke of the oar, made the scene a magical one; while the bugle calls and regimental bands on the different boats increased the effect. Joe's boat, the Daniel Webster No. 2, lies further away from us up towards Cheeseman's Creek. . . .

G's Journal.

Next morning Mr. Olmsted hailed the steamer which carried the 16th New York, to "let the Colonel know that his wife was on board among the nurses." He received an acknowledgment from the Colonel in the form of a check for one thousand dollars for the Sanitary Commission, and what was still better, Mr. O. said, a note of hearty appreciation of the Commission's work for the soldiers. Joe soon came over to the steamer himself, and Lenox Hodge, who was with a Philadelphia detail of surgeons on the steamer Commodore, also came on board.

G. to Mother.
May 1, '61.

We are in sight of the abandoned rebel quarters at Ship Point, now used as a hospital, on low, filthy ground surrounded by earth-works, rained on half the time and fiercely shone on the other half, a death place for scores of our men, who are piled in there covered with vermin, dying with their uniforms on and collars up, dying of fever. Of course there is that vitally important thing, medical etiquette, to contend with here as elsewhere, and so it is:—" Suppose you go ashore and ask whether it would be agreeable to have the ladies come over, just to walk through the hospital and talk to the men?" So the ladies have gone to talk with the men with spirit lamps and farina and lemons and brandy and clean clothes, and expect to have an improving conversation!

While we are lying here off Ship Point, New Orleans has surrendered quietly, and round the corner from us Fort Macon has been taken. What is it to us so long as the beef tea is ready at the right moment? We have been getting the beds made on our side of the cabin; only 25 are ready, but in two of them a lieutenant and private of the 16th are lying, brought over from the shore yesterday—Eliza's game. She has taken them vigorously in hand, stealing clean clothes from the Wilson Small and treating them to nice breakfasts and teas. Dr. Haight, of New York, has just put his head in to know if Miss Woolsey has any rice ready. "No. She has used it all up on the man in the bunk-ward, with the dysentery." Ask the cook—cook won't boil it; so Miss W. lights her spirit lamp and boils it, and boils it. She has her reward—two men, each with his little plate of it—Was it good?—"Yes, beautiful."

E's Journal about this time.

Before we were up this morning, Joe came over to the Webster to ask us to go down to Fortress Monroe for the day with him, General Slocum and Colonel Bartlett of the 27th New York. Finding I was not likely to be wanted, I accepted gladly, Georgy preferring to go over to Ship Point again. The sail down was only about two and a half hours, and we came upon the fleet almost before we knew it. A great deal of shipping was lying off Old Point Comfort, and in the midst lay the "Minnesota," and the "Vanderbilt," with her great steel prow, prepared to meet and run down the Merrimac; and just off the Rip Raps we saw the "Galena," the "Naugatuck," and the "Monitor." We landed at once and began our sight-seeing with a great space covered by some three hundred enormous cannon lying side by side like giant mummies in Egypt. Then we went directly to the Fortress itself unchallenged, and meeting Captain, now Colonel, Whipple, A. A. G., were taken to his nice little house and office just put up within the pretty enclosure of the fort, and then to General Wool's headquarters. The old General was alone and very polite, said he remembered Uncles Gardiner and Sam Howland, and took me for a daughter and therefore Joe's sister. He read us the despatches he was just sending to Washington announcing the fall of Fort Macon and the retreat of Beauregard from Corinth to Memphis. He insisted on taking us through his pretty garden and gave me a lovely bunch of lilacs and tulips, jonquils, wall-flower, etc., which the old gentleman picked himself (mostly without stems) and presented with very gallant little speeches.

Captain Whipple took us over the moat and on the ramparts, and to the wonderful water battery where the great guns stand ready to belch forth at any moment on the Merrimac or any other enemy. The monsters "Union" and "Lincoln" stand by themselves and point towards Sewall's Point. Even the lighthouse is on its guard and has its faces towards the enemy darkened with canvas.

Got back to the ship all right and found nothing had occurred.

A. H. W. to G. and E.

NEW YORK, May 1st, 1862.

My Dear Girls: Never were two creatures pounced on and whirled out of sight more completely than you. Fate seems to descend and wrap you from the vision and the reach of your family, and every event only carries you farther off. Do write us when you can and help us to realize what and where you are! . . . We hear from Mrs. Buck or somebody that the Daniel Webster is expected here the last of this week, on her first trip with wounded and sick, but I should hardly think it could load so soon. Is it to come through the canals, as the "Richard Welling" is coming with the Vermont wounded? Perhaps we shall see you too! That will be famous if you come on in her to New York. . . . We have got sponges, lots of towels, doylies, castile soap, etc., etc. together, and are all ready to put them up and send them to you at any moment. If you find you don't need them on board, keep them for the use of the 16th. We *must* do something for that, as *our* regiment. . . . There are three times as many ladies as are needed at the hospital, 194 Broadway, and Jane's work finished, she will not go again. . . . Mrs. Buck, Jane and Miss Caroline Murray are to have Thursday each week as their day at the Park Barracks. Young Dr. Schauffler *lives* there, and the notice is posted all over the city, so that disabled soldiers returning (singly sometimes) may see it and know that there is rest for them and surgical treatment, all freely provided, and Mrs. Stetson of the Astor House, who is one of the committee, engages to have beef tea, broth, gruel, etc., always ready in case they are called for, and to have *any* delicacy quickly prepared.

H. L. H. writes:
Ship Point, May 3, '62.

Dear Georgy: The 8th Illinois Cavalry arrived several days ago. They are disembarking to-day. Cannot the Daniel Webster take the sick off from Ship Point? They will be doing a great service if they can.

G's Journal.
May 4.

Mr. Olmsted decided to do it, and the " D. W." sailed with 190 sick from the deserted camps within a range of some miles—eighteen, the poor fellows say who were jolted down to the shore over corduroy roads. The loads began arriving at 5.30 this morning, and we refitted the state-rooms which had been made up twice already, all along of the men nurses turning in and rioting in boots in the nice clean beds. No objection to the "relief-watch" lying down gently on the outside of the beds, but why should they pull out the under-quilts and pin them up for state-room doors? E. and I discovered all sorts of candle ends tucked away or stuck in cakes of soap, with every facility for setting the ship on fire—also the work of the men nurses.

Mrs. Griffin and Mrs. Lane were, meantime, in the pantry getting breakfast for the sick.

G. to Mother.

OFF SHIP POINT.

<small>Yorktown abandoned by the rebels.</small>

It was the Wilson Small (a little steamboat chartered by the Commission to run up the creeks and bring down sick and wounded), that came alongside with our first patients, thirty-five in number, typhoid cases, from Ship Point, who were slung through the hatches on their stretchers. . . . We women arranged our days into three watches, and then a promiscuous one for any of us, as the night work might demand.

After breakfast, Sunday, on the Webster, we all assembled in the forward ward, and Dr. Grymes read the simple prayers for those at sea and the sick. Our poor fellows lay all about us in their beds and listened quietly. As the prayer for the dying was finished, a soldier close by the doctor had ended his strife.

We crawled up into our bunks that night amid a tremendous firing of big guns, and woke up in the morning to the announcement that Yorktown was evacuated! Franklin was in McClellan's tent when the news came, and he says McClellan did not know what to make of it.

A little tug has just passed, calling out to each transport to be ready to move in ten minutes if the order is given; probably to go round to Yorktown, and be ready to push up the river in case our men advance. A tug from Baltimore came alongside just now with contrabands and workmen for the "Ocean Queen," which the Commission has secured, and E. and I will probably go over to her this evening.

A. H. W. to G. and E.

NEW YORK, May 2nd.

My Dear Girls: We have received this morning your letter of Monday and Tuesday (Georgy's) written at intervals and mailed off Ship Point. What a strange life you are leading on board a hospital ship, sewing hospital flags, dispensing medicines, etc., etc. You two have always been together in the queerest and most varied circumstances, and in all parts of the world, from the heart of the Mammoth Cave to the top of the Pyramids of Egypt, in peace; and now, in war. You did not inclose the ward-list, but "Dr. Woolsey," we feel confident, is a joke on Georgy. She deserves a title of the sort, I am sure. You thought of everything it seems, even to a flat-iron. . . . We seem to be sitting at home impotent and imbecile. It costs us no trouble to order home a few pieces of mosquito bar from Holmes', or a few dozen towels from Milliken's—and even these are sitting under the piano waiting. We have screwed the bandage-roller on again, and the little table stands with strips of cotton and pins and labels just as it stood one year ago, when Georgy fired away with it day after day,—between the folding doors of the parlors.

Mother came home yesterday from Philadelphia, leaving Hatty at the Hodge's. Aspinwall, wife and baby are there. We think Mother looks well. She brought a few of Joe's photographs. What a keen, alert, decided look he has, as becomes a Colonel and a man who has done a year's military duty! Soon after Mother, came Mary, Robert and May to dine and spend the night. This happened very nicely, as it was Mother's first evening at home after Washington. . . .

What great events are happening! Awhile ago, two such things as the fall of New Orleans and of Fort Macon in one week would have crazed us with surprise and delight. We are almost *blasés* in such matters. . . . It is a good joke and commentary on the southern doctrine of "State rights" that the Governor of North Carolina has been arrested in Richmond, Virginia, for "Unionism"!

From H. L. H. (sent on board the hospital ship to G.)
CHEESEMAN'S LANDING, FRIDAY.

Dear Georgy: I hope to see you and Eliza to-day. . . . We received all the wounded from the assault on the lunette alluded to, except one too badly hurt to move (who has since died, they tell me) and a few so slightly injured as to be retained for future service. The "boys" here say that Thomas Archer, your servant's brother, did not belong to their Company H, but to Company A, and that he was among those left behind on account of his injuries being slight.

So far our patients, with hardly an exception, have been a superior class of men, and it has been a great pleasure to attend to them.

Dr. Tripler was here yesterday, and I was glad to hear of the probable removal of not only the 200 sick at Ship Point, but of 400 scattered elsewhere, to Boston, New York or Philadelphia.

Mother to G. and E.
NEW YORK, SUNDAY P. M.

My Dear Girls: I have an unexpected opportunity of writing, or rather of getting my letter to you. Dr. Gurden Buck was telegraphed this morning, through the Sanitary Commission, to leave for Yorktown on board the "Ocean Queen," and he is off for Baltimore at 5 o'clock this P. M., to take ship there. In the meantime just as we came in from church, a telegram arrived from you, dear E., to Charley, asking if he would like the "Clerkship" of the "Daniel Webster," and if so to come on. . . . Charley accepts the clerkship, and will be ready when the "Daniel Webster" comes here. Right upon the top of this excitement of a telegram from Yorktown to us! comes another to Mrs. McClellan at the 5th Avenue Hotel, telling her that Yorktown has been evacuated by the rebels, leaving all their large guns, and much else besides! The newsboys are out already with their extras, and the Aspinwalls are at the door wishing to know why we don't unfurl our flag! which is all rolled up round the stick. Cousin William has been in to tell us of the news direct from Mrs. McClellan, and the whole city is at once commencing its rejoicings. How eagerly we shall look for your account, and how anxious to know what your movements will be. Why are they telegraphing for so many surgeons from here, and Philadelphia, and other towns, when there has been no battle, as we understand? I suppose the army is to push on after the retreating rebels. . . . I wish I were down there with you, and have a great mind to offer my services to Dr. Buck as head nurse or matron of the "Daniel Webster." . . . Jane has gone off with her Sunday treat to the hospital, of jelly and oranges; Abby and Carry have gone to church again, and Charley is out making enquiry about the boats and trying to find out whether the "Daniel Webster" is expected here, and *when*.

Your things are all ready to go by him, and we have offered Dr. Buck any stores he may wish. We have piles of elegantly rolled bandages which he may be glad to have.

J. S. W. to J. H.
    8 BREVOORT PLACE, 3d May, Chi Alpha night.

So you three have met again, Georgy, Eliza and the Colonel. . . . It must have been a jolly meeting for you all on the floating Hospital, and Eliza says you showed symptoms of illness immediately on seeing the comfortable beds. But it is rather a perilous position for the girls. It is no longer *visiting*, but *living*, in an atmosphere of infection, day and night, typhoid, rubeola, gangrene, and what not. They will be in for anything going, and the service in a crowded transport will make terrible draughts on the sympathies of all concerned. We hear surmises that the Daniel Webster will come round to New York. If so, I sincerely hope the girls will come in her if possible, if it is only for a day. What an excellent thing to have these boats systematically provided, and to have *ladies* on board. It will go far to humanize the horrid vehicles. Heavy reproaches belong *some-*

where for the want of foresight and humanity in the government arrangements of the kind. I have seen it. Send your sick men, if you have any, on a Sanitary Commission transport. Fully *half* the complaints about the Vermonters of Lee's Mills are strictly correct, and half are half too many for toleration. The men are in comparative paradise now in "our" (!) hands, though one or two will die in consequence of careless treatment,—Government doings. Somebody says of the barbarisms of the Chinese Tae-Pings: "if you want to complete the picture, transfer them to America and prefix the adjective Red."

We have been having a Chi Alpha (the Clergymen's Social Club) for Mr. Prentiss, while he was moving. I say "we" although *our* participation was through the key-hole alone. The last of the mild elderly gentlemen has taken his hat and cane, and the family have rushed down and wildly consumed vast quantities of sandwiches, chicken salad, and the loveliest fried oysters! Don't you wish you had some? . . .

One of the entertainments, not edible, was a "James Projectile," weight 58 lbs., brought in the self-sacrificing and gallant hat box of Chas. Johnson, sent by Frank Bacon as a receipt in full, I suppose, for the few little matters we have sent him from time to time,—filled and covered with the red brick dust made by the great breach.*

>"The slave shouts in the barracoon
>As through the breach we thunder!"

But never, Chas. Johnson says, *never* was there such a disgusted set of men as the Connecticut Seventh, when the white flag went up; they had set their hearts on storming the place, and everything was ready. He went through the casemates with F. B. on his rounds among the patients, his own and those left to his care by Colonel Olmsted, and gave us a very interesting picture of the scene, too long and circumstantial to write out in a letter. He was very much pleased with Dr. Bacon, "so exactly the man for the place," he said; so utterly cool, so gentle, and so untiring in care and patience. One young fellow they came to, had lost his leg, and the Doctor was trying to soothe him to sleep without an anodyne—" What part of Connecticut are *you* from?" asked Charles J.; "I'm a Georgian, sir. Yes, sir (kindling up), I fired the last gun from this fort, sir!" "Yes," said the Doctor quietly, in his mesmeric way, "he

F. B. with wounded rebels at Fort Pulaski.

---

* On the newel post at your uncle Frank's house in New Haven stands this projectile, fired from the battery by which he stood during the attack on Fort Pulaski. It went through the wall, and was taken out of the rubbish inside the fort by him and sent North to your grandmother.

stood by his gun till a shot dismounted it and hurt him. But try now to go to sleep, and if you find you cannot, I'll give you something to help you." "O, if I could have one drink of milk, Doctor!" "I'll see; perhaps I can get you a little." So he gave the candle (in a bottle) to Charles, and was gone for a quarter of an hour, coming back with a little milk in the bottom of a cup, which the young Georgian eagerly swallowed. The story is getting too long—and there were two or three others to match—but what I observe is, that a man of less fine fibre, instead of taking up the talk of the poor Georgian, would have "improved the occasion" to him.

Did you notice that to-day, in the transactions of the Board of Brokers, when the "Government Sixes touched par," for the first time since the rebellion, that the brokers were all on their feet in a minute giving three tremendous cheers? . . . Mother seriously announces just here, that two of the tea spoons, used by the clergymen this evening, are missing, and mentions the name of Rev. Dr. ———!

Sunday.—A day of great events. At 1 P. M., Cousin William came in to tell us he had seen a man who had seen a man (literal) who had read McClellan's telegram to his wife, announcing the evacuation of Yorktown. The man, once removed, was Barlow, and Mr. A.

considered it perfectly reliable. At two the extras were out in a swarm, and Colonel Betts and one or two others came in most kindly, bringing papers and congratulations. It is a blessed respite in our anxiety about you, for we were afraid of a severe battle if there had been any battle at all. It is good news for all who have friends in the army. . . . It becomes us at any rate now to thank God and take courage and draw a much longer breath than we've drawn for a month.

Apropos of your Uncle Frank's "improving the occasion" at Fort Pulaski—he *did* improve it in giving the *rebel surgeon* a merited rebuke. "Good-bye, my poor fellows," the surgeon had said, "I don't know what will happen to you *now*. I shall have to leave you to *this* gentleman." "You need not have any apprehensions, sir," F. B. answered; "these are not the first wounded Georgians I have had to care for;" and then he told him of the wounded rebels he had looked after at the battle of Bull Run. The fellow melted at once and said those men and Colonel Gardner came into his hands directly from F. B.'s, and he had heard of the kindness shown them.

E's Journal.

ON THE YORK RIVER, May 5.

Before we were up this morning, though that was very early, the army fleet (including Joe's transport) was off up York river to cut off the retreat of the rebels. Our last load of sick came on board the Webster this morning early, and by nine o'clock she was ready to sail for the North, so G. and I, with Messrs. Knapp and Olmsted, and our two doctors, Wheelock and Haight, were transferred by the Wilson Small to the great "Ocean Queen," lying in the bay. We sailed up to Yorktown, standing on deck in the rain to enjoy the approach to the famous entrenchments. Gloucester Point alone, with its beautiful little sodded fort, looked very formidable, and the works about Yorktown are said to be almost impregnable. The rebels left fifty heavy guns behind them and much baggage, camp equipage, etc.

A. H. W. to G. and E.

NEW YORK, May 7th, 1862.

My dear Girls : I hadn't time to write a long letter, but must send off a note to say that the Daniel Webster came to the dock at dusk yesterday. Charley went down at once, thinking there was a possible chance of your being on board, or at all events, some of the 16th sick. Mrs. Griffin, who came up to care for the men, had gone, and several of the officers had landed, but the men were to remain till morning. . . . I am thankful you were not on board, for your own sakes. *Five men* died and more are dying to-day, and will die in the act of being landed. . . . McClellan's despatches to-day are not very hopeful. " He will do the best he can "— the " rebels out-number him greatly," " are fighting fiercely ; will contest every inch of the way ; strongly intrenched," etc., etc. Yesterday he called it a " brilliant success." . . . Your letter, Georgy, to Charley, of Saturday and Sunday, is received this morning. It furnishes us the missing links in the story, and will instruct Charley whom to apply to about his duties and his passage, etc. We felt that your telegram, with merely your signature, did not authorize him to go aboard and assume duty. . . . Mrs. Griffin sent us your penciled note as soon as she landed, with one from herself, saying she had left you well—" lovely and active," I think were her expressions. She asked if I knew anything about Mrs. Trotter's decision as to going to the front. The latter was here yesterday. She said she should love dearly to go, but she believed she couldn't, her mother couldn't spare her just now.

Later. . . . Charley went down yesterday and saw Mr. Strong, and was inducted as *Purser* of the ship Daniel Webster. Mr. Strong gave him a sum of money, and he has been on

C. W. W. joins the Sanitary Commission.

board to-day paying the medical cadets and the contrabands. Came home just now for a lunch and has gone down again to finish. He thinks he may have to sleep on board. The vessel is not cleaned up or ready yet. . . . They *may* get off to-morrow afternoon. Mrs. Trotter is to send up to-night to see what we have heard. She is going to join the Daniel Webster on its return trip.

E. W. H. to J. H.

May 7th, '62.

<small>The Ocean Queen.</small>

My dear Joe: Down in the depths of the Ocean Queen, with a pail of freshly-made milk punch alongside of me, a jug of brandy at my feet, beef tea on the right flank, and untold stores of other things scattered about, I write a hurried note on my lap, just to tell you that we keep well, but have been so busy the past 48 hours that I have lost all track of time. You had scarcely left us the other day when our first installment of sick came aboard—*150 men*—before anything whatever was ready for them. We had only just taken possession of the ship, as you saw, and not an article had been unpacked or a bed made. With two spoons, and ten pounds of Indian meal (the only food on board) made into gruel, G. and I managed, however, to feed them all and got them to bed. They have come in the same way ever since, crowded upon us unprepared, and with so few to do for them; and we have now nearly 600, and more coming to-night. . . . Until to-day we have had only our small force who were detached from the Webster, and I may say without vanity that G. and I, and the two young doctors, Wheelock and Haight, have done *everything*. We women have attended to the feeding of the 400 or 500, and those two young fellows have had the responsibility of their medical care! Last night, however, a large party of surgeons, dressers and nurses arrived from New York, and though to-day things have been frightfully chaotic, they will settle down soon and each one will have his own work to do. . . . G. and I look after the special diet and the ordering of all the food. Beef tea is made by the ten gallons and punch by the pail. I was so busy yesterday morning that I didn't know when you left, and only saw the last of the fleet far up York river.

G's Journal.

Lenox Hodge happened to have come over from his hospital station on shore to call on us, just as the first patients arrived for the Ocean Queen, and, being the only doctor on hand at the time, was pressed into the service. He superintended the lowering into the forward cabin of all the very sick. He told us to have wine and water ready for the weakest, and I in the front cabin, and E. in the back, went round with brandy and water and gave it to every man who looked faint. By the time this was done, the gruel was ready, and it was good to see how refreshed the poor fellows were. E. and I were almost alone at the time these first men came. Messrs. Olmsted and Knapp were away on business, and the two young doctors had gone ashore; we should have been completely at a loss without Len. Tug after tug followed, and 800 men were put on board in the next three days.

G. to Mother.

"OCEAN QUEEN."

It seems a strange thing that the sight of such misery should be accepted by us all so quietly as it was. We were simply eyes and hands for those three days. Strong men were dying about us; in nearly every ward some one was going. Yesterday one of the students called me to go with him and say whether I had taken the name of a dead man in the forward cabin the day he came in. He was a strong, handsome fellow, raving mad when brought in, and lying now, the day after, with pink cheeks and peaceful look. I had tried to get his name, and once he seemed to understand and screeched out at the top of his voice, John H. Miller, but whether it was his own name or that of some friend he wanted, I don't know. All the record I had of him was from my diet-list, "Miller, forward cabin, port side, No. 119, beef tea and punch."

Last night Dr. Ware came to me to know how much floor-room we had. The immense saloon of the after-cabin was filled with mattresses so thickly placed that there was hardly stepping room between them, and as I swung my lantern along the row of pale faces, it showed me another strong man dead. E. had been working hard over him, but it was useless. He opened his eyes when she called "Henry" clearly in his ear, and gave her a chance to pour brandy down his throat, but he died quietly while she was helping some one else. We are changed by all this contact with terror, else how could I deliberately turn my lantern on his face and say to the Doctor behind me, "Is that man dead?" and stand coolly, while he listened and examined and pronounced him dead. I could not have quietly said, a year ago, "That will make one more bed, Doctor." Sick men were waiting on deck in the cold though, and every few feet of cabin floor were precious; so they took the dead man out and put him to sleep in his coffin on deck. We had to climb over another soldier lying up there, quiet as he, to get at the blankets to keep the living warm.

From the "Ocean Queen" we, with the rest of the Sanitary Commission Staff, were transferred to the "Wilson Small," which became from this time our home and Headquarters' boat.

A. H. W. to G. and E.
8 BREVOORT PLACE, SATURDAY.

My Dear Girls: How little we know where you are and what worlds of work you are doing. It is hard to keep still, I know, where so much ought to be done. . . . Yesterday Charley and the Webster were to sail and we had a carriage and all went down with the traps—box of brandy, trunk of towels, etc., bundle of airbeds, bundle of fans, and a basket with a few eatables—some fresh eggs which had just arrived from Fishkill, and three or four bottles of ale, which I hope Eliza will drink; she sometimes used to take a glass of it at home. As for Georgy, I do not expect to have her take anything of that sort, after what mother tells me of the fate of the boxes of claret you took to Washington. One box was still unopened, and, so far as *she* knew, Georgy had never touched a drop. . . . We found Mrs. Trotter on board. The other ladies soon came —Mrs. Griffin, Miss Katharine P. Wormeley, Mrs. Blatchford and Mrs. H. J. Raymond. . . .

The vessel is a fifth-rate bed-buggy concern, I should say, and the hold where the men were put seemed miserable in spite of your pains, but for which it would have been *very* forlorn. Charley was so busy running hither and thither that we hadn't much chance at him. I was sorry we had not packed a great hamper of cooked food for him and Mrs. Trotter. Another time we will do better. They expect to be back by Wednesday with as many sick as they can carry, and judging from the number they brought packed on the Ocean Queen, they will stow them with deadly closeness. We saw Dr. Grymes and liked his looks and manner. He startled us by telling us that the Ocean Queen was coming up the bay with over a thousand sick, *four hundred typhoid cases.* Couldn't do without *you*, he said; "only ladies down there to come—of course they are on board." Mrs. Griffin, too, was convinced of it and sent back by us a big bundle of tins she had bought for Georgy. We left the Webster at four, when they were to sail at any moment, and drove down to the pier where they said the Ocean Queen was to lie. She was not due till six, so we came home. What with the news from West Point, Va., *without details*, and with the idea that you were the only women on the Ocean Queen to see after the nurses and the sick, and Charley's departure, we were sufficiently sobered and excited, a compound of both. This morning Uncle Edward reports us the *Herald's* news from West Point, that it was only a skirmish and that the loss of the 16th was two killed, beside wounded. . . . At ten o'clock Dr. Buck landed on the Ocean Queen, came up to his house and sent us word that you were *not on board*. This morning he has been in for a moment, and says you were indefatigable and indispensable at the front; far more useful in staying than in coming up, that he didn't know where you went when you left the Ocean Queen, but that you were "all right" with Mr. Olmsted somewhere, and taken care of. . . . Eleven hundred, Dr. Buck said, came on the Ocean Queen. So many of them are *virulent fever* cases, men who must die, that there is great perplexity what to do with them. The City Hospital, North building, is fast filling up, and the air is so infectious that Mrs. Buck thinks it unsafe to enter it. The Commissioners propose that these new cases should go to Ward's Island. The government barracks on Bedloe's and Riker's Islands won't be ready for some days, and I dread having the Daniel Webster or some other transport bring a thousand more before these have been decently housed. . . . Mother has driven out to Astoria with Uncle E. Carry has gone to Park Barracks with flowers and cologne sent from Astoria, and Jane is at the City Hospital with oranges for fever men. *She* goes into the fever ward, considering it duty, and undertakes too much for her nerves, but you needn't tell her so. Carry and I are going this afternoon to see a "Mr. Woolsey," who was sent to St. Luke's, sick of fever.

A. H. W. to G. and E.
FRIDAY, May 16.

We have hundreds of dollars sent to us to spend "for the soldiers." Mr. Wm. Aspinwall, for one, sent Jane a cheque for $250. Now how shall we lay it out, so as to be most useful? Dr. G. said it made him heartsick, as it would us, to see the destitution and suffering of those men brought in at Yorktown. It makes me heartsick to think of it, and the only comfort is in knowing that if the condition of the men is horrible as it is, what would it be if nothing were done— if there were no Sanitary Commission. Take away all that voluntary effort has done for the army and what light would the government appear in before the world? Shamefully inefficient and neglectful!

Dr. Grymes shook Mother warmly by the hand to-day as we went on board the Daniel Webster, and said, "We can't do without your children. We fight for them down there, to know whether they shall go up on the boats or stay at Yorktown, but on the whole, they are more useful where they are. Your son, too, is very busy and is indispensable." I hope you will all three manage soon to be together and have the comfort of each other's help, and keep each other in check from doing too much. Jane says she has awful dreams about Georgy, that the other night a message came that she was ill with hasty typhoid fever followed by paralysis from over-exertion! There, Georgy, is a catalogue of evils for you.

Uncle Edward is ready to do anything on earth. He sent by the Daniel Webster 75 canton flannel shirts which he thought would be useful for typhoid men brought in from camp. Up here, he says, they are sure to be taken care of after a while. He bought also eighty dollars worth of cotton pocket handkerchiefs, half of which I sent by Mrs. Trotter; etc., etc. He brought here for Jane to dispose of six jugs of very old port wine, each half a gallon, which he had decanted himself. Jane says *that* shall be distributed under her own eye. . . .

We saw *your* red flag, I suppose it was, that you spent Sunday in making, flying at the peak of the Daniel Webster. . . . After the hundred canton flannel bed gowns were all made they told us they were too long for sick men and too heavy for fever patients. . . . Mother is extremely anxious to go on one of these trips of the Daniel Webster, and urges my consent! I generally evade the subject, for I think it would be too severe service. Don't you need stepladders for climbing to upper berths? Have you got them?

We, G. and E. had, by Mr. Olmsted's orders remained on the " Wilson Small " instead of going North, in order to help in the reception of wounded men from the front, the fitting up of the hospital transports and the trans-shipment of patients. Some of the twenty women who had just arrived from New York went up in charge of the Ocean Queen and other transports as they filled up.

We were all assigned to duty by Mr. Olmsted wherever he thought we fitted in best, and his large printed placards put up on the steamers gave orders for the "watches" and hours for "relief," meals, etc., etc., so that the work went on as in a city hospital.

G's Journal.

WILSON SMALL, May 7, '62.

The Merrimac is out; and the Monitor and Naugatuck are fighting her. The Galena has run up the James towards Richmond. We are lying along the dock at Yorktown quietly, where four days ago the rebels were ducking themselves in the water.

Battle of West Point, Va.; 16th N. Y. engaged.

Franklin's division has moved up to West Point with large reinforcements, and has been fighting at the point of the bayonet. Captain Hopkins steamed alongside this morning and called out the news, just down from West Point, on business, in the Mystic. Two of the 16th are killed, and Captain Curtis wounded in the chest. . . . We took on board the Small 20 to 30 from this fight. Had beds made on the cabin floor, and each man carefully put into a clean one as his stretcher came aboard, Captain Curtis among them. Several were amputations, and two died on the boat. Everything was done for them; beef tea and brandy given, and a capital surgical nurse was in charge. It was pleasant to see Mr. Olmsted come quietly into the cabin now and then. I would look round and he would be there sitting on the floor by a dying German, with his arm round his pillow—as nearly round his neck as possible—talking tenderly to him, and slipping away again quietly. He only came when the ward was quiet, and no one round to look at him.

E's Journal.

May 14.

I can't keep the record of events day by day, but last Friday we came down again from West Point to Yorktown, and G. and I went to Fortress Monroe on two hospital ships, G. on the

Knickerbocker with the sick of Franklin's Division, and Miss Whetten and I on the Daniel Webster No. 2, with two hundred of the Williamsburg wounded. Since the day of the battle they had lain in the wet woods with undressed wounds. Some one had huddled them on to a boat without beds or subsistence, and then notified the Sanitary Commission to take care of them; and we were detailed to attend to them on the way to Fortress Monroe, with basins, soap, towels, bandages, etc. We washed and fed them all, Moritz going round with buckets of tea and bread. The poor fellows were very grateful, but we had a terribly hard experience. One man had lost both legs and had one arm useless, but was as cheerful and contented as possible. Colonel Small, of the 26th Pennsylvania, was wounded and lying in the dining room. Just before midnight I went in to see Colonel Fiske, sick with typhoid fever, lying on the bare slats of a berth with only his blanket under him and a knapsack for a pillow. We made him tolerably comfortable and left him much happier than we found him.

Sunday morning the sick were all carefully removed by Dr. Cuyler to the shore hospital at Fortress Monroe, and we ran back to Yorktown, where we found Charley, just arrived on the Daniel Webster from New York, transferred to the Small.

From Mother.

8 BREVOORT PLACE, May 13th.

My Dear Girls: I have just come up to my own room from breakfast, and from the reading of your most welcome and satisfactory letter, my dear Eliza, written off West Point; and now before anything calls off my attention, or any visitors arrive to "sit the morning," I have seated myself to thank you both, Georgy for her's of the 8th, received on Saturday, and yours E., this morning. It is very thoughtful and kind in you to write at all, and I wonder how you can do it in the midst of *such scenes!* and yet how miserable it would be for *us* if we did not hear directly from your own pens of your welfare. I am as much and more at a loss than yourself where to begin to tell you all I want to say.... Miss H. and a lady friend were ushered in upon me this morning, the latter wishing to know *all* the particulars about the *position* of lady nurses down at Yorktown, and what was particularly required of them, as she had started from home with a "strong impulse" to offer her services. All I could tell her was that "a desire to be useful, plain common sense, energetic action, fortitude, and a *working apron*, were some of the absolute essentials!—not to be a looker-on, but a doer—to take hold with a good will and a kind heart. She left with a feeling that perhaps she could be quite as useful without going down

to Yorktown! I have no doubt she can. . . .
Charley must have seen you before this. He
will tell you all about his getting off and our
being on board with him. He took a quantity
of things for himself and you girls, which I
hope you may find useful. I told him to help
himself from the long basket, and use anything
he wanted for himself or others on the voyage.
The fruit, I was afraid, might not keep. The
fresh eggs were from Fishkill, especially for you,
E. I long to hear from Charley all about his
trip, and I wonder much whether he will come
back in the boat or stay behind. I think it will
be better, perhaps, for him to make the trip back
here, and then return to stay with you. But
this you will, of course, arrange among you.
. . . So you have both seen Fortress Monroe,
and landed, in spite of Stanton and his strict
rules! I am glad of it. You are certainly
highly favored girls, and I must give way to a
little motherly feeling and say you deserve it
all. You cannot imagine what our anxieties
have been since the commencement of McClellan's move to push the enemy to the wall. The
evacuation of Yorktown took us by surprise,
and somehow or other we do not seem to get up
the proper degree of enthusiasm about it. The
subsequent doings, with the destruction of the
much dreaded Merrimac, have not called forth
the jubilant demonstrations throughout the com-

munity here that I supposed such news would produce. They seem to be waiting for the *occupation of Richmond* to burst out with a joyous and prolonged expression of their feelings. Think of our troops being so near the desired "on to Richmond!" We can scarcely realize all that has happened since our parting that Sunday morning. Oh! how lonely and sad I felt when I turned away from the window to the empty room, and the deserted little beds in the corners at the Ebbitt House. But Hatty and I *made the most of each other*. I did not leave her that day. . . . A young gentleman sent in his card last evening,—Julian T. Davies—and followed in. He came to see Mrs. Howland, as her name and Miss Woolsey's were mentioned as having arrived here in the Ocean Queen. Mr. Hone had called for the same reason, and Mrs. Russell, I believe. Young D. said the report that Colonel Howland was wounded went up one aisle of the church in Fishkill, and immediately after, the *contradiction* went up the other, but he called to know *what* we had heard from you. You cannot tell what a relief and comfort your letter this morning gives us. I drove out on Saturday to Astoria with your Uncle E. Took an early dinner there, and then went up to Mary's and sat with her till six o'clock. Found her perfectly well, and the children lovely. . . . Abby mails you the daily papers constantly; they must be taken by other eager hands. Do let us know if any men from the 16th are brought here. We would like to find them out. Jane is untiring in her visits and attentions at the Hospitals—Abby at her shirt-making and cutting out for others to make, and doing all sorts of good things in the intervals, and doing all the running for the family generally. We cannot prevail on her to take time or money to buy herself a spring bonnet or dress. My love to Charley. I do not write him, as he may be on his way back. Hatty is still in Philadelphia. I am so glad you have Lenox Hodge at hand. It is a real comfort to think of it—tell him so, with my love. Give a great deal of love to our own Joe from us all. We shall be so anxious now to hear all the time. We grasp at every paper. . . . Farewell, dear girls, with a kiss to each, and to Charley two, if with you. We look anxiously for the Daniel Webster. Dr. Buck came and told us all about you—exalted praises!

A. H. W. to G. and E.

May 14.

My dear Girls: Since Mother wrote you yesterday the Daniel Webster has come in again. Fred Rankin called last night with a message from Mrs. Trotter, whom he met in the street on the way from the steamer to take the cars for home. He told us that Charley had stayed down at Yorktown. It may have been necessary for him to do so, in the service, or at the request of the Sanitary Commission, but we feel disappointed that he did not finish up the round trip and return in the steamer. . . .

"Capture of Richmond" has been cried every day for a week by the "Express; 4th Edition" boys!

Mrs. Trotter sent word that she had a very pleasant and satisfactory trip and should sail again on Friday; that most of the men improved on the voyage. They were *all* to be landed at 194 Broadway, F. Rankin thought. Among them, in the newspaper list, we see *Capt. Parker, Co. D, 16th New York.* Carry has just started down town, and a boy with her, carrying a quantity of flannel shirts for convalescents and some cotton ones for the City Hospital. She will stop at all the depots, the Hospital, Park Barracks and 194, and at the two latter will enquire for Captain Parker. She has stuck some handkerchiefs and cologne in her pocket, and I think delights at the prospect of sallying forth unwatched to "find some wounded soldiers." . . . Last night Mother made a white flannel shirt, which has gone down to be put in use at once. She sighs for the quiet of Washington and the companionship of G. and E., whom she *admires*, and who, she is afraid, are making themselves sick. . . .

Do take care of yourselves and let us know what *we* can do. I am having long, white, flannel hospital shirts made, and have bought and sent off all I could find at the employment societies of cotton night-gowns and red volunteer shirts.

Charley's hurried letters from Headquarters of the Sanitary Commission no doubt gave the account of his arrival and his work as purser on the Daniel Webster, and as clerk in the Quartermaster's Department later. We have nothing left but an occasional mention of letters as received. Aunt E. among others says, "Charley's long, interesting letter reached us to-day," and in a letter of F. L. Olmsted's to the Rev. Dr. Bellows his name occurs in this paragraph :—

OFF YORKTOWN, May 15.

... It is now midnight. Knapp and two supply boats started five hours ago for the sick at Bigelow's Landing. Two of the ladies are with him; the rest are giving beef tea and brandy and water to the sick on the Knickerbocker, who have been put into clean beds. Drs. Ware and Swan are in attendance, aided most efficiently by Wheelock and Haight. Mr. Collins is executive officer on the boat, and *Mr. Woolsey, clerk*, taking charge of the effects of the soldiers."

And later from Miss Wormeley:

"We all take the greatest interest in Charley's letter. He writes well, just what he sees and thinks about and throws genuine light on other accounts."

G. to Mother.

STEAMER KNICKERBOCKER.

On the "Knickerbocker."

If my letter smells of "Yellow B." sugar, it has a right to, as my paper is the cover of the sugar-box. Since I last wrote I have been jumping round from boat to boat, and Saturday came on board the Knickerbocker at Mr. Olmsted's request, with Mrs. Strong and some others, to put things in order, and, privately, to be on hand to "hold" the boat, which had been made over to the Commission, over the heads of the New Jersey delegation. Dr. Asch was on board, and we had the New Jersey dinner table abolished and 56 Sanitary Commission beds made on the dining-room floor that night. The 200 wounded and sick brought down to Fortress Monroe under our care were transferred to the shore hospital, where we stole some roses for our patients on the Small. Saw regiments embarking for Norfolk, which surrendered the next day. Saw Mr. Lincoln driving past to take possession of Norfolk; and by Tuesday had the boat all in order again, with the single exception of a special-diet cooking-stove. So we went ashore at Gloster Point and ransacked all the abandoned rebel huts to find one, coming down finally upon the sutler of the "Enfants Perdus," who was cooking something nice for the officers' mess over a stove with *four* places for pots. This was too much to stand; so under a written authority given to "Dr. Olmsted" by the quartermaster of this department, we proceeded to rake out the sutler's fire and lift off his pots, and he offered us his cart and mule to drag the stove to the boat and would take no pay! So through the wretched town filled with the débris of huts and camp furniture, old blankets, dirty cast-off clothing, smashed gun-carriages, exploded guns, vermin and filth everywhere, and along the sandy shore covered with cannon-balls, we followed the mule,—a triumphant procession, waving our broken bits of stove-pipe and iron pot-covers. I left a polite message for the Colonel "Perdu," which had to stand him in place of his lost dinner. I shall never understand what was the matter with that sutler, whose self-sacrifice was to secure some three hundred men their meals promptly.

We set up our stove in the Knickerbocker, unpacked tins and clothing, filled a linen-closet in each ward, made up beds for three hundred, set the kitchen in order, and arranged a black hole with a lock to it, where oranges, brandy and wine are stored box upon box; and got back to Yorktown to find everybody at work fitting up the "Spaulding." I have a daily struggle with the darkeys in the kitchen, who protest against everything. About twenty men are fed from one pail of soup, and five from a loaf of bread, unless they are almost well, and then no amount of food is enough.

One gets toughened on one's fourth hospital ship and now I could stop at nothing; but it is amusing to see the different ways taken to discover the same thing. Dr. McC.: "Well-my-dear–fellow–is–anything–the–matter–with–your–bowels–do–your–ears–ring–what-'s-your-name?" Dr. A.: "Turn over my friend, have you got the dia*ree*?" Dr. A. was in a state of indignation with Miss Dix in the shore hospital at Yorktown. She has peculiar views on diet, not approving of meat, and treating all to arrowroot and farina, and by no means allowing crackers with gruel. "*Them* does not go with this," as Dr. A. gracefully puts the words into Miss Dix's mouth.

www.ingramcontent.com/pod-product-compliance
Lightning Source LLC
Chambersburg PA
CBHW020302240426
43673CB00039B/680